AGAINST EQUALITY

AGAINST EQUALITY

QUEER
REVOLUTION
NOT MERE
INCLUSION

EDITED BY
RYAN CONRAD

AK PRESS
EDINBURGH · OAKLAND · BALTIMORE

Against Equality
Queer Revolution, Not Mere Inclusion
Edited by Ryan Conrad

All essays © by their original authors
This edition © 2014 AK Press (Edinburgh, Oakland, Baltimore)

ISBN: 978-1-849351-84-3
e-ISBN: 978-1-849351-85-0
Library of Congress Control Number: 2013952047

AK Press   AK Press UK
674-A 23rd Street   PO Box 12766
Oakland, CA 94612   Edinburgh EH8 9YE
USA   Scotland
www.akpress.org   www.akuk.com
akpress@akpress.org   ak@akedin.demon.co.uk

The above addresses would be delighted to provide you with the latest AK Press distribution
catalog, which features several thousand books, pamphlets, zines, audio and video recordings,
and gear, all published or distributed by AK Press. Alternately, visit our websites to browse
the catalog and find out
the latest news from the world of anarchist publishing:
www.akpress.org | www.akuk.com
revolutionbythebook.akpress.org

Printed in the United States on recycled, acid-free paper.

Against Equality covers by Chris E. Vargas | www.chrisevargas.com
Layout by Kate Khatib | www.manifestor.org/design

Contents

Part 3: Prisons Will Not Protect You

Acknowledgments

This project would not have been possible without the endless hours of writing and editing done by all our contributors and those that continue to take a chance on publishing our work. Many thanks to *UltraViolet*, *The Bilerico Project*, *QueerCents*, *Maximum Rocknroll*, the *Gay and Lesbian Review*, *Common Dreams*, *CounterPunch*, *No More Potlucks*, *The Guide*, Pink Triangle Press, *Windy City Times*, *Alternet*, *Upping the Anti*, *Workers World Paper*, the National Center for Reason and Justice, Queers for Economic Justice, PolitiQ-queers solidaires!, the Sylvia Rivera Law Project, South End Press, and the numerous personal blogs on which our work has been posted and re-posted. Additional gratitude goes to Yasmin Nair and Deena Loeffler for their many hours of proofreading and exquisite humor. Lastly, we are so grateful to AK Press for collaborating with us, believing in our projects, supporting our work through distribution, and taking us on for publication.

Against Equality
Queer Revolution, Not Mere Inclusion

RYAN CONRAD, KARMA CHÁVEZ, YASMIN NAIR, AND DEENA LOEFFLER
FOR AGAINST EQUALITY

WE WRITE AT A MOMENT of historical coincidence. On June 26, 2013, the Supreme Court made its decision in the *United States v. Windsor* case, determining that the Defense of Marriage Act (DOMA) is unconstitutional. On that same day, the Court ruled that proponents of California's Proposition 8, which banned same-sex marriage, did not have constitutional standing to defend the law in the courts, making same-sex marriage again legal in California.

Around the same time, Against Equality (AE) finalized and announced our collaboration with AK Press to publish our three existing anthologies as the volume you now hold in your hands.

We at AE are, by no means, implying that significant judicial decisions related to gay issues are equivalent to an independent publisher deciding to publish a queer radical book. We simply want to note that what we believe will go down in history as the greatest marker of gay assimilation in the U.S. came at the same time, ironically, as queer radical history began to reach greater mainstream visibility. While we, archivists of queer politics, take no credit for the decades and even centuries of truly insurgent queer radical work that precede us, we cannot help but underscore the significance of this political moment for this and other reasons.

The DOMA and Prop 8 decisions were handed down by the same Supreme Court that effectively rendered the 1965 Voting Rights Act null and void the previous day. A week earlier, the same court also dealt a significant blow to Miranda Rights, deciding that if an accused remains silent before their Rights are read to them, prosecutors can use that silence against them.

There was some consternation that the same court could render such seemingly incongruent decisions. How could nine justices collectively (even with recorded minority dissent) conclude that gay marriage was an inalienable right? "[Proposition 8] directly subverts the principle of equality at the heart of the Fourteenth Amendment, and is an affront to the inalienable right to pursue one's own happiness that has guided our nation since its founding," according to the Cato Institute's Ilya Shapiro. How could the Supreme Court conclude that marriage needed legal protection and encouragement, but that voting was a right now easily accessed by a Black and Brown population that had, according to its summation, come so far that it no longer needed a jurisprudential Act to deter infringement?

The level of disenfranchisement is greater than ever at this historical moment. Several states have already moved to institute voter identification laws and other restrictions with the end of Voting Rights Act protections. Escalating poverty and consistent underemployment and unemployment mean that the United States now faces greater inequality than ever before, with wealth concentrated in the pockets and bank accounts of a very elite few. In many rural areas and major urban centers, like Chicago, public schools are being gutted in favor of private or charter schools, denying youth the chance at a quality public education and also denying workers the opportunity for jobs with union protection.

There are clear connections between economic disenfranchisement, serious impediments to voting rights and education, and the furthering of a neoliberal economy that depends upon highly selective resource concentration. But what commentators and most of the left, in their desperate attempt to valorize "gay rights," have still failed to consider is this: These decisions are deeply entwined in each other, and one indubitably leads to the other. We contend that the rise in a particular notion of "gay rights" (a term never espoused by the Chief Justice Roberts's court) is particularly dependent upon erasure of the political and economic rights of the most marginal.

Ironically, but not surprisingly, both gay cases centered on wealthy gay interests. The plaintiff in United States v. Windsor was Edith Windsor, an 84-year-old lesbian whose partner died in 2009, leaving her with estate taxes of nearly $400,000. To the average person, gay or straight, that number is large enough to strike profound fear in the heart. Most people are unlikely to die with that much savings, or to ever see that kind of amount accrue in their lifetimes, let alone to have to pay that much tax.

Publicity generated by major gay rights organizations and promoted relentlessly by neoliberal media outlets like the *New York Times* led people to believe that Windsor was a slightly impoverished and beleaguered widow who scrappily fought a system that tried to deprive her of precious resources. The unvarnished truth was omitted: by her own admission, she is "mildly affluent." Our own research, culled from several news reports and a list of her assets found in scattered sources, indicates that Windsor is worth somewhere close to $10,000,000. It's true that in New York City, where Windsor maintains one of her two active residences, $10,000,000 is a sum that classifies her as only comfortably well-off. But even in NYC, and certainly elsewhere, Windsor is, like a Jane Austen character, possessed of good fortune and unlikely to find herself scraping by with food stamps and coupons. Yet Windsor has become an icon for gays and lesbians who will never achieve or hope to leave such sizeable estates behind. Posters and t-shirts proclaiming "I AM Edith Windsor" circulated at Pride events held shortly after the decisions.

Edith Windsor was a strategic choice—someone who was presentable and sympathetic enough to the public and the courts, but not a multi-millionaire like, say, the political figure David Mixner or Chicago's reclusive gay media mogul, Fred Eychaner, a man with a massive fortune who commands private meetings with President Barack Obama. It's unlikely that someone truly poor would have had a case that merited attention—not because they wouldn't have been sympathetic but because the average gay or lesbian person will never have a partner leave a vast enough estate to warrant such a large tax bill.

In other words, what the court was arguing for was not the right of gays to marry, but for wealthy gays and lesbians (only *Forbes* dared to name Windsor as such) to keep their fortunes. For that reason, a court as invested in maintaining the neoliberal status quo—and whose agenda is not very different than Barack Obama's—is also interested in ensuring that racially and economically disenfranchised people in this country suffer further resource depletion and less access to essential rights and services.

This Against Equality anthology reminds us and the world that there is a queer radical/left history that has not been co-opted into meaningless support for "gay rights" at the cost of furthering neoliberalism. It exists to document our resistance to a gay agenda that has actively erased radical queer history by rewriting recent events into a narrative of progress, one where gays and lesbians flock towards marriage, military service, hate crime legislation, and the prison industrial complex.

In the last decade alone, the gay rights movement has achieved notable victories: The spread of gay marriage, federal hate crime legislation, and the end of the U.S. military's Don't Ask Don't Tell policy (DADT). All this has come at considerable cost. For instance, the bolstering of marriage in this country has meant a furthering of the idea that health care and immigration rights are marital benefits not deserved by individuals. Even in the United Kingdom, where the National Health Service (NHS) has been a lodestar for the rest of the world, the rise of gay marriage as a way to privatize benefits comes with greater pushes to dismantle or at least radically alter the NHS—which was greatly responsible for economic recovery in the United Kingdom after World War II.

Hate crime legislation, which purports to provide fairness for minority communities, does nothing to address root causes of violence, and increases the scope of the prison industrial complex through extended sentencing. The end of DADT comes with the expansion of bloodthirsty imperialism and neocolonialism by the United States. At this time, American gay soldiers are celebrating Pride weekend in Afghanistan even as the same army continues blasting out the innards of a country already eviscerated by ruinous U.S. foreign policy.

Collectively, this anthology collects and presents forceful reminders that queer resistance is not only against the oppression of people defined as queer, but against all disenfranchisement, and that this resistance is not merely a pale version of free love but deeply embedded in the political legacies of Emma Goldman and Voltairine de Cleyre, among many others. The resistance archived here does not merely shout out for sexual liberation, as important as that might be, but insists upon a radical political and economic reorientation of the world.

The contents of these pages range from personal to analytic but their driving force is structural change. The stories of experiences gathered here do not simply provide personal testimony, but also sharpen the critiques presented.

Since our inception, AE has been criticized for our critiques, and accused of not providing alternatives. Our continued response is that the structures of assimilation are so tenacious that they need, first and foremost, hard and insistent critiques in order to dismantle the authority and power they have accrued over the years. Additionally, every contributor to this anthology and every member of the small Against Equality collective is connected to projects that radically alter the political landscape. Whether we work on grassroots organizing against privatization of Chicago schools, the prison industrial complex, HIV/AIDS discrimination laws in Canada, health disparities in under-served communities, or ties between militarization and queer immigrant discourses in Arizona, our individual and collective work persistently points out alternatives to the privatized state and the brutality of the prison industrial complex and the military. In other words, we critique like our lives depend upon it.

Contrary to what our progressive/left critics proclaim, action is—or can be—a form of analysis. When gay marriage supporters publicly trot out weeping children clinging to their gay or lesbian parents or insist that their lives are more "real" than ours, they obfuscate the ways that such strategies are necessarily born out of their own analysis: an analysis that determines, for instance, the manipulative extent to which the public can be wooed by such melodramatic and homonormative affect.

WHO IS AGAINST EQUALITY?

Against Equality is a small, all-volunteer, anti-capitalist collective that maintains an online archive of radical queer and trans critiques of the holy trinity of mainstream gay and lesbian politics: gay marriage, gays in the military, and hate crime legislation. In 2009, a classist and urban-centric gay marriage campaign in rural Maine resulted in a successful referendum that repealed a recently passed law permitting gay marriage. AE began as a blog by Ryan Conrad, initially designed to air frustrations and anger at marriage campaign politics. After receiving massive amounts of support and sensing a need for a record of queer resistance against mainstream gay politics, the blog was quickly transformed to its current form, as a collectively organized online archive of written and visual materials from across the globe.

As an anti-capitalist collective, we are quite skeptical of the nonprofit model employed by multi-million dollar organizations like the Human Rights Campaign and The National Gay and Lesbian Task Force. By functioning as anti-profit, not simply nonprofit, we try to strike a balance between valuing our own labor and making our work as financially accessible as possible. All our publications and other cultural production (postcards, pins, tote bags, etc.) are kept as affordable as possible while we cheat, steal, and talk our way out of the thousands of dollars of debt we have accrued over the years. Though foregoing nonprofit status and fiscal sponsors has rendered us ineligible for grants, it allows us to be more directly accountable to our community instead of to funders. We've deliberately eschewed a nonprofit structure, preferring to operate as a collective. Not being beholden to a board or conventional funders has meant that we've struggled financially, but that also keeps us focused on our work, not on endless grant writing, fundraising, and board development.

While AE members often write and make cultural work about our shared politics, we are first and foremost an archive. We are not an organization, we do not have an office, we do not have a phone, we do not have a volunteer/intern coordinator, and we all have other jobs—often two! Collective members maintain the archive in addition to their local community activism. We see the intellectual work in our archive as informing our activism, and our activism informing our intellectual work. Both are forms of labor, and both are absolutely necessary for our movements to grow and deliver concrete beneficial changes for our entire community.

We do not publish new writing on our website, but archive pieces that have been previously published elsewhere, online or in print. AE is committed to archiving radical work from all parts of our collective queer history, which is messy and complex. Online, we archive pieces without censorship or exegesis because we believe that an unclouded historical overview is preferable to one that is apologetic or revisionist—after all, our collective began as an effort to combat the erasure of queer radical history and activism by the mainstream gay and lesbian community. To that end, we recognize that sometimes the pieces we archive demonstrate language or ideology that is not seamlessly in line with what we might consider preferable today. Rather than revise or erase, we retain these pieces as part of our ongoing effort to document queer history as what it was, not what we wish it would have been. In the same way, we also ask that any submissions to the archive remain exactly as they originally appeared, without revisions to language or politics. Within the pages of this anthology, the only changes to previously published material are editorial decisions to combine a writer's multiple pieces into one as well as to include a few authors' afterthoughts on how their pieces have been received since their original publication.

WHAT THIS BOOK IS

This anthology is the result of four years of editing and archiving work by the AE collective, work that began in 2009. From 2010 to 2012, AE released a pocket-sized book every year on each of the three themes in our online archive. We compiled what we thought were some of the most compelling and diverse online critiques and put them into print. The pieces that make up these books range greatly in form and content. From deeply personal to scholarly, from anti-urbanist to prison abolitionist, the current small volume spreads out in many directions, building coalition-like critiques across many social and economic justice movements.

Each volume from our pocket-sized series, *Against Equality: Queer Critiques of Gay Marriage* (2010), *Against Equality: Don't Ask to Fight Their Wars* (2011), and *Against Equality: Prisons Will Not Protect You* (2012), comprises a section of this book. By putting them into a single volume, we are able to greatly reduce our financial burden of keeping this self-published series widely available in print. In addition, by combining all three volumes, we also hope to encourage those who may be interested in only one area of our archive to engage with the other themes. Thanks to the generous support of AK Press, we are able to make this possible.

This book is an archival anthology. All the pieces found herein have been previously published elsewhere. The majority of these pieces were published exclusively online and appear in print for the first time in AE's books. The only original content found in our books is the set of three introductions, all of which appeared in the original publications and that now serve as section introductions to this book.

WHAT THIS BOOK DOES

This anthology is meant to serve as an introduction to the diverse array of radical queer and trans critiques leveled against mainstream gay and lesbian politics. Our hope is that by engaging with the ideas in this book, readers can go on to build broader and more nuanced critiques that best reflect the specificity of their own communities. This collection is by no means exhaustive or complete, but represents what we found to be some of the best and most convincing arguments assembled in our online archive.

Beyond the immediate purpose of building a larger, more critically engaged community of radical queer and trans folks, we see the relevance of this collection as even more important today than ever before. As mentioned, the United States saw the repeal of DOMA in the summer of 2013, the end of DADT in autumn 2011, and the passage of federal hate crime laws in the 2010 National Defense Authorization Act; we want to be sure that voices of resistance are not erased and written out of history. These essays are like bread crumbs, laying out different pathways to justice and resistance for those who dare to imagine a more just world. When people look back on these desperately conservative gay times, we hope our collective voices can be an inspiration to those who come after us—those that look to our queer histories, just like we did, as a site of rejuvenation, excitement, and hope.

WHY PUBLISH?

It feels like the entire publishing industry is collapsing in upon itself, save for a few niche indie presses and a couple of mega-conglomerates, yet AE has chosen to publish books anyway. Perhaps seemingly initially foolish or financially reckless, we find ourselves committed to the printed word for a number of important reasons.

While it may be surprising for city dwellers to learn that not everyone has high-speed Internet access or seamless cell-phone coverage, rural queers know all too well what it means to be on the losing side of the digital divide. Rural poverty aside, even if many small-town queer and trans people wanted to purchase high-speed Internet access or cell-phone data plans, such consumer options are often not available. Quite simply, the fiber optic cables and cell phone towers do not exist. Telecommunication companies will not entertain the idea of putting them up because it is not profitable to do so in sparsely populated areas. Regional libraries and schools often become the main lifeline to online access, and these spaces are surveilled and policed in ways that make it difficult and uncomfortable, if not outright dangerous, to access queer and trans materials online.

Aside from those who do not have online access due to lack of infrastructure, there are others who simply are not interested in investing many hours learning how to use computers, let alone learn how to efficiently navigate through endless amounts of Internet garbage in order to access what we've culled together in our publications. Whether they are older individuals who have not worked on computers most of their lives or those of a new generation who would rather go without, publishing in print form means greater access.

Lastly, in terms of access, there are a large number of queer and trans people left behind by nearly all of our so-called gay and lesbian community organizations: incarcerated LGBTQs. With little, but more often no Internet access, incarcerated members of the LGBTQ community are left out of conversations that happen largely online. Through our publications and free-books-to-prisoners policy, we extend these conversations to many who have never and will never be granted online access. It is imperative that we, as a radical queer and trans social- and economic-justice movement, not abandon our friends and family held captive by the state, regardless of the harm they may or may not have caused.

Beyond access to online versus physical print media, there is an important point to be made regarding what we refer to as "seizing the means of production of knowledge." Our three pocket-sized anthologies were self-published. This allowed us to work outside the typical academic or publishing industry timeline and also allowed AE, as an activist group with no profit motive, to maintain full control over the project. It allowed us to take online op-eds and blog posts, then put them into print where they became official knowledge; once in book form, the ideas presented together became reputable source material for scholarly research. University instructors are now teaching our work across the United States, Canada, and perhaps beyond. It is doubtful that this would have ever happened if these pieces remained a series of disconnected online materials. In short, once our work became official knowledge, the ideas and critiques presented in this anthology were gradually approached with more seriousness and given more weight. Instead of being isolated extremists nestled in the far corners of the Internet, we were a coherent and defiant set of voices demanding greater attention to the failures of mainstream gay and lesbian equality politics.

And, of course, there is always the bookness of a book. Though we make this collection available as an e-book due to demand from those overseas who find shipping costs prohibitive, there is still that irreplaceable feeling one gets when folding down the corner of a page and writing notes with a pencil. The feeling of gathering for a book club discussion where well-worn pages are smudged with traces of shared meals, and discussed, reworked, challenged, and built upon. The feeling of passing on a cherished book to a lover, friend, or the next generation of queer and trans people who will look to this moment for traces of resistance like we did with previous decades. The feeling one just does not get from gathering around the glowing screen of a laptop or tablet. Plus, it's much easier to cruise someone on the beach or in the park by checking out their book than trying to guess what's on their e-reader.

CONCLUSION

We hope that readers will consider this collection a small part in the construction of a radical queer present. In our view, this anthology and our online archive provide access to resources for revitalizing queer political imaginations, even as those resources are imperfect. It is vitally important to draw upon the resources of the past in order to create more life chances for queer and trans folks here, now, and in the future. Rather than bemoaning our neoliberal, desperate futures, we want to reinvigorate the queer political imagination with fantastic possibility

AGAINST EQUALITY

EQUALITY

QUEER CRITIQUES
OF
GAY MARRIAGE

EDITED BY RYAN CONRAD

INTRODUCTION BY YASMIN NAIR

Against Equality, Against Marriage
An Introduction

YASMIN NAIR

A PROGRESS NARRATIVE

THE HISTORY OF GAY MARRIAGE supposedly goes something like this: In the beginning, gay people were horribly oppressed. Then came the 1970s, where gays—all of whom looked like the men of The Village People—were able to live openly and have a lot of sex. Then, in the 1980s, many gay people died of AIDS—because they had too much sex in the 1970s. This taught them that gay sex is bad. The gays who were left realized the importance of stable, monogamous relationships and began to agitate for marriage and the 1,000+ benefits it would bring. Soon, in the very near future, with the help of supportive, married straight people—and President Obama—gays will gain marriage rights in all fifty states, and they will then be as good and productive as everyone else.

This is, obviously, a reductive and, yes, tongue-in-cheek history. But it is also, sadly, exactly the reductive history that circulates in both the straight and gay media. In a 2009 column commemorating the fortieth anniversary of the Stonewall riots, the liberal Frank Rich of *The New York Times* described the events thus: "The younger gay men—and scattered women—who acted up at the Stonewall on those early summer nights in 1969 had little in common with their contemporaries in the front-page political movements of the time." Rich ignored, willfully or not, the fact that Stonewall was initiated largely by unruly drag queens and transgender people, the sort who would have been avoided by the "gay men" who achieve such prominence in his sanitized version of gay history, one that reads like something from the press offices of the conservative National Gay and Lesbian Task Force (NGLTF) or the ultra-conservative Human Rights Campaign (HRC). Rich went on to draw an arc directly from Stonewall to the contemporary gay rights movement, as if its history were simply an upwards movement towards marriage. He even made the outrageous claim that AIDS was made much worse because those who struggled with the disease and were activists in the period were people "whose abridged rights made them even more vulnerable during a rampaging plague." In other words, if only they had the rights bestowed upon them by marriage, gays would not have suffered quite so much.

Rich concluded that, "full gay citizenship is far from complete." By that, of course, he meant that only marriage could guarantee "full" citizenship. He dismissed the complexity of gay history (which did not begin with Stonewall) and ignored the fact that much of gay liberation was founded on leftist and feminist principles, which included a strong materialist critique of marriage. Or that AIDS activism in the 1980s called for universal health care, the demand for which has been abandoned by the gay mainstream in favor of the idea that gays should simply be given health care via marriage.

Rich's views are widely echoed in a world where the default liberal/progressive/left position on gay marriage is an uncritical and ahistorical support of it as a magic pill that will cure all the ills facing contemporary gays/queers. 2008 saw a spate of suicides by teens who killed themselves after relentless bullying by peers for supposedly being gay. This led straights and gays alike to assert that the legalization of gay marriage would remove the stigma of being gay by conferring normality upon queer/queer-identified teens. Gay marriage would supposedly prevent such tragic moments. But if we follow this idea to its logical end, it becomes apparent that what appears to be a wish to bestow dignity upon queers is in fact deeply rooted in a fear and loathing of the unmarried, and a neoliberal belief that the addition of private rights tied to the state's munificence will end all social problems.

In a December 2009 blog for *The Nation* titled "On the New York Senate Marriage Equality Vote," Melissa Harris-Lacewell wrote about the extreme harassment suffered by her lesbian niece at her school, which eventually led to her transferring out. Bizarrely, Harris-Lacewell connected the lack of "marriage equality" to her niece's troubles: "Each time we refuse to recognize LGBT persons as first class citizens, deserving of all the rights and protections of the state, we make the world more harsh, more dangerous, and more difficult for my niece and for all gay and transgender young people. They deserve better." On the way to this strange formulation, she conceded that "marriage equality" will not solve the systemic problems of violence and institutional discrimination, but on this she was firm: "marriage equality" would make life better and easier for LGBTs. What is so puzzling is that Harris-Lacewell is purportedly on the left and writes for a magazine whose leftist credentials are well established.

Yet, surely, if a teen is unhappy or commits suicide because he/she is gay and cannot bear to live in a homophobic world, or because he/she is relentlessly taunted by peers for looking/acting gay, surely the problem, the very great problem, lies in the shocking cruelty of a world that will not tolerate any deviation from the norm. When we decide that the solution to such cruelty is to ensure that queer/queer-seeming teens should appear normal via gay marriage, are we not explicitly condoning and even creating a world where discrimination is acceptable? Are we not explicitly telling queer teens and adults that non-conformity can and should lead to death?

WHOSE EQUALITY? AT WHAT COST?

Such convoluted pieces of logic overdetermine today's relentless quest for gay marriage, a quest that is portrayed in terms of an attainment of "full citizenship" (begging the question: who has half citizenship, exactly?) and in terms of "full equality." But who gains "equality" under these circumstances? And at what cost? One of the biggest arguments for gay marriage is that it would allow gays and lesbians to access the over one thousand benefits that straight married people can access. Well-known feminists like Gloria Steinem give their stamp of approval to gay marriage with the rationale that "we" (feminists) have changed marriage for the better. Yet, while it may be true that women can no longer be raped with impunity by their husbands, the basic nature of marriage is unchanged: it remains the neoliberal state's most efficient way to corral the family as a source of revenue, and to place upon it the ultimate responsibility for guaranteeing basic benefits like health care. Furthermore, if millions of people are excluded from the 1,000+ benefits simply because they are NOT married, surely it does not matter that "we" have changed the institution when we now choose to ignore the inequalities perpetuated by marriage? Surely we ought not to be for a society where basic benefits like health care are only granted to those who get married? Surely the point is not to change an archaic institution but to change, you know, the world?

The history of gay marriage is now used to overwrite all of queer history as if the gay entrance into that institution were a leap into modernity, as if marriage is all that queers have ever aspired to, as if everything we have wrought and seen and known were all towards this one goal. Americans are fond of judging modernity in the Islamic world by the extent to which women there are allowed to toss away their veils. In the U.S. landscape of "gay rights," marriage is the veil: the last barrier between gays and lesbians and "full citizenship." Opening it up to them is considered the last sign of gay modernity, still to be attained. Liberals and lefties alike, straight and gay, look at gay marriage in countries like Spain and Argentina as the ultimate mark of civilization. They note approvingly that South Africa guarantees a constitutional right to gay marriage, but they have nothing to say about the fact that the same country has over five-million people living with HIV and no similar guarantee for health care.

Gay marriage is seen as the core of a new kind of privatized and personal endeavor—the rights of LGBT *individuals* to enter into a private contract. This ignores the fact that the U.S. is the only major industrialized nation to tie so many basic benefits like health care to marriage. Gay marriage advocates are fond of pointing to Norway or Canada as prime examples of countries where gay marriage is legal, as examples to emulate. They ignore one basic fact: in all these countries, citizens were guaranteed rights like health care long before they legislated marriage. Simply put: in Canada, getting divorced does not put you at risk of losing your health care and dying from a treatable condition. I am not suggesting Canada's public health program is perfect and not under constant threat from the conservative Harper regime, but the fact is that health care is not a basic right in the United States. Tiny differences, but extreme consequences.

Over the same period of years that the gay marriage fight has gathered steam, roughly two and a half decades, the U.S. has also slid into an increasingly fragile economic state. Over 45 million Americans are uninsured (the new health care "reform" is likely to prove too onerous for most). On the queer front, we have seen an increase in the policing, surveillance, and arrests in cases of public displays of sexuality, made especially resonant in the recent case of DeFarra Gaymon, who was shot to death by the police in a park in Newark, supposedly during an undercover sting operation and while supposedly engaging in public sex. HIV/AIDS rates are not only rising, those infected with the virus are now among the newly criminalized. A dearth of funds is causing the closure of resources and safe spaces for queer homeless youth.

This section of the anthology is impelled by the failure of both the gay rights movement and the so-called left to address the nightmare of neoliberalism that faces us today. We see this as the moment to move beyond the idea that marriage could ever be part of a radical vision for change. The essays in this section, by writers, activists, and academics on the left, highlight the harmful role of marriage in a neoliberal state that emphasizes issues of identity and the family in order to deflect attention away from the attrition of social services and benefits. Focusing on the family as the arbiter of benefits also ignores the fact that the exclusion of queer people from the normative family structure is marked by physical and psychological violence. When queers criticize the State's emphasis on the normative family, we do so because we know only too well the violence of exclusion and because, for many of us, our identities as queer people have been marked and shaped, not always in unproductive ways, by that violence.

In short, the family is the best way to advance capitalism, as the base unit through which capitalism distributes benefits. Through our reliance on the marital family structure, emphasized and valorized by the push for gay marriage, we allow the state to mandate that only some relationships and some forms of social networks count. If you are married, you get health care. If you are not, go and die on your sad and lonely deathbed by yourself; even the state will not take care of you. If you are married, you get to be the good immigrant and bring over your immediate and extended family to set up a family business and send your children to the best schools after years of perseverance and hard work (at least theoretically). If you are not, you can be deported and imprisoned at the slightest infraction and not one of the kinship networks that you are a part of will count in the eyes of the state. In other words, a queer radical critique of the family is not simply the celebration of an outsider status, although it is often that, but an economic critique. A queer radical critique of gay marriage exposes how capitalism structures our notion of "family" and the privatization of the social relationships we depend on to survive.

In a neoliberal economy, gay identity becomes a way to further capitalist exploitation. In an essay titled "Professional Homosexuals," Katherine Sender writes about gays and lesbians in a high-tech firm trying for years to form a gay and lesbian employee group; such groups were banned for fear they would "function as trade unions." Eventually, the firm allowed such a group to form; it was concerned with the "recruitment … and productivity of gay and lesbian employees." None of which had to do with them as workers. The point is this: today, capitalism does not seek to exclude gays and lesbians—instead, it seeks to integrate them into its structure of exploitation as long as they don't upset the status quo.

This section of the anthology insists that we stop looking for "equality" in the narrow terms dictated by neoliberalism, where progress means an endless replication of the status quo. It insists that we stop acquiescing to the neoliberal demand that our identities should dictate what basic rights are given to us. Against Equality is unapologetic and even, at times, angry. We are not only putting gay marriage advocates on notice, but their "straight allies" as well. In the course of our work, over the last many years, our critics have often accused us of having no "solutions." Our response, then and now, is that the critique, one that has often been silenced or made invisible, is a necessary part of the process of finding solutions that erase the economic inequality that surrounds us all. Our work is not intended to be prescriptive—unlike marriage, we do not guarantee eternal happiness of the married kind—but to agitate for a much needed dialogue on these matters. Our point, as will be evident from the essays that follow, is that the idea of marriage as any kind of solution for our problems perpetuates the very inequalities that gay marriage advocates claim to resolve.

Open Letter to LGBT Leaders Who Are Pushing Marriage Equality

KATE BORNSTEIN

TO THE LEADERS, MEMBERSHIP, AND supporters of The Human Rights Campaign, The National Gay and Lesbian Task Force, and statewide groups supporting marriage equality as your primary goal,

Hello. I'm Kate Bornstein, and I've got a great deal to say to you, so you deserve to know more about me: I write books about postmodern gender theory and alternatives to suicide for teens, freaks, and other outlaws. I'm a feminist, a Taoist, a sadomasochist, a femme, a nerd, a transperson, a Jew, and a tattooed lady. I'm a certified Post Traumatic Stress Disorder survivor. I'm a chronic over-eater who's been diagnosed with anorexia. I'm sober, but I'm not always clean. I've got piercings in body parts I wasn't born with. I'm also an elder in the community you claim to represent, and it is with great sorrow that I must write: you have not been representing us.

This piece originally appeared on Kate Bornstein's blog (katebornstein.typepad.com) on December 4, 2009.

Let's talk about a love that unites more people than have ever before been united by love. Let's defend some real equality.

The other day, New York State's lesbian and gay bid for marriage equality went down in flames, enough flames to make people cry. Thousands of lesbians, gay men, bisexuals, and transgender people and their allies spent a lot of money and heart-filled hours of work to legalize marriage equality, with little to show for it. That sucks, and I think the reason it didn't work is because marriage equality is an incorrect priority for the LGBTQetc communities.

Marriage equality—as it's being pushed for now—is wasting resources that would be better deployed to save some lives. There are several major flaws with marriage equality as a priority for our people:

Marriage as it's practiced in the USA is unconstitutional... if you listen to Thomas Jefferson's interpretation of separation of church and state. The way it stands now, if you're an ordained leader in a recognized religion, the U.S. government gives you a package of 1,500–1,700 civil rights that only you can hand out to people. And you get to bestow or withhold these civil rights from any American citizen you choose, regardless of that citizen's constitutionally granted rights. The government has no constitutional right to hand that judgment call over to a religious body.

Marriage equality—as it's being fought for now by lesbian and gay leaders who claim they're speaking for some majority of LGBTQetc people—will wind up being more marriage inequality. Single parents, many of whom are women of color, will not get the 1,500–1,700 rights they need to better and more easily raise their children. Nor will many other households made up of any combination of people who love each other and their children.

When lesbian and gay community leaders whip up the community to fight for the right to marry, it's a further expression of America's institutionalized greed in that it benefits only its demographic constituency. There's no reaching out beyond sexuality and gender expression to benefit people who aren't just like us, and honestly... that is so 20th-century identity politics.

Marriage is a privileging institution. It has privileged, and continues to privilege people along lines of not only religion, sexuality and gender, but also along the oppressive vectors of race, class, age, looks, ability, citizenship, family status, and language. Seeking to grab oneself a piece of the marriage-rights pie does little if anything at all for the oppression caused by the institution of marriage itself to many more people than sex and gender outlaws.

The fight for "marriage equality" is simply not the highest priority for a movement based in sexuality and gender. By simple triage, the most widespread criminality against people whose identities are based in sex and gender is violence against women. Women still make up the single-most oppressed identity in the world, followed closely by kids who are determined to be freaky for any reason whatsoever.

Lesbian and gay leaders must cease being self-obsessed and take into account the very real damage that's perpetrated on people who are more than simply lesbian women and/or gay men, more than bisexual or transgender even. Assuming a good-hearted but misplaced motivation for all the work done on behalf of fighting for marriage equality, it's time to stop fighting on that front as a first priority of the LGBTQetc movement. It's time to do some triage and base our priorities on a) who needs the most help and b) what battlefront will bring us the most allies.

I'm asking that you fight on behalf of change for someone besides yourself. Please. I promise the rewards of doing that will revisit you threefold. Who needs the most help is easy: women. To lesbian and gay leaders, I ask you to ally yourselves with the centuries-old feminist movements and their current incarnations. You want to get a bill passed through Congress? Take another run at the Equal Rights Amendment. Unlike gay marriage, the ERA stands a better chance of making it into law, given the Obama Administration and our loosely Democratic majority in congress.

Stopping the violence against women and freaky children, and backing another run at the ERA have got a good chance of creating a national front, lots of allies. On the home front of sex and gender, there's plenty of room for change that doesn't require millions of dollars and thousands of hours.

Looking into the community of people who base their lives on sexuality and gender, there's a lot of door-opening to do. Beyond L, G,

B, and T, there's also Q for queer and Q for questioning. There's an S for sadomasochists, an I for intersex, an F for feminists, and another F for furries. Our community is additionally composed of sex educators, sex workers, adult entertainers, pornographers, men who have sex with men, women who have sex with women, and asexuals who have sex with no one but themselves. You want to create some real change? Make room for genderqueers, polyamorists, radical faeries, butches, femmes, drag queens, drag kings, and other dragfuck royalty too fabulous to describe in this short letter.

There are more and more people to add to this ever-growing list of communities whom you must own as family and represent in your activism. You cannot afford—politically, economically, or morally—to leave out a single person who bases a large part of their identity on being sex positive or in any way a proponent of gender anarchy.

That's what I have to say to you. That and thank you for the good hearts you've clearly demonstrated in your activism. I'm asking you to open your hearts further is all.

The best way to engage me in a conversation or recruit me to help is to contact me through Twitter. I look forward to talking with you, and I hope we can work together on the terms I've outlined above.

Warmly, and with respect,

Your Auntie Kate

Marriage is Murder
On the Discursive Limits of Matrimony

ERIC A. STANLEY

So, what is wrong with gay marriage?

IN ORDER TO ANSWER THAT question we must first understand what this thing called marriage is. Marriage is essentially a financial and legal contract that allocates the movement of property, power and privilege from one person to another. Historically it has been a way of consolidating family power amongst and between men, through women. In more recent times marriage in the United States has functioned to solidify the American middle class. Marriage does this through concentrating wealth and power through family lines and inheritance (both in terms of money and power). Because of marriage's ability to discipline class structures it is now, and always has been, a primary structure of a capitalist economy. In reality most people marry within their own socioeconomic class.

This piece was originally written for an action at the Republican National Convention in 2004 and a zine, entitled "Married to the State: A Shotgun."

Marriage, earlier through miscegenation laws, and currently through racist "values," also contains wealth through racist ideologies of matrimony. Because of these realities there has been a long history of critique of the institution of marriage launched by feminists of color, white feminists, and queer people among others.

What about gay marriage? Isn't gay marriage going to change all of this?

NO. The current push towards gay marriage is, in fact, not going to subvert the systems of domination we all live through. Ironically, the gay marriage movement is standing on these same legacies of brutality for their slice of the wedding cake. Take for example the "Freedom to Marry" stickers created by the Freedom to Marry organization. Not only are these stickers falsely equating the intervention of the State into one's life (marriage) with "freedom" (when was the last time the State helped you to become more "free"?) they are trying to work this idea through horrifying star-spangled stickers. Instead of critiquing the ways U.S. imperialism has rendered most transgender people, queer people, people or color etc. as expendable through its countless wars here and abroad, the Freedom To Marry stickers simply disguise these histories and reproduce this red-white-and-blue national theme for every married gay and guilt-filled liberal to wear with PRIDE.

If straight people can marry, why should gay people not have the same privilege?

What we are calling for is an abolishment of State sanctioned coupling in either the hetero or homo incarnation. We are against any institution that perpetuates the further exploitation of some people for the benefit of others. Why do the fundamental necessities marriage may provide for some (like health care) have to be wedded to the State sanctioned ritual of terror known as marriage?

Won't gay marriage help couples stay together where one person is not a U.S. citizen?

The way immigration is being used by the gay marriage movement is not only un-thought-out but also relies on racist notions of the "white man saving his brown lover." Although it is true that because of the U.S. policies on immigration some lesbian and gay couples may be split, gay marriage does not at all question these systems that allow some people into the country (white) while excluding others (people of color). Where are the gay marriage "activists" when the INS is actively raiding and deporting whole families? (Such as it is currently doing just blocks away from the Castro in San Francisco's Mission District.) Also missing from the picture of immigration that gay marriage advocates are painting is the reality that there are queer couples in the U.S. where neither person is a U.S. citizen. How will gay marriage help them stay in the U.S. if that is what they want to do? Gay marriage will not challenge "citizenship" but simply place some bodies within its grasp while holding others out.

I agree with your argument, but isn't gay marriage a step in the right direction?

This liberal model of "progression" is one of the primary ways many of us are ideologically trapped into a reformist way of thinking. To understand how gay marriage, like voting, will never lead to liberation we can look to the histories of many "social justice movements" that only address oppressions on a level of the symptomatic. Gay marriage and voting are symbolic gestures that reinforce structures while claiming to reconfigure them. This scheme will undoubtedly become apparent with "marriage equality" advocates. As they have positioned gay marriage as the last great civil rights battle, will they continue to fight after the Honeymoon?

Won't gay marriage help get health care to more people?

It may help some people get health care but for the vast majority of Americans with NO health care it will do nothing. And within the rhetoric of the gay marriage movement, working towards health care for all (people and animals) is nowhere to be found. This argument

29

also relies on the false assumption that one person would already have health care.

So if you are against gay marriage then you are allying with the Christian Right and the GOP!

NO. This is amongst the most troubling aspects of this current epidemic of gay marriage. The way the marriage movement is framing any critique of their precious institution is either you are one of us (gay married) or you are one of them (homophobe). This helps to silence the much needed debate and public discourse around such issues. It seems as if everyone has been shamed into submission and subsequent silence by the marriage movement. Even in allegedly "progressive" circles any mention of the implicit links between marriage, misogyny, and racism in the U.S. gets shut down by a "gay married."

Ironically, if you look at the rhetoric of the Freedom to Marry movement and the Republican Party, their similarities are frighteningly apparent. In their ideal world we would all be monogamously coupled, instead of rethinking the practice of "coupling." They want us working our jobs, not working towards collective and self-determination, remembering anniversaries not the murder of trans-people, buying wedding rings not smashing capitalism. The vision of the future the Republicans and the gay marriage movement have offered will render most of us already in the margins of the picture (trans-people, sex workers, queers of color, HIV positive people, non-monogamous people etc.) as the new enemy of the régime of married normalcy they hope to usher in.

I Still Think Marriage is the Wrong Goal

DEAN SPADE AND CRAIG WILLSE

A LOT OF STORIES ARE circulating right now claiming that Black and Latino voters are to blame for Prop 8 passing. Beneath this claim is an un-interrogated idea that people of color are "more homophobic" than white people. Such an idea equates gayness with whiteness and erases the lives of LGBT people of color. It also erases and marginalizes the enduring radical work of LGBT people of color organizing that has prioritized the most vulnerable members of our communities.

Current conversations about Prop 8 hide how the same-sex marriage battle has been part of a conservative gay politics that de-prioritizes people of color, poor people, trans people, women, immigrants, prisoners and people with disabilities. Why isn't Prop 8's passage framed as evidence of the mainstream gay agenda's failure to ally with people of color on issues that are central to racial and economic justice in the U.S.?

This statement was originally published on Facebook in 2008 and was then circulated online via makezine.enoughenough.org.

Let's remember the politics of marriage itself. The simplistic formula that claims "you're either pro-marriage or against equality" makes us forget that all forms of marriage perpetuate gender, racial, and economic inequality. It mistakenly assumes that support for marriage is the only good measure of support for LGBT communities. This political moment calls for anti-homophobic politics that centralize anti-racism and anti-poverty. Marriage is a coercive state structure that perpetuates racism and sexism through forced gender and family norms. Right wing pro-marriage rhetoric has targeted families of color and poor families, supported a violent welfare and child protection system, vilified single parents and women, and marginalized queer families of all kinds. Expanding marriage to include a narrow band of same-sex couples only strengthens that system of marginalization and supports the idea that the state should pick which types of families to reward and recognize and which to punish and endanger.

We still demand a queer political agenda that centralizes the experiences of prisoners, poor people, immigrants, trans people, and people with disabilities. We reject a gay agenda that pours millions of dollars into campaigns for access to oppressive institutions for a few that stand to benefit.

We are being told marriage is the way to solve gay people's problems with health care access, immigration, child custody, and symbolic equality. It does not solve these problems, and there are real campaigns and struggles that would and could approach these problems for everyone, not just for a privileged few. Let's take the energy and money being put into gay marriage and put it toward real change: opposing the War on Terror and all forms of endless war; supporting queer prisoners and building a movement to end imprisonment; organizing against police profiling and brutality in our communities; fighting attacks on welfare, public housing, and Medicaid; fighting for universal health care that is trans and reproductive health care inclusive; fighting to tax wealth not workers; fighting for a world in which no one is illegal.

Is Gay Marriage Anti-Black???

KENYON FARROW

I WAS IN ATLANTA ON business when I saw the Sunday, Feb. 29th edition of the *Atlanta Journal Constitution* that featured as its cover story the issue of gay marriage. Georgia is one of the states prepared to add some additional language to its state constitution that bans same sex marriages (though the state already defines marriage between a man and a woman, so the legislation is completely symbolic as it is political).

What struck me about the front-page story was the fact that all of the average Atlanta citizens who were pictured that opposed gay marriages were black people. This is not to single out the *Atlanta Journal Constitution*, as I have noticed in all of the recent coverage and hubbub over gay marriage that the media has been really crucial in playing up the racial politics of the debate.

For example, the people who are in San Francisco getting married are almost exclusively white whereas many of the people who are shown opposing it are black. And it is more black people than typically shown

This piece was originally published on March 5, 2004 and has been re-posted on numerous websites.

in the evening news (not in handcuffs). This leaves me with several questions: Is gay marriage a black/white issue? Are the Gay Community and the Black Community natural allies or sworn enemies? And where does that leave me, a black gay man, who does not want to get married?

SAME-SEX MARRIAGE AND RACE POLITICS

My sister really believes that this push for gay marriage is actually not being controlled by gays & lesbians. She believes it is actually being tested in various states by the Far Right in disguise, in an effort to cause major fractures in the Democratic Party to distract from all the possible roadblocks to re-election for George W. in November such as an unpopular war and occupation, the continued loss of jobs, and growing revelations of the Bush administration's ties to corporate scandals.

Whatever the case, it is important to remember that gay marriage rights are fraught with racial politics, and that there is no question that the public opposition to same-sex marriages is in large part being financially backed by various right-wing Christian groups like the Christian Coalition and Family Research Council. Both groups have histories and overlapping staff ties to white supremacist groups and solidly oppose affirmative action but play up some sort of Christian allegiance to the black Community when the gay marriage issue is involved.

For example, in the 1990s the Traditional Values Coalition produced a short documentary called *Gay Rights, Special Rights*, which was targeted at black churches to paint non-heterosexual people as only white and upper class, and as sexual pariahs, while painting black people as pure, chaste, and morally superior.

The video juxtaposed images of white gay men for the leather/S&M community with the voice of Dr. Martin Luther King's "I Have a Dream" speech, leaving conservative black viewers with the fear that the Civil Rights Movement was being taken over by morally debased human beings. And since black people continue to be represented as hyper-sexual beings and sexual predators in both pop culture and the mass media as pimps & players, hoochies & hos, rapists of white women & tempters of white men, conservative black people often cling to the other image white America hoists onto black people as well—asexual and morally superior (as seen in the role of the black talk show host and the role of the black sage/savior-of-white people used in so many Hollywood movies, like *In America* and *The Green Mile*, which are all traceable to Mammy and Uncle Remus-type caricatures).

Since the Christian Right has money and access to corporate media, they set the racial/sexual paradigm that much of America gets in this debate, which is that homos are rich and white and do not need any such special protections and that black people are black—a homogeneous group who, in this case, are Christian, asexual (or hetero-normative), morally superior, and have the right type of "family values." This, even though black families are consistently painted as dysfunctional and are treated as such in the mass media and in public policy, which has devastating effects on black self-esteem, and urban and rural black communities' ability to be self-supporting, self-sustaining, and self determining.

The lack of control over economic resources, high un/underemployment, lack of adequate funding for targeted effective HIV prevention and treatment, and the large numbers of black people in prison (nearly 1 million of the 2.2 million U.S. prison population) are all ways that black families (which include non-heterosexuals) are undermined by public policies often fueled by right wing "tough on crime" and "war on drugs" rhetoric.

Given all of these social problems that largely plague the black community (and thinking about my sister's theory), one has to wonder why this issue would rise to the surface in an election year, just when the Democratic ticket is unifying. And it is an issue, according to the polls anyway, that could potentially strip the Democratic Party of its solid support from African-American communities.

And even though several old-guard civil rights leaders (including Coretta Scott King, John Lewis, Revs. Al Sharpton and Jesse Jackson) have long supported equal protection under the law for the gay, lesbian, bisexual, and transgender community (which usually, but not always means support of same-sex marriage), the right wing continues to pit gay marriage (and by extension, gay civil rights) against black political interests, by relying on conservative black people to publicly speak out against it (and a lot has been written about how several black ministers received monies from right-wing organizations to speak out against same-sex marriages in their pulpits).

But many black leaders, including some I've been able to catch on television recently despite the right-wing's spin on the matter, have made the argument that they know too well the dangers that lie in "separate but equal" rhetoric. So, if many of our black leaders vocally support same-sex marriage, how has the Christian Right been able to create such a wedge between the black community and the gay community?

HOMOPHOBIA IN BLACK POPULAR CULTURE

Some of the ways that the Christian right-wing has been so successful in using same-sex marriage as a wedge issue is by both exploiting homophobia in the black community and also racism in the gay community. In regards to homophobia in the black community the focus of conversation has been about the Black Churches' stance on homosexuality.

It has been said many times that while many black churches remain somewhat hostile places for non-heterosexual parishioners, it is also where you will in fact find many black gays and lesbians. Many of them are in positions of power and leadership within the church—ushers, choir members/directors, musicians, and even preachers themselves.

But let me debunk the myth that the Black Church is the black community. The black community is in no way monolithic, nor are black Christians. The vast majority of black people who identify as "Christian" do not attend any church whatsoever. Many black Americans have been Muslim for over a century and there are larger numbers of black people who are proudly identifying as Yoruba, Santero/a, and atheists as well.

The black community in America is also growing more ethnically diverse, with a larger, more visible presence of Africans, West Indians, and Afro-Latinos amongst our ranks. We have always been politically diverse, with conservatives, liberals, radicals, and revolutionaries alike (and politics do not necessarily align with what religion you may identify as your own). It is also true that we are and have always been sexually diverse and multi-gendered. Many of our well-known Black History Month favorites were in fact Gay, Bisexual, Lesbian, or Transgender.

Despite our internal diversity, we are at a time (for the last thirty years) when black people are portrayed in the mass media—mostly through hip-hop culture—as being hyper-sexual and hyper-heterosexual to be specific. Nowhere is the performance of black masculinity more prevalent than in hip-hop culture, which is where the most palpable form of homophobia in American culture currently resides.

This of course is due largely to the white record industry's notions of who we are, which they also sell to non-black people. Remember pop culture has for the last 150 years been presenting blackness to the world—initially as white performers in blackface, to black performers in blackface, and currently to white, black, and other racial groups performing blackness as something that connotes sexual potency and a propensity for violent behavior, which are also performed as heterosexuality.

And with the music video, performance is as important (if not more) than song content. As black hip-hop artists perform gangsta and Black Nationalist revolutionary forms of masculinity alike, so follows overt homophobia and hostility to queer people, gay men in particular. Recently, DMX's video and song "Where the Hood At?" contained some of the most blatant and hateful homophobic lyrics and images I have seen in about a decade.

The song suggests that the "faggot" can and will never be part of the "hood" for he is not a man. The song and video are particularly targeted at black men who are not out of the closet, and considered on the "down low." Although challenged by DMX, the image of the "down low" brother is another form of performance of black masculinity, regardless of actual sexual preference.

But it's not just "commercial" rap artists being homophobic. "Conscious" hip-hop artists such as Common, Dead Prez, and Mos Def have also promoted homophobia through their lyrics, mostly around notions of "strong black families," and since gay black men (in theory) do not have children, we are somehow anti-family and antithetical to what a "strong black man" should be.

Lesbians (who are not interested in performing sex acts for the pleasure of male voyeurs) are also seen as anti-family, and not a part of the black community. A woman "not wanting dick" in a nation where black dick is the only tangible power symbol for black men is seen as just plain crazy, which is also expressed in many hip-hop tunes. None of these artists interrogate their representations of masculinity in their music, but merely perform them for street credibility. And for white market consumption.

It cannot be taken lightly that white men are in control of the record industry as a whole (even with a few black entrepreneurs), and control what images get played. Young white suburban males are the largest consumers of hip-hop music. So performance of black masculinity (or black sexuality as a whole) is created by white men for white men. And since white men have always portrayed black men as sexually danger-ous and black women as always sexually available (and sexual violence against black women is rarely taken seriously), simplistic representa-tions of black sexuality as hyper-heterosexual are important to main-taining white supremacy and patriarchy, and control of black bodies.

Black people are merely the unfortunate middlemen in an exchange between white men. We consume the representations like the rest of America. And the more that black people are willing to accept these representations as fact rather than racist fiction, the more heightened homophobia in our communities tends to be.

RACE AND THE GAY COMMUNITY

While homophobia in the black community is certainly an issue we need to address, blacks of all sexualities experience the reality that many white gays and lesbians think that because they're gay, they "un-derstand" oppression, and therefore could not be racist like their het-erosexual counterparts. Bullshit.

America is first built on the privilege of whiteness, and as long as you have white skin, you have a level of agency and access above and beyond people of color, period. White women and white non-heteros included. There is a white gay man named Charles Knipp who roams this nation performing drag in blackface to sold-out houses, north and south alike. Just this past Valentine's Day weekend, he performed at the Slide Bar in NY's east village to a packed house of white queer folks eager to see him perform "Shirley Q Liquor," a welfare mother with nineteen kids.

And haven't all of the popular culture gay images on TV shows like *Will & Grace*, *Queer as Folk*, etc., been exclusively white? No matter how many black divas wail over club beats in white gay clubs all over America (Mammy goes disco!) with gay men appropriating language and other black cultural norms (specifically from black women), white gay men continue to function as cultural imperialists the same way straight white boys appropriate hip-hop (and let's not ignore that white women have been in on the act, largely a result of Madonna bringing white women into the game).

There have always been racial tensions in the gay community as long as there have been racial tensions in America, but in the 1990s, the white gay community went mainstream, further pushing non-hetero people of color from the movement.

The reason for this schism is that in order to be mainstream in America, one has to be seen as white. And since white is normative, one has to interrogate what other labels or institutions are seen as normative in our society: family, marriage, and military service, to name a few. It is then no surprise that a movement that goes for "normality" would then end up in a battle over a dubious institution like marriage (and hetero-normative family structures by extension).

And debates over "family values," no matter how broad or narrow you look at them, always have whiteness at the center, and are almost always anti-black. As articulated by Robin D.G. Kelley in his book *Yo Mama's Dysfunktional*, the infamous Moynihan report is the most egregious of examples of how the black family structure has been portrayed as dysfunctional, an image that still has influence on the way in which black families are discussed in the media and controlled by law enforcement and public policy.

Since black families are in fact presented and treated as dysfunctional, this explains the large numbers of black children in the hands of the state through foster care, and increasingly, prisons (so-called "youth detention centers"). In many cases, trans-racial adoptions are the result. Many white same-sex unions take advantage of the state's treatment of black families; after all, white queer couples are known for adopting black children since they are so "readily" available and also not considered as attractive or healthy compared to white, Asian, and Latino/a kids.

If black families were not labeled as dysfunctional or de-stabilized by prison expansion and welfare "reform," our children would not be removed from their homes at the numbers they are, and there would be no need for adoption or foster care in the first place. So the fact that the white gay community continues to use white images of same-sex families is no accident, since the black family, heterosexual, same sex or otherwise, is always portrayed as dysfunctional.

I also think the white gay community's supposed "understanding" of racism is what has caused them to appropriate the language and ideology of the Black Civil Rights Movement, which has led to the bitter divide between the two communities. This is where I, as a black gay man, am forced to intervene in a debate that I find problematic on all sides.

BLACK COMMUNITY AND GAY COMMUNITY— NATURAL ALLIES OR SWORN ENEMIES?

As the gay community moved more to the right in the 1990s, they also began to talk about Gay Rights as Civil Rights. Even today in this gay marriage debate, I have heard countless well-groomed, well-fed white gays and lesbians on TV referring to themselves as "second-class citizens." Jason West, the white mayor of New Paltz, NY, who started marrying gay couples was quoted as saying, "The same people who don't want to see gays and lesbians get married are the same people who would have made Rosa Parks go to the back of the bus."

It's these comparisons that piss black people off. While the anger of black heteros is sometimes expressed in ways that are in fact homophobic, the truth of the matter is that black folks are tired of seeing other people hijack their shit for their own gains, and getting nothing in return. Black non-heteros share this anger of having our blackness and black political rhetoric and struggle stolen for other people's gains.

The hijacking of Rosa Parks for their campaigns clearly ignores the fact that white gays and lesbians who lived in Montgomery, AL and elsewhere probably gladly made many a black person go to the back of the bus. James Baldwin wrote in his long essay "No Name in the Street" about how he was felt up by a white sheriff in a small southern town when on a visit during the civil rights era.

These comparisons of "Gay Civil Rights" as equal to "Black Civil Rights" really began in the early 1990s, and largely responsible for this was the Human Rights Campaign (HRC) and a few other mostly-white gay organizations. This push from the HRC, without any visible black leadership or tangible support from black allies (straight and queer), to equate these movements did several things: 1) Pissed off the black community for the white gay movement's cultural appropriation, and made the straight black community question non-hetero black people's allegiances, resulting in our further isolation. 2) Gave the (white) Christian Right ammunition to build relationships with black ministers to denounce gay rights from their pulpits based on the HRC's cultural appropriation. 3) Created a scenario in their effort to go mainstream that equated gay and lesbian with upper-class and white.

This meant that the only visibility of non-hetero poor people and people of color wound up on *Jerry Springer*, where non-heteros who are poor and of color are encouraged (and paid) to act out, and are therefore only represented as dishonest, violent, and pathological.

So, given this difficult history and problematic working relationship of the black community and the gay community, how can the gay community now, at its most crucial hour, expect large scale support of same-sex marriage by the black community when there has been no real work done to build strategic allies with us? A new coalition has formed of black people, non-hetero and hetero, to promote same-sex marriage equality to the black community, and I assume to effectively bridge that disconnect, and to in effect say that gay marriage ain't just a white thing. Or is it?

IS GAY MARRIAGE ANTI-BLACK?

I, as a black gay man, do not support this push for same-sex marriage. Although I don't claim to represent all black gay people, I do believe that the manner in which this campaign has been handled has put black people in the middle of essentially two white groups of people, who are trying to manipulate us one way or the other. The Christian right, which is in fact anti-black, has tried to create a false alliance between themselves and blacks through religion to push forward their homophobic, fascist agenda.

The white gay civil rights groups are also anti-black, however they want black people to see this struggle for same-sex unions as tantamount to separate but equal Jim Crow laws. Yet any close examination reveals that histories of terror imposed upon generations of all black people in this country do not in any way compare to what appears to be the very last barrier between white gays and lesbians' access to what bell hooks describes as "christian capitalist patriarchy."

That system is inherently anti-black, and no amount of civil rights will ever get black people any real liberation from it. For, in what is now a good forty years of "civil rights," nothing has intrinsically changed or altered in the American power structure, and a few black faces in inherently racist institutions is hardly progress.

Given the current white hetero-normative constructions of family and how the institutions of marriage and nuclear families have been used against black people, I do think that to support same-sex marriage is in fact, anti-black (I also believe the institution of marriage to be historically anti-woman, and don't support it for those reasons as well).

At this point I don't know if I am totally opposed to the institution of marriage altogether, but I do know that the campaign would have to happen on very different terms for me to support same-sex marriages. At this point, the white gay community is as much to blame as the Christian Right for the way they have constructed the campaign, including who is represented, and their appropriation of black civil rights language.

Along with how the campaign is currently devised, I struggle with same-sex marriage because, given the level of homophobia in our society (specifically in the black community), and racism as well, I think that even if same-sex marriage becomes legal, white people will access that privilege far more than black people. This is especially the case with poor black people who, regardless of sexual preference or gender, are struggling with the most critical of needs (housing, food, gainful employment), which are not at all met by same-sex marriage.

Some black people (men in particular) might not try to access same-sex marriage because they do not even identify as "gay" partly because of homophobia in the black community, but also because of the fact that racist white queer people continue to dominate the public discourse of what "gay" is, which does not include black people of the hip-hop generation by and large.

I do fully understand that non-heteros of all races and classes may cheer this effort for they want their love to be recognized, and may want to reap some of the practical benefits that a marriage entitlement would bring—health care (if one of you gets health care from your job in the first place) for your spouse, hospital visits without drama or scrutiny, and control over a deceased partner's estate.

But, gay marriage, in and of itself, is not a move towards real and systemic liberation. It does not address my most critical need as a black gay man to be able to walk down the streets of my community with my lover, spouse, or trick, and not be subjected to ridicule, assault, or even murder. Gay marriage does not adequately address homophobia or transphobia, for same-sex marriage still implies binary opposite thinking, and transgender folks are not at all addressed in this debate.

WHAT DOES GAY MARRIAGE MEAN FOR ALL BLACK PEOPLE?

But what does that mean for black people? For black non-heteros, specifically? Am I supposed to get behind this effort, and convince heterosexual black people to do the same, especially when I know the racist manner in which this campaign has been carried out for over ten years? And especially when I know that the vast majority of issues that my community—The Black Community, of all orientations and genders—are not taken nearly this seriously when it comes to crucial life and death issues that we face daily like inadequate housing and health care, HIV/AIDS, police brutality, and the wholesale lockdown of an entire generation in America's grotesquely large prison system.

How do those of us who are non-heterosexual and black use this as an opportunity to deal with homophobia, transphobia, and misogyny in our communities, and heal those larger wounds of isolation, marginalization and fear that plague us regardless of marital status? It is the undoing of systems of domination and control that will lead to liberation for all of ourselves, and all of us as a whole.

In the end, I am down for black people who oppose gay marriage—other folks "in the life" as well as straight, feminists, Christians, Muslims, and the like. But I want more than just quotes from Leviticus or other religious and moral posturing. I want to engage in a meaningful critical conversation of what this means for *all* of us, which means that I must not be afraid to *be* me in our community, and you must not be afraid *of* me. I will struggle alongside you, but I must know that you will also have my back.

Marriage is Still the Opiate of the Queers

KATE AND DEEG

"We want the abolition of the institution of the bourgeois nuclear family. We believe that the bourgeois nuclear family perpetuates the false categories of homosexuality and heterosexuality by creating sex roles, sex definitions and sexual exploitation. The bourgeois nuclear family as the basic unit of capitalism creates oppressive roles of homosexuality and heterosexuality... It is every child's right to develop in a non-sexist, non-racist, non-possessive atmosphere which is the responsibility of all people, including gays, to create."
—"Third World Gay Liberation Manifesto," New York City (circa 1970)

"The struggle for civil rights within the context of this society can, at best, result in second class status and toleration by a wretched straight society. The struggle for democratic or civil rights assumes that the system is basically okay, and that its flaws can be corrected through legal reform.... We

---

This piece, which includes a reprint of another text by the same authors from 1996, originally appeared in the April 2004 issue of UltraViolet.

demand the right of all lesbians and gay men, and children to live in the manner we choose."

—"Gay Liberation, Not Just Gay Rights!" LAGAI, Lavender Left (Los Angeles) and Lesbian and Gay Liberation and Solidarity Committee (New York), 1987

A specter is haunting Amerikkka.

The specter of gay marriage.

Every few years, it seems, we have a new wave of push and counter-push on the marriage issue, and we are always in the same unpleasant position. We demand all civil rights for queer people.

But marriage isn't a civil right. It's a civil wrong.

Just because George W., Pete KKKnight and the KKKristian RR-Right don't want us to get married, doesn't mean we have to want to.

In 1996, we held our legendary First Ever Mass Gay Divorce on Castro Street, where a good time was had by all at the dish breaking booth and the Go Your Separate Ways Travel Agency. At that time, we wrote the following flier:

> Remember us? We are lesbians and gay men, the people who choose love, and sex, over societal acceptance, over physical security, over the almighty buck.

> We pursue our love into the cities and towns where we find each other. What a wonderful variety of relationships we have—from anonymous or casual sex in baths, bathrooms and beaches, to long-term monogamy and everything (and everyone) in between. We say, "the state can't tell us who, or how, to love." We say, "Get your laws off my body." So how exactly does that become a plea to the state to marry us? Will having state-defined relationships make us better lovers? It hasn't done much for hets.

> We always thought that one of the good things about being a lesbian, or gay man, is that you don't have to get married. Many of us have parents who are or were married, and really, it's nothing to write home about.

The heterosexual nuclear family is the most dangerous place to be. A woman is beaten every fifteen seconds. One girl in three is sexually molested by the time she reaches maturity. According to the National Coalition to Prevent Child Abuse, one million children were abused last year, and 1,000 were killed. 46 percent of the murdered children were not yet one year old.

We're here today because we were lucky enough to survive these odds.

When our gay leaders talk about how gay marriage will support the institution of marriage in this society, we have to agree. We would oppose it for this reason alone. It is interesting that while assimilationists clamor for gay marriage, the right wing is trying to hold straight marriages together by eliminating no-fault divorce. Strange bedfellows?

Gay marriage might give some married gay people access to health care, tax breaks, and immigration rights. But shouldn't our community be fighting for us all to have access to health care, whatever our "marital status?" The same for immigration. Somehow, in these right-wing times, money, goods, and jobs are free to flow across the border, but not people. Shouldn't everyone be able to live where they want to, who made these borders anyhow? And why should any married people pay less taxes? What assimilationist gays are really asking is that the heterosexuals share some of their privilege with queers who want to be like them.

There is a basic conflict here, between those who see the gay movement as a way to gain acceptance in straight society, and lesbians and gay men who are fighting to create a society in our own image. A decent and humane society where we can be free. We do not want the crumbs from this society's table, and we are not fighting for a place at it. We want to overturn the fucking table.

Assimilation is NOT liberation

We couldn't have said it better. Oh, yeah, we did say it.

The origins of the LGBTQ movement are revolutionary. The rebellions at Stonewall and San Francisco City Hall were led by drag queens and butches who rejected heterosexual roles and restrictions, who were inspired by the revolutionary example of the Black Panthers and the Women's International Terrorist Conspiracy from Hell (WITCH). Now, some of the same people who participated in those fabulous outpourings of anti-establishment rage tripped over each other on the way to City Hall to have their love blessed by Gavin Newsom, successor to Dan White and Dianne Feinstein, darling of the developers, persecutor of the homeless, and the cause of Gay Shame getting beaten and busted by the cops on more than one occasion.

For many older lesbian and gay couples, who recall the days when they could not go to a bar without fear, the chance for official sanction of their love feels like a chance for acceptance after a lifetime of oppression. We respect their choice. But we continue to demand that we honor all our relationships, not just the ones that mimic straight capitalist society.

We remind queer people everywhere that we did not survive the early days of the AIDS epidemic because of the relationships between one man and one man, but because of the strong love of our communities: the health care teams of gay men, lesbians, fag hags and chosen families who spent days and weeks hanging around the intensive care units of Kaiser and Pacific Presbyterian Medical Center, refusing to leave when told "family only," fighting bitterly with biological family members who showed up trying to cram their loved ones into a box and whisk them back to Iowa or New Jersey to be buried with crosses or talismans.

According to a 2004 General Accounting Office report, there are 1,138 federal rights and responsibilities that are automatically accorded to married people. Why should we fight for 1,138 rights for some people, instead of all rights for all people? If Freedom to Marry and the Human Rights Campaign Fund (of course, what can you expect from the folks who brought you the equals sign?) put the resources they have already spent on the "right" to get married into fighting for health coverage for all residents of this rich country (not "virtually all Americans" as "promised" by future president John Kerry) and housing for all the queer youth kicked out by their families and living on the streets, we would have a much better world by now.

Every so-called communist organization in town is suddenly joining the battle cry for marriage. Huh? Have they forgotten their Engels? It is testimony to the fundamental homophobia of the left that they are only comfortable fighting for the most puritan of queer rights. Where were they when the bathhouses were being closed? The left has never recognized queer liberation as the truly revolutionary movement that it is. It is time they did.

The right-wingers say marriage is a sacred religious institution. We agree. The state has no business getting involved in religious institutions, from sanctioning personal unions to legislating what schoolgirls should wear on their heads.

Of course, we too will be fighting to defeat the anti-queer marriage amendments. How can we not? But we resent having to do it, and we will not allow it to distract us from our real needs: equality, justice, self-determination, and self-actualization for ALL. Just because you are not someone's significant other, does not mean you are insignificant.

The Marriage Fight is Setting Us Back

JOHN D'EMILIO

EVEN BEFORE THE MORNING PAPER was delivered to my door, I had a long string of e-mails from news groups and organizations announcing the decision in the New York same-sex marriage case. Once again, a major defeat. Over the next weeks, a few more piled up. In the last dozen years, in almost every one of the fifty states, overwhelming majorities in state legislatures or lopsided votes in ballot referenda have reaffirmed that marriage is the union of a man and a woman.

Even the few victories for seekers of the right to marry have morphed into defeats. Legislators and voters undid favorable court opinions in Hawaii and Alaska. And, thanks to the insistence of marriage activists that only the real thing will do, the enactment of civil unions in Vermont and Connecticut and marriage-type rights in California and New Jersey have come to seem like a consolation prize, a spruced-up version of inferiority.

Please, can we speak the truth? The campaign for same-sex marriage has been an unmitigated disaster. Never in the history of organized

This piece originally appeared in the November–December 2006 issue of The Gay and Lesbian Review.

queerdom have we seen defeats of this magnitude. The battle to win marriage equality through the courts has done something that no other campaign or issue in our movement has done: it has created a vast body of new antigay law. Alas for us, as the anthropologist Gayle Rubin has so cogently observed, "sex laws are notoriously easy to pass.... Once they are on the books, they are extremely difficult to dislodge."

While outrage and shock over judicial defeats make for good quotes in the press, this disaster should surprise only those activists and ideologues who are utterly convinced of their own rectitude and wisdom. Their determination to get marriage has blinded them to the glaring flaws in the strategy of making marriage equality the prime goal of the gay and lesbian movement, and litigation the main way to achieve it. For one thing, the federal courts and many state courts have grown steadily more conservative for a generation. Did any one really believe that the courts in this era would lead the way on marriage equality?

Then, too, our ever more right-of-center Supreme Court, to which this issue must finally come, has not generally led in struggles for social justice. Rather, it has tended to intervene as a new social consensus develops. Decisions like *Brown v. Board of Education* and *Roe v. Wade* do not prove that social movements should turn to the courts to deliver justice. Instead they show that litigation produces the desired results only after a lot of groundwork outside the courts has been laid. What groundwork for same-sex marriage had been laid when the first cases went forward in the 1990s? What groundwork had been laid for the more recent cases that marriage activists pushed forward *after* countless legislatures and hordes of voters reaffirmed that marriage is the union of a man and a woman?

But putting aside the tactical stupidity of the marriage activist, if there's a single overarching reason why their determined focus on same-sex marriage has disturbed me, it is this: in the deepest, most profound sense, the campaign for marriage equality runs *against history*.

The last half-century has seen one of the most remarkable social transformations in U.S. history. A group of people despised by virtually everyone, hounded and pursued by government officials and law enforcement agents, condemned by every significant religious tradition, and pathologized by scientific experts now has taken its place among the panoply of groups—ethnic, racial, religious—that claim recognition and legitimacy in public life. A group of people who, five decades ago, went to great lengths to mask their sexual identity from anyone who didn't share it now goes to great lengths to display it in every possible venue—at family gatherings and alumni reunions, in occupational associations and workplaces, at school and in places of worship, in massive parades and international athletic competitions. This is quite extraordinary.

How did this happen? As someone who has researched, written about, and participated in our political movement for more than thirty years, I have a bias toward attributing the change to the power of organized collective activism. Lots of individuals saying "this is intolerable and has to change" and then banding together to do something about it has been vital.

AIDS, too, has had something to do with it. Within a few concentrated years it drove out of the closet huge numbers of us, who in turn built a vast network of organizations, engaged with a broad range of institutions, and made demands of public officials. AIDS proved a much more effective mobilizer of people than either the call of sexual freedom or the lure of smashing patriarchy.

But when I put my activist bias aside, the only way to really understand the remarkable transformation in queer life since the 1950s is to move beyond specific events, campaigns, and motivators—beyond Stonewall, Anita Bryant, AIDS. Instead, I have to acknowledge that over the last half-century we have been carried along in the wake of some deep and broad transformations in the patterns of everyday life in the U.S. Think, for a minute, of 1950s television: *Father Knows Best*, *Leave It to Beaver*, *The Donna Reed Show*—all those happy white families, living in nice houses, with mom tending the home and dad at work. Pregnancy out of marriage was a scandal to be hidden away. Divorce was a shameful failure. Childlessness was a pitiable tragedy. In this environment, faggots and dykes were beyond the pale, regarded as deviant and dangerous.

Starting in the 1960s, all this began to change. Divorce became increasingly commonplace. Even with greater access to abortion, large numbers of women had children outside of marriage. The number of single-parent households grew. Cohabitation of unmarried men and women became so widespread that the Bureau of the Census began to categorize and count the phenomenon. Women's participation in the paid labor force skyrocketed. Birth rates sank to replacement levels. The living arrangements of heterosexual Americans became bewilderingly varied. Over the course of a lifetime an individual might move in with a partner, break up with that partner and find another, get married, have a child, get divorced, cohabit with someone else who also had a child (or didn't), break up again, cohabit again, marry again, and become a stepparent. Throughout this saga, all the adults involved were working for a living.

A succinct way of describing these changes is this: *Since the early 1960s, the lives of many, many heterosexuals have become much more like the imagined lives of homosexuals.* Being heterosexual no longer means settling as a young adult into a lifelong coupled relationship sanctioned by the state and characterized by the presence of children and sharply gendered spousal roles. Instead, there may be a number of intimate relationships over the course of a lifetime. A marriage certificate may or may not accompany these relationships. Males and females alike expect to earn their way. Children figure less importantly in the lifespan of adults, and some heterosexuals, for the first time in history, choose not to have children at all.

These changes are not aberrational, not temporary, and not reversible. Neither a decline in morality nor the cultural turbulence of the 1960s explains them. They were not caused by a media culture that exploits sex. Instead, these changes are joined at the hip with the revolutionary growth in economic productivity and technological innovation to which capitalism has given rise and that now have their own momentum. These new "lifestyles" (a word woefully inadequate for grasping the deep structural foundations that sustain these changes) have appeared wherever capitalism has long historical roots. The decline in reproductive rates and the de-centering of marriage follow the spread of capitalism as surely as night follows day. They surface even in the face of religious traditions and national histories that have emphasized marriage, high fertility, and strong kinship ties.

If you need more evidence that the new shape of social life is not a passing heterosexual phase, look at the pathetic failure of efforts to reverse these trends. Since the mid-1970s, the most dynamic and aggressive force in American politics has been the evangelical Christian Right. It has the numbers, the money, the organization, the passion. It can send people into voting booths like no other group in the U.S. Evangelical conservatives have made issues of family and sexual morality the centerpiece of their message and their mobilizations. Because of them, abortions are harder to get, an abstinence-only message dominates sex education, and pre-marital counseling has become the rage. Yet the birth rate remains low, the young are still having sex and cohabiting, and divorce is commonplace.

Grasping the revolutionary change in the lives of heterosexuals in the last half-century lets us put a whole different spin on the transformation in the status of gays and lesbians in the U.S. in the same time period. The huge steps toward visibility, toward acceptance, toward integration, toward equality—and they have been huge—have come, fundamentally, because the life course of heterosexuals has become more like ours. We've made gains not because we've shown heterosexuals that we are just like them, or because we've persuaded them to respect our "differences," but because many of them have become so much like us that they find us less threatening, less dangerous, less strange. In other words, for the last several decades, our lives have been flowing with the powerful current of social and cultural change. We have been swimming with history, not against it.

And then along comes same-sex marriage. Or, rather, along come some yearning couples, plus a band of activists to support them, single-minded in their pursuit of marriage equality. They confuse ordinarily intelligent queers by purveying the line that full dignity, full respect, and full citizenship will come only when gays and lesbians have achieved unobstructed access to marriage.

It doesn't surprise me that, on balance, the results have been grim. Had we tried to devise a strategy that took advantage of the force of historical trends, we would, as a movement, have been pushing to further de-center and de-institutionalize marriage. Once upon a time, we did. In the 1980s and early 1990s, imaginative queer activists invented such things as "domestic partnership" and "second-parent adoption" as ways of recognizing the plethora of family arrangements that exist throughout the United States. AIDS activists pressed for such things as universal health insurance that would have decoupled perhaps the most significant benefit that marriage offers. (A great irony: universal health care, which has seemed so remote in the conservative era that Reagan ushered in, could more successfully have been fought for state-by-state than could same-sex marriage.)

I don't think it's too much to ask that our organizational leadership, especially at the national level, pursue intelligent strategies. Nor is it too much to ask that they have the courage to say "this isn't working" and make a major course correction. We're already going to have to live with the negative results of their misjudgments for a long time. Please stop throwing good money after bad. And, please, make history be something that works for us instead of racing into the wind against history.

Postscript: Since I drafted this essay, the Washington State Supreme Court has issued a ruling upholding the state's ban on same-sex marriage. Gay leaders have once again expressed shock and anger at the decision and have pledged to keep fighting for marriage equality. Fortunately, the same day as the Washington decision, a group of queer activists who are mostly outside the network of "mainstream" GLBT organizations have released a document, "Beyond Same-Sex Marriage: A New Strategic Vision for All Our Families and Relationships, " that calls for a shift in direction. Over 200 activists and intellectuals have signed it (full disclosure: I'm one of the signatories). Could this be a new beginning?

Against Equality, In Maine and Everywhere

RYAN CONRAD

IN THE AFTERMATH OF THE losing battle for gay marriage rights in Maine, many local queer and trans activists have been left wondering how we even got here in the first place. And the more troubling question is: who is going to clean up this mess? How did gay marriage become "the issue" in Maine and how did so many LGBTA folks get duped into making this campaign their top priority, emotionally, financially and otherwise, by the shallow rhetoric of equality? If we, as a radical queer community, are to prevent the de-prioritization and de-funding of critical queer and trans community issues/organizations/services, the campaign in Maine must be dissected and used as a case study to learn from. Our queerest futures depend on it!

MAINE IN CONTEXT: MATERIAL CONDITIONS/ POLITICAL POSITIONINGS

Maine is one of the poorest states in the country with a majority of its manufacturing outsourced overseas and its agricultural industries

This piece originally appeared online at The Bilerico Project *(bilerico. com) and in print with* UltraViolet *in late fall of 2009.*

struggling to keep up with the rising costs of doing business. The state ranks 43rd out of all states when measuring average annual income and has the 15th highest unemployment rate in the nation.[1] To say that the economy in Maine is struggling is an understatement, and employment/poverty is a major concern for working class queer and trans folks.

Maine is also the largest New England state, covering an area greater than all the other New England states combined with a population about the same size as Rhode Island. Maine's overwhelmingly white population and most of its wealth is concentrated along the coast, particularly in the southern part of the state. As in many other states in the U.S., this creates a dichotomy of rural poor versus urban wealth that is often translated to conservative versus liberal. It's not that there aren't rich people from Boston buying second homes in the rural areas down east or abject poverty in small cities like Lewiston and Waterville, but the overwhelming trend points towards a paradigm of rural poverty in most of the state. Organizing a truly statewide campaign across such a large, rural, poor area is particularly challenging.

Under these material conditions queer and trans folks in Maine have been fighting for their lives. For over a decade the state struggled to pass and uphold an addendum to the state's human rights act that gave non-discrimination protections to LGBT folks in housing, employment, and credit. The non-discrimination law, once vetoed by the governor after passing legislation in 1993 and overturned twice by referendum in 1998 and 2000, was finally upheld in referendum in 2005 by a narrow margin.[2] The stranglehold of the conservative Christian right appeared to be weakening over the last two decades, but the bitter taste of defeat at the polls in the past still hadn't left our mouths upon entering the gay marriage referendum.

Outside of the political arena, queer and trans folks in Maine have continued to face anti-queer violence in their communities, in their homes, and on the streets of even the most gay-friendly towns. The gruesome murder of Scott A. Libby in Raymond in 2009,[3] the gay bashing of a man in Portland to the point of unconsciousness in 2008,[4] and the complete destruction of two lesbians' home and car in Poland in 2006 serve as just a few examples.[5] They don't just want us to not get married, they want us dead!

THIS WEDDING CAKE IS ROTTEN

Gays and lesbians of all ages are obsessing over gay marriage as if it's going to cure AIDS, stop anti-queer/anti-trans violence, provide all uninsured queers with health care, and reform racist immigration policies. Unfortunately, marriage does little more than consolidate even more power in the hands of already privileged gay couples engaged in middle class hetero-mimicry.

Let's be clear: the national gay marriage campaign is NOT a social justice movement. Gay marriage reinforces the for-profit medical industrial complex by tying access to health care to employment and relational status. Gay marriage does not challenge patent laws that keep poor/working-class poz folks from accessing life-extending medications. Gay marriage reinforces the nuclear family as the primary support structure for youth even though nuclear families are largely responsible for queer teen homelessness, depression, and suicide. Gay marriage does not challenge economic systems set up to champion people over property and profit. Gay marriage reinforces racist immigration laws by only allowing productive, "good", soon-to-be-wed, non-citizens in while ignoring the rights of migrant workers. Gay marriage simply has nothing to do with social justice.

AN OPPORTUNISTIC NATIONAL STRATEGY

The national strategy for gay marriage is much larger and more insidious than most expect. Maine was used as a pawn in a much larger scheme to pressure the federal government to take up the issue. Even though LGBTQ-identified Mainers spoke loud and clear about their priorities at both the statewide symposium convened by the Maine Community Foundation's Equity Fund in 2007 and in a pre-election poll put out by the Family Affairs Newsletter (FAN) in January 2009, somehow we still found ourselves in the midst of a $6-million campaign for someone else's priority. The FAN found that nearly 70% of their readers did not identify marriage as their top priority issue[6] and the symposium's 4,000-word summary only mentions gay marriage in one sentence positively.[7] Gay marriage is mentioned twice in the document, but in the second instance it is referenced negatively by youth at the conference who saw the gay marriage issue as pressuring them to live up to unwanted heteronormative expectations.[8]

Most of the rights and privileges cited by the talking heads of the gay marriage movement are actually doled out by the Federal government and not individual states, thus the needed pressure from regional blocks on the federal government. These 1,138 rights are cited by the General Accounting Office of the United States Government and largely pertain to the transfer of property and money.[9] If Maine had won with the popular vote, there would have been a greater opportunity to push the federal government to move on the issue as an entire regional block would be able to apply more serious pressure than through the piecemeal process of states legislating in favor of gay marriage across the country here and there.

This national influence was seen in Portland on election night when both the executive director from the Human Rights Campaign (Joe Solmonese) and the National Gay and Lesbian Task Force (Rea Carey) showed up to give the crowd a pep talk. Even more telling was the $400,000+ dollars contributed by the HRC and NGLTG combined, as well as in-kind staff time.[10] If the NGLTF or HRC were interested in improving the lives of queer and trans Mainers, they would have given this kind of funding to issues actually outlined as critical at the statewide symposium and not to a bunch of power-consolidating homo-politicos in Portland.

More money continued to roll in from other gay marriage groups in Massachusetts, Vermont, California, Colorado, Oregon, and New Jersey;[11] all recent gay marriage winners or soon-to-be-pawns in the state-by-state game to pressure the feds, whether the issue is a local priority or not.

FOLLOWING THE MONEY

The gay-marriage campaign has been sucking up resources like a massive sponge, corralling everyone to give up their last dollar and free time, leaving little sustenance for other queer groups doing critical work in our communities. An Equality Maine campaign letter had the audacity to claim that gay marriage is "the fight for our lives." I wonder whose lives they are talking about, when AIDS service organizations and community health/reproductive clinics across the state have been tightening their belts and desperately trying to crunch numbers so that more queer folks don't end up unemployed, uninsured, or worse yet, dead. These organizations include clinics like Western Maine Community Action Health Services; AIDS service organizations like Down East AIDS Network, Eastern Maine AIDS Network, Maine AIDS Alliance, the Frannie Peabody Center; and queer/trans youth support groups like Out as I Want to Be, Outrageously Supportive, Outright L/A and PRYSM.

In addition, over the last few years we have seen the Maine Speak Out Project and the Charlie Howard Memorial Library close their doors in Portland while the few remaining LGBT youth advocacy groups across the state scrounge just to keep their doors open after most of them folded in the late nineties. The Department of Education has also announced that it will no longer be funding HIV Prevention Outreach Educators as of June 2010. A particularly horrifying scenario for the queer community here, as queer men account for 67% of people living with HIV in Maine.[12]

While essential services are disappearing, organizations are closing, and new gaps in services for aging LGBTQ folks are being identified, the marriage campaign in Maine is spending money with abandon. The "No on 1" group spent close to $6 million over the duration of the campaign,[13] taking in $1.4 million in donations in the first three weeks of October alone.[14] In a state with a tanking economy, this kind of reckless spending on a single issue campaign that isn't even a top priority for most LGBT folks is blatant and unrestrained classism at its worst.

To put this budget in perspective, the largest funding source for LGBT organizations in the state is the Equity Fund, which only distributes $40,000 a year amongst the numerous LGBT applicant organizations.[15] At the current fiscal rate, it would take the Equity Fund about 135 years to catch up with the spending accrued in one year by the Maine's gay marriage campaign. Imagine what kind of change could be made if that $6 million was used to support organizational capacity building and programming of those organizations providing essential services and advocacy that the Equity Fund supports with their meager budget. This kind of long-term approach to advocating real change seems like an obvious preference to throwing money down the drain in single-issue legislative campaigns.

CULTURAL CHANGE VS. LEGISLATIVE CHANGE

Changing a law in a book does much less to create an atmosphere of safety for queer and trans folks than long-term cultural change. In fact, in Maine the gay marriage law and referendum has conjured more re-actionary anti-queer violence than before. This can be seen quite clearly in Maine where the platform for people to air their homophobic grievances became massively public. This overwhelming outpouring of homophobic vitriol via every kind of media outlet and public forum imaginable has had a terrible impact on LGBT youths' mental health in particular. One needs no further proof than volunteering at one of the few remaining queer and trans youth advocacy organizations in the poorer part of the state like I do in Androscoggin County. Here youth have been utterly demoralized, openly gay bashed in school and town newspapers, and some even banned from starting a Gay Straight Alliance in their Somerset County High School because of homophobic school staff citing the gay marriage campaigns as too controversial.

The focus of this campaign was to win the referendum by getting out the vote in winnable parts of the state, ie. metro-Portland and the coast, leaving the already most vulnerable queers in the rural parts of the state to fend for themselves while the campaign drums up homophobic fervor across the inland counties. Those abandoned by the faux statewide campaign in the rural parts of the state have no support organizations to turn to once the campaign is over as they do not exist or barely do. Furthermore, even if gay marriage had passed, would it even be safe to get gay married in most of the state? Quite clearly, no. And again, power and privilege remain among those who already had them to begin with.

Some suggest that gay marriage is part of a progress narrative and that it is a step in the right direction towards more expansive social justice issues. This largely ignores a critique of power. Once privilege is doled out to middle class gay couples, are they going to continue on to fight against racist immigration policies, for universal health care, for comprehensive queer/trans inclusive sex education, or to free queers unjustly imprisoned during rabidly homophobic sex-abuse witch hunts?[16] Doubtful is an overstatement. It's more likely they will be enjoying summer vacations at an expensive bed and breakfast in Ogunquit while the rest of us are still trying to access basic rights like health care and freedom of movement. Let's be real: privilege breeds complacency.

QUEER FUTURES AGAINST EQUALITY

The for/against dichotomy setup by the gay marriage movement and the homophobic legislative pandering of the Christian right is an absolute distraction.

If we are to imagine queer futures that don't replicate the same violence and oppression many of us experience on an everyday basis as queer and trans folks, we must challenge the middle class neo-liberal war machine known as the national gay marriage campaign. We must fight the rhetoric of equality and inclusion in systems of domination like marriage and the military, and stop believing that our participation in those institutions is more important than questioning those institutions legitimacy all together. We need to call out the national marriage campaign as opportunistic and parasitic. We must challenge their money mongering tactics to assure our local, truly community based LGBT organizations aren't left financially high and dry while offering the few essential services to the most marginalized of our community. Let Maine be an early example of why we must continue to fight against equality.

NOTES

1. U.S. Census Bureau, *2009 Statistical Abstract: State Rankings*.
2. http://www.equalitymaine.org/the-issues/non-discrimination.
3. http://scottlibby.blogspot.com.

4. "Suspect Sought in Alleged Hate Crime," *Portland Press Herald*, 10 September 2008, http://news.mainetoday.com/updates/032723.html.
5. "Couple Calls Vandalism a Hate Crime," WGME 13, 19 July 2006, http://www.wmtw.com/news/9543231/detail.html?rss=port&psp=new.
6. *Family Affairs Newsletter*, Bangor, 15 January 2009.
7. *LGBT Symposium 2007: Strengthening Communities, Building Alliances Summary Report*, 2008.
8. Ibid.
9. General Accounting Office, "Categories of Law Involving Marital Status," 1997, http://gao.gov/archive/1997/og97016.pdf.
10. *Follow the Money*, http://www.followthemoney.org/database/StateGlance/committee.phtml?c=3925.
11. Ibid.
12. "Maine Comprehensive HIV/AIDS Prevention Plan 2004–2008," HIV Epidemiological Data Provided by Maine Bureau of Health, 2003.
13. *Follow the Money*, http://www.followthemoney.org/press/ReportView.phtml?r=404.
14. Miller, Kevin. "MoneyFueling Battle Over Gay Marriage," *Bangor Daily News*, 24 October 2009.
15. "Summary of Recent Grants from the Equity Fund 2008," http://www.mainecf.org/grants/recentgrants/equitygrants.aspx
16. Bernard Baran Justice Committee, http://www.freebaran.org.

Who's Illegal Now?

Immigration, Marriage, and the Violence of Inclusion

YASMIN NAIR

IF YOU SPENT ANY TIME at all this past summer walking down a busy street in a city like Chicago, you would have run into one of the countless young people representing the Human Rights Campaign (HRC). Without a doubt, he or she was wearing what seems to be the designated uniform of the legions of (paid) recruits for "marriage equality": an American Apparel t-shirt with the words "Legalize Gay" emblazoned across it.

If you were the sort of unthinking liberal/progressive towards whom this shirt was aimed, you would have nodded in assent and eagerly signed on to whatever petition/membership drive was waved at you by the HRC representative. Yes, you would have thought, in your well-meaning if somewhat clueless and ahistorical way, we must "legalize gay." But anyone with a modicum of sense and, oh, a sense of

Versions of this piece originally appeared on Queercents *(queercents.com) and* The Bilerico Project *(bilerico.com) in May 2009.*

history would have wondered, as I do: who, exactly, is illegal here? Does the admonition make either grammatical or political sense?

Are gays now illegal? Are the streets now filled with police roaming the streets in Humvees, guns drawn and mouths tightly clenched, looking for gays to throw into a giant gay gulag? Is it now forbidden to be a man who wears pink? Are men driven out of hairdressing salons and interior design firms? Are we now forbidden from watching *Glee*? I mean, no, really, who's illegal now?

As it turns out, the ubiquitous t-shirt (go to any gay event and the damn thing appears on at least a dozen torsos within spitting distance) has an interesting history, one that is implicated in the sordid machinations of the "marriage equality" movement and which shamelessly exploits the hard-won civil rights battles of this country.

The t-shirt first popped up into view immediately after the passage of Proposition 8 in California, and was featured on the AA website in a range of colors, including teal and pink (how gay!), with the words "Repeal Prop 8" directly below "Legalize Gay." The promotional material went on to say: "In the fall of 2008, Proposition 8 passed in California, striking down the legalization of same-sex marriage. Now the decision rests in the hands of California's Supreme Court, with state lawmakers declaring the vote unconstitutional. Equal rights for all—repeal Prop 8."

Now that Prop 8 has been struck down, the slogan has become the unofficial motto of the HRC, which shamelessly pretends that it was originally crafted for it by AA when, in fact, what it means is that the current manifestation of the shirt as seen on its own website, with a tiny version of the HRC equals sign, was designed by AA. This is, of course, typical of the HRC, which would, if it could, claim that it was there at the dawn of time when gays were created.

But the "Legalize Gay" t-shirt provides more than a catchy slogan for the "marriage equality" movement. The words serve to first perpetuate a fiction of illegality (we are to assume that "gay" is now "illegal") and then yoke marriage to both a domestic history of civil rights battles and the contentious issue of immigration. The specious connection to marriage is easy to locate, as we saw above, while the one to immigration is more complicated—but both are made in equally problematic ways.

The t-shirts are a variation on AA's "Legalize L.A." t-shirts, part of the company's attempt to market itself as an immigrant-rights-friendly entity. Founded in 1997 by Dov Charney, AA became famous for being the largest U.S. clothing manufacturer based entirely in this country. In other words, AA does not outsource its manufacturing, pays its workers between $11–$18 an hour, and claims to be sweatshop free. But the company is also anti-union—and management has reportedly gone about strenuously and aggressively busting any attempts to form one. Which begs the question: how can any corporation be worker-friendly and anti-union? In early 2010, AA was subjected to an Immigration and Customs Enforcement (ICE) raid on its workers, of whom 2,500 were found to be undocumented (ICE puts the number closer to 1,500). More recently, in the summer of 2010, AA has seen its profits drop steeply. Charney has blamed the company's financial woes on his loss of employees due to the ICE crackdowns. Predictions for AA's economic health are, at the time of this writing, dire.

Charney's woes hardly end at the business side of the corporation. He has, from the outset, been sharply criticized for what many consider sexist advertisements, featuring young and thin models in various enticing poses (how and why these are any different from what appears in the pages of *Vogue* magazine is a mystery that has never been addressed by his critics). More significantly, he has faced sexual harassment charges from former female employees. Through it all, Charney has managed to skate on his bad boy image but the allure of that reputation may be fading in light of his financial troubles. Sure, we like our bad boys—but we also want them to be *successful* bad boys.

AA was teetering towards a downslide around the time of Proposition 8, so it is not outlandish to assume that the "Legalize Gay" t-shirt was just one more way for it to curry favor with a population of consumers that most marketing experts define as upwardly mobile to well-off, buying into the stereotype that "gay" is a class identity unto itself.

The slogan "Legalize Gay" presents a visible and entirely fictitious suggestion that to be gay is illegal while simultaneously erasing the very troubling ways in which the undocumented labor that makes the t-shirts is literally rendered illegal. In fact: after *Lawrence v. Texas*, sodomy is no longer illegal. In 1991, U.S. Attorney Janet Reno lifted the ban on gay and lesbian immigrants. While several states still lack explicit anti-discrimination laws against the LGBT population, to be gay is not illegal—you cannot be hauled away for being discovered as gay. Sure, gays and lesbians might not be allowed to marry in several states but this has not meant that those with otherwise unblemished records can no longer leave their houses, or buy cars, or keep their jobs.

Do people wearing this t-shirt have a clue what it really means to be illegal? To be, for instance, an "illegal alien" who gets swept up in an Immigration and Customs Enforcement raid and is deported soon thereafter? To be unable to travel freely because they lack the proper documentation? To pay for their school tuition and rent in cash because they lack social security numbers?

It is not just the undocumented whose lives are effectively erased by this t-shirt, but the millions who are being funneled into the prison industrial complex in order to increase its profits. According to Bob Libal, co-author of *Operation Streamline: Drowning Justice and Draining Dollars along the Rio Grande*, Texas alone has diverted an estimated 1.2 billion federal dollars "into warehousing the undocumented in predominantly for-profit private jails and detention centers, while they await trial or serve sentences prior to deportation." Over the last decade or so, more of the undocumented are detained, often indefinitely, for non-violent and petty crimes, and the increased numbers inflate the perception that the undocumented are inherently criminal while expanding the prison industrial complex. The numbers have exploded because the PIC has been relentlessly creating new categories of "illegal aliens," and putting people in jail for longer periods of time.

The "Legalize Gay" t-shirt allows the wearer to smugly pose as "illegal" while cluelessly erasing the reality that millions are actually made illegal in the terms dictated by draconian laws around immigration and the prison industrial complex, which create new and ever-shifting categories of illegality for immigrants.

While the t-shirt erases the reality of immigration, "marriage equality" advocates are also attempting to appropriate the issue of immigration reform with a focus on the Uniting American Families Act (UAFA). Groups like Immigration Equality (IE) will pay scant attention to other matters which affect queer immigrants, like the now-lifted

ban on HIV-positive people or asylum on the basis of sexual orientation, and their slight attention to these serves as a smokescreen for their
emphasis on the UAFA, a piece of legislation which essentially seeks
to provide the benefits of marriage to gay and lesbian citizens and permanent residents and their non-citizen partners. Under U.S. law, and
under specific legal circumstances, a citizen or permanent resident is
allowed to sponsor their spouse for immigration. Given that gay marriage is not federally recognized, gays and lesbians cannot do the same;
the UAFA seeks to correct that by replicating the visa requirements
for same-sex partners. It essentially substitutes the phrase "permanent
partnership" for "spouse" wherever applicable in immigration law.

The UAFA was first introduced as the Permanent Partners Act of
2000 and eventually re-named, presumably to add more affect by
evoking the specter of families torn apart. It has frequently died in
committee but was recently galvanized by the situation of Shirley Tan
and her family. Tan came here in 1986 as a tourist, and overstayed her
visa in order to remain with her partner Jay Mercado who was, like her,
originally from the Philippines. Mercado is currently a citizen, but Tan
is still undocumented. They have been domestic partners for a while,
according to a *People* article, and even wed in 2004. Tan gave birth to
their twin sons who are both citizens. In 1995, Tan applied for asylum
because, in 1979, according to her, a cousin shot her in the head and
killed her mother and sister. In 2002, ICE (Immigration and Customs
Enforcement) served Tan with an order of deportation, but the couple
claim to never have received it. Finally, in 2009, ICE agents showed up
at the couple's Pacifica, California home and arrested her. At the time
of this writing, Tan has been able to obtain stays on her deportation
while she waits to hear about the fate of the UAFA.

Immigration Equality and other supporters of the UAFA have made
Shirley Tan and her family members the poster children for a piece of
legislation that, they claim, would guarantee that binational couples
like the Tan-Mercados are able to stay together. In the process, they
have continued to emphasize the sheer American-ness of Tan and her
family (Her kids play soccer! She's a stay-at-home mom! She sings in
the choir!) while, in not-so-subtle ways, marking her as the preferable
alternative to those *other* nasty "illegals." In the same *People* article,

Rachel Tiven of IE was quoted as saying, "*They* are exactly the kinds of immigrants you want in this country" (emphasis mine). Right. The others can just rot in hell. You know the ones they mean—the day laborers who move from job to job, underpaid and overexploited; the low-paid workers who build suburban houses for us on the cheap as opposed to living in them; and so on.

As queer immigration rights activists or as people concerned with the same, our concerns should be with comprehensive immigration reform (CIR). The current immigration crisis has come about because the United States feeds on cheap labor and the exploitation of millions, the very people it chooses to dispose of quickly and crudely via the mechanisms of raids and deportations. It does this because it knows that there is more cheap labor to be had because of the conditions of "free trade" it has created, conditions that guarantee a breakdown in the economies of countries like Mexico. These conditions, in turn, guarantee the flow of people desperate to find a living here.

The UAFA does not change the paradigms of immigration and, in fact, completely ignores the issues of labor that have created the current crisis. It goes so far as to erase the domestic labor performed by women (or men) like Tan in favor of a fantasy narrative about the nuclear family with a single bread-winner. It fixates on an emotional and affective problem, posited as a problem of true love—what could be truer than decades of living together and children? It is a quick-fix solution for a privileged few and does nothing to address the larger economic crisis that is immigration in the United States.

The UAFA is now being presented as *the* immigration cause for LGBT people. But if queers are to speak about immigration in any form, we need to understand the larger context in which such bills operate. The UAFA will not benefit every gay and lesbian couple, and it will be a distraction from CIR. It makes a grand symbolic gesture, but it is also most likely an exercise in futility that will not, in fact, even benefit many binational couples. While it is not explicitly a marriage bill, it is in fact one that compels people to conjoin in the same way as married partners—but only if you have the economic resources.

For instance, if you or your partner entered the country illegally and without inspection, chances are that spousal sponsorship won't help anyway. But, and this is a huge complication that can enter even for straight couples: under certain circumstances, even a spouse can be subject to a 10-year ban, which means that she/he will have to return to the country of origin and not return for a decade.

Is your head spinning yet?

What it comes down to is this: under very narrow circumstances, Shirley Tan's case could be replicated in a straight binational marriage, but each case is unique and not all straight marriages are automatic routes to citizenship. Tan's case is somewhat complicated because she also sought to gain asylum, a petition that was denied. But even if all things were equal, there is the issue of economics. The UAFA deems it necessary that the sponsoring partner show proof of ample resources, which leaves poorer people out of the picture. In fact, IE and HRC representatives at an immigration conference I attended spoke about the need to show the economic costs if binational couples decided to leave the United States for a country like Canada that recognizes their relationships—they might just up and leave! This is the supposed trump card—if gay and lesbian couples are not allowed to be together, several of them with lucrative businesses will just take them to countries like Canada. So there.

Of course, if you don't have the resources, tough luck. And good lawyers who won't just take your money and run can be hard to find. In addition, the speed with which your immigration application goes through the system depends a lot on your country of origin. What most people do not know is that immigration law is incredibly arcane and subject to the whims of issues as fickle as shifting relations between the United States and other countries. So, if your partner is from a country like, say the Netherlands or France, the chances are that your passage will be easier. If you are from Iran or Pakistan—well, how easy do think your application will be?

What is also left out of the whole spouse/permanent partnership issue is the fact that such relationships are also likely to be rife with abuse. The UAFA specifically requires that partners demonstrate financial interdependency. Partnerships, like straight marriages, will be subject to a two-year period during which much of the power rests with the sponsoring partner. If you are on your spouse's H1-B (on an H-4, the visa that allows you to enter the country as a "spousal dependent"), you cannot get a social security number and you cannot apply for jobs; in many states you will not even be permitted a valid drivers license. *The Hindu*, an Indian newspaper, has written about the abuse of women on their husbands' H-4 visas. The abuse is so widespread that immigration rights activists are currently trying to reform the process so that the dependent spouse might gain some measure of dignity and independence. Is this the kind of situation we feminist queers fought for? Do we seriously believe that the pure love between gays and lesbian couples makes it impossible for such abuse to occur?

Do we really think love will be enough?

So where does this leave Shirley Tan and others like her? It absolutely makes sense that we agitate on their behalf. If there is a petition to sign, sign it. If there is a march in your town, go ahead and march. At the very least, the law needs to change so that it is more flexible and grants people like Tan the leeway to be in the country they now call home. But, at the same time, ask yourself, as either a queer or a straight citizen, about those millions of undocumented who don't have the resources to leave. Consider those millions of undocumented immigrants who might be in binational relationships but whose families are not considered ideal because they lack the money and respectability that the law demands.

The fact is that the UAFA doesn't really stand much of a chance because Republicans and Democrats alike worry that it's a way of writing gay marriage into federal law. And, let us be blunt about it: it is, even if its supporters insist otherwise. This is marriage by another name, and it demands that couples tie themselves to a shockingly retrograde form of economic dependency which feminists have long been fighting against. I happen to be against gay marriage for reasons that have to do with my position on the left, but there are plenty of people on the right who do not want it for different reasons. If the UAFA is forced into CIR, there's a chance that CIR itself will suffer because this legislation might well become the proverbial straw that breaks the camel's back as far as these conservatives are concerned. Gays and lesbians in binational couples and their supporters will be able to make an emotional and symbolic point about the discrimination they suffer, but the costs to

CIR may be irreparable. So, go ahead and protest for Shirley Tan and others like her. But if you cannot or will not protest on behalf of the millions of others who don't fit the cozy and unrealistic idea of "family" as well, don't protest at all.

Queer Kids of Queer Parents Against Gay Marriage!

MJ KAUFMAN AND KATIE MILES

IT'S HARD FOR US TO believe what we're hearing these days. Thousands are losing their homes, and gays want a day named after Harvey Milk. The U.S. military is continuing its path of destruction, and gays want to be allowed to fight. Cops are still killing unarmed black men and bashing queers, and gays want more policing. More and more Americans are suffering and dying because they can't get decent health care, and gays want weddings. What happened to us? Where have our communities gone? Did gays really sell out that easily?

As young queer people raised in queer families and communities, we reject the liberal gay agenda that gives top priority to the fight for marriage equality. The queer families and communities we are proud to have been raised in are nothing like the ones transformed by marriage equality. This agenda fractures our communities, pits us against natural

---

This piece originally appeared online as a blog at queerkidssaynomarriage. wordpress.com in October 2009. This version includes a note from both the authors after the original piece.

allies, supports unequal power structures, obscures urgent queer concerns, abandons struggle for mutual sustainability inside queer communities, and disregards our awesomely fabulous queer history.

Children of queers have a serious stake in this. The media sure thinks so, anyway. The photographs circulated after San Francisco mayor Gavin Newsom's 2004 decision to marry gay couples at City Hall show men exchanging rings with young children strapped to their chests and toddlers holding their moms' hands as city officials lead them through vows. As Newsom runs for governor these images of children and their newly married gay parents travel with him, supposedly expressing how deeply Newsom cares about families: keeping them together, ensuring their safety, meeting their needs. These photos, however, obscure very real aspects of his political record that have torn families apart: his disregard for affordable housing, his attacks on welfare, his support for increased policing and incarceration that separate parents from children and his new practice of deporting minors accused—not convicted—of crimes. As young people with queer parents we are not proud of the "family values" politic put forth by these images and the marriage equality campaign. We don't want gay marriage activism conducted in our name—we realize that it's hurting us, not helping us.

We think long-term monogamous partnerships are valid and beautiful ways of structuring and experiencing family, but we don't see them as any more inherently valuable or legitimate than the many other family structures. We believe in each individual and family's right to live their queer identity however they find meaningful or necessary, including when that means getting married. However, the consequences of the fight for legal inclusion in the marriage structure are terrifying. We're seeing queer communities fractured as one model of family is being hailed and accepted as the norm, and we are seeing queer families and communities ignore and effectively work against groups who we see as natural allies, such as immigrant families, poor families, and families suffering from booming incarceration rates. We reject the idea that any relationship based on love should have to register with the state. Marriage is an institution used primarily to consolidate privilege, and we think real change will only come from getting rid of a system that continually doles out privilege to a few more, rather than trying to reform it. We know that most families, straight or gay, don't fit in with the standards for marriage, and see many straight families being penalized for not conforming to the standard the government has set: single moms trying to get on welfare, extended family members trying to gain custody, friends kept from being each other's legal representatives. We have far more in common with those straight families than we do with the kinds of gay families that would benefit from marriage. We are seeing a gay political agenda become single-issue to focus on marriage and leave behind many very serious issues such as social, economic, and racial justice.

HOW THE MARRIAGE AGENDA IS LEAVING BEHIND AWESOME QUEER HISTORY.

We're seeing the marriage equality agenda turn its back on a tradition of queer activism that began with Stonewall and other fierce queer revolts and that continued through the AIDS crisis. Equality California keeps on sending us videos of big, happy, gay families, and they're making us sick: gay parents pushing kids on swings, gay parents making their kids' lunches, the whole gay family safe inside the walls of their own homes. Wait a second, is it true? It's as if they've found some sort of magical formula: once you have children, your life instantly transforms into a scene of domestic bliss, straight out of a 1950s movie. The message is clear. Instead of dancing, instead of having casual sex, instead of rioting, all of the "responsible" gays have gone and had children. And now that they've had children, they won't be bothering you at all anymore. There's an implicit promise that once gays get their rights, they'll disappear again. Once they can be at home with the kids, there's no reason for them to be political, after all!

Listening to this promise, we're a bit stunned. Whoever said domesticity wasn't political? Wasn't it just a few years ago that the feminists taught us that the personal is political? That cooking, cleaning, raising children, and putting in countless hours of physical, emotional, and intellectual labor should not mean withdrawing from the public sphere or surrendering your political voice? After all, we were raised by queers who created domestic lives that were always politically engaged, who raised kids and raised hell at the same time. What makes Equality California think that an official marriage certificate is going to make us any less loud and queer? Oh wait. We remember. It's that sneaky thing about late liberal capitalism: its promise of formal rights over real restructuring, of citizenship for those who can participate in the state's economic plan over economic justice for all. Once you have your formal rights (like a marriage license), you can participate in the market economy and no longer need a political voice. Looking around at the world we live in, we're unconvinced.

We're also seeing another alarming story surface: If gays are ready to get married and have children, the AIDS crisis must be over! Gay men shaped up after AIDS hit, or at least the smart ones did. Those responsible enough to survive realized that they wanted children, and promptly settled down into relationships that were monogamous and that, presumably, carried no risk of HIV contraction. Come on. We reject all the moralizing about parenthood, responsibility, and sexual practice that goes on in this story. Besides the obvious fact that the AIDS crisis is not over, in the U.S. or abroad, we realize that parenthood and non-monogamy aren't mutually exclusive. The gay marriage movement wants us to believe that you need a sperm donor or an adoption agency to have children, but we know that there are more ways to make queer families than any of us can imagine. We refuse the packaged and groomed history that writes out the many HIV+ individuals in our lives and communities who are living healthily, loving in monogamous and non-monogamous relationships, and raising children. We challenge our queer communities to remember our awesomely radical history of building families and raising children in highly political, inventive, and non-traditional ways.

HOW MARRIAGE EQUALITY FRACTURES OUR COMMUNITY AND PITS US AGAINST OUR STRONGEST ALLIES.

We believe that the argument for gay marriage obscures the many structural, social, and economic forces that break families apart and take people away from their loved ones. Just for starters, there's the explosion in incarceration levels, national and international migration for economic survival, deportation, unaffordable housing, and lack of access to drug rehabilitation services. The argument for gay marriage also ignores the economic changes and cuts to social services that make it nearly impossible for families to stay together and survive: welfare cuts, fewer after-school programs, less public housing, worse medical care, not enough social workers, failing schools, the economic crisis in general.

We choose solidarity with immigrant families whom the state denies legal recognition and families targeted by prisons, wars, and horrible jobs. We reject the state violence that separates children from parents and decides where families begin and end, drawing lines of illegality through relationships. We see this as part of a larger effort on the part of the state to control our families and relationships in order to preserve a system that relies on creating an underclass deprived of security in order to ensure power for a few. We know that everyone has a complex identity, and that many queer families face separation due to one or more of the causes mentioned here, now or in the future. We would like to see our queer community recognize marriage rights as a short-term solution to the larger problem of the government's disregard for the many family structures that exist. As queers, we need to take an active role in exposing and fighting the deeper sources of this problem. We won't let the government decide what does and does not constitute a family.

The way that the marriage agenda phrases its argument about health care shows just how blind it is to the needs of the queer community. It has adopted marriage as a single-issue agenda, making it seem like the queer community's only interest in health care is in the inclusion of some members of two person partnerships in the already exclusive health care system. Health care is a basic human right to which everyone is entitled, not one that should be extended through certain kinds of individual partnerships. We know this from queer history, and if we forget it, we will continue to let our community live in danger. The question of universal health care is urgent to queers because large groups of people inside our communities face incredible difficulty and violence receiving medical care, such as trans people who seek hormone treatment or surgery, people who are HIV positive, and queer and trans youth who are forced to live on the street. Instead of equalizing access to health care, marriage rights would allow a small group of people who have partnered themselves in monogamous configurations to receive care. If we accept the marriage agenda's so-called solution, we'll leave out most of our community.

Perhaps because the gay marriage movement has forgotten about the plurality and diversity of queer communities and queer activism, it has tried to gloss over its shortcomings by appropriating the struggles of other communities. We reject the notion that "gay is the new black," that the fight for marriage equality is parallel to the fight for civil rights, that queer rights and rights for people of color are mutually exclusive. We don't believe that fighting for inclusion in marriage is the same as fighting to end segregation. Drawing that parallel erases queer people of color and makes light of the structural racism that the civil rights movement fought against. The comparison is made as if communities of color, and black communities in particular, now enjoy structural equality. We know that's not true. We would like to see a queer community that, rather than appropriating the narrative of the civil rights movement for its marriage equality campaign, takes an active role in exposing and protesting structural inequality and structural racism.

Rather than choosing to fight the things that keep structural racism intact, the liberal gay agenda has chosen to promote them. The gay agenda continually fights for increased hate crimes legislation that would incarcerate and execute perpetrators of hate crimes. We believe that incarceration destroys communities and families, and does not address why queer bashings happen. Increased hate crimes legislation would only lock more people up. In a country where entire communities are ravaged by how many of their members get sent to jail, where prisons are profit-driven institutions, where incarceration only creates more violence, we won't accept anything that promotes prison as a solution. Our communities are already preyed upon by prisons—trans people, sex workers, and street kids live with the constant threat of incarceration. We believe that real, long-term solutions are found in models of restorative and transformative justice, and in building communities that can positively and profoundly deal with violence. We challenge our queer communities to confront what we are afraid of rather than locking it up, and to join members of our community and natural allies in opposing anything that would expand prisons.

The gay marriage agenda also supports the expansion of the army, seemingly forgetting about all of the ways that the army creates and maintains violence and power. The gay marriage agenda fights to abolish the "don't ask don't tell" policy, promoting the military's policy and seeking inclusion. We've thought long and hard about this, and we can't remember liking anything that the U.S. military has done in a really long time. What we do remember is how the military mines places where poor people and people of color live, taking advantage of the lack of opportunities that exist for kids in those communities and convincing them to join the army. We think it's time that queers fight the army and the wars it is engaged in instead of asking for permission to enter.

MARRIAGE DOESN'T PROMISE REAL SECURITY.

As the economy collapses, as the number of Americans without a job, without health care, without savings, without any kind of social security net increases, it's easy to understand how marriage has become an instant cure-all for some. Recognizing that many in our community have lived through strained or broken relationships with their biological families, through the darkest days of the AIDS epidemic in the United States, through self-doubt about and stigmatization of their relationships, we understand where the desire for the security promised by marriage comes from. However, we see the promotion of gay marriage as something that tries to put a Band-Aid over deeper sources of insecurity, both social and economic. With marriage, the state is able to absolve itself of responsibility for the well-being of its citizens, as evidenced by the HRC's argument that with gay marriage, the state could kick more people off of welfare. If the HRC got its way, the queers who do not want, or are not eligible for, marriage would be even less secure than before. We're frightened by the way the marriage agenda wants to break up our community in this way, and we're committed to fighting any kind of politics that demonizes poor people and welfare recipients. We challenge our queer communities to build a politics that promotes wealth redistribution. What if, rather than donating to the HRC campaign, we pooled our wealth to create a community emergency fund for members of our community who face foreclosure, need expensive medical care or find themselves in any other economic emergency? As queers, we need to take our anger, our fear, and our hope and recognize the wealth of resources that we already have, in order to build alternative structures. We don't need to assimilate when we have each other.

WE'RE NOT LIKE EVERYONE ELSE.

Everywhere we turn, it seems like someone wants us to support gay marriage. From enthusiastic canvassers on the street to liberal professors in the academy, from gay lawyers to straight soccer moms, there's someone smiling at us, eager to let us know how strongly they support our "right to marry," waiting for what should be our easy affirmation. And there seems to be no space for us to resist the agenda that has been imposed upon us. We're fed up with the way that the gay marriage movement has tried to assimilate us, to swallow up our families, our lives, and our lovers into its clean-cut standards for what queer love, responsibility, and commitment should look like. We reject the idea that we should strive to see straight family configurations reflected in our families. We're offended by the idea that white, middle-class gays—rather than genderqueers, poor people, single moms, prisoners, people of color, immigrants without papers, or anyone whose life falls outside of the norm that the state has set—should be our "natural" allies. We refuse to feel indebted or grateful to those who have decided it's time for us to be pulled out from the fringe and into the status quo. We know that there are more of us on the outside than on the inside, and we realize our power.

We write this feeling as if we have to grab our community back from the clutches of the gay marriage movement. We're frightened by its path and its incessant desire to assimilate. Believe it or not, we felt incredibly safe, happy, taken care of, and fulfilled with the many queer biological and chosen parents who raised us without the right to marry. Having grown up in queer families and communities we strongly believe that queers are not like everyone else. Queers are sexy, resourceful, creative, and brave enough to challenge an oppressive system with their lifestyle. In the ways that our families might resemble nuclear, straight families, it is accidental and coincidental, something that lies at the surface. We do not believe that queer relationships are the mere derivatives of straight relationships. We can play house without wanting to be straight. Our families are tangled, messy, and beautiful—just like so many straight families who don't fit into the official version of family. We want to build communities of all kinds of families, families that can exist—that do exist—without the recognition of the state. We don't believe that parenting is cause for an end to political participation. We believe that nurturing the growth, voice, and imagination of children as a parent, a family, and a community is a profoundly radical act. We want to build networks of accountability and dependence that lie outside the bounds of the government, the kinds of networks that we grew up in, the kinds of networks that we know support single-parent families, immigrant families, families who have members in the military or in prison, and all kinds of chosen families. These families, our families, work through our collective resources, strengths, commitments, and desires, and we wouldn't change them for anything.

***

The above essay was written in October 2009. The marriage equality movement was gaining steam in advance of the National Equality March and we were frustrated by the way images of children with gay parents were being used in the media. When we first shared our essay, we never expected our words to spread so quickly or so far. It was written for our friends and fellow activists, and we had no idea what a large audience would read it. Since sharing this essay, our relationship to it has changed, in different ways for both of us. Below are first Katie's and then Martha's words about our relationship to the essay.

***

Since we shared the essay, we've heard a lot of generous and smart feedback from people who see gay marriage as very important for their families, emotionally and otherwise. We know that for many people, marriage, and the benefits it can give, can be a form of survival. We believe that people can experience an immediate need for the benefits marriage would provide and a simultaneous hope for more expansive solutions.

When we wrote about solidarity with other communities, we did so knowing that no lines exist between all of these communities, that all of us are members of more than one community, that our communities bleed into others, that they are all inextricably connected. Since writing the essay, though, both of us have become uncomfortable with using the term "solidarity." We don't want to mark out the groups with whom we should be strategically sharing power as separate from us, because we know that groups tend to overlap in identity. We often find that when we claim "solidarity" with one group or another, the use of that word obscures a more personal connection we have to the struggle in which we're engaged.

We see queerness as fundamentally about honoring and validating relationships built on love and an individual's right to build the lives they want for their bodies, desires, and needs. Because of this, we see many social justice struggles as intrinsically queer, and as crucial for queer individuals and communities. Queer struggles throughout history have shown us how imaginative and creative good, effective organizing is—and that is why we are excited, not resigned, about all of the possibilities we have as queers. It isn't that we think there's not enough energy for anything more than one fight—it's that we think that queers, as people who occupy all sorts of places that aren't even supposed to exist, have the power to build activism that can truly challenge the structures of power, and that is a part of a larger activism fought by all who exist outside of formal recognition.

—Katie Miles (2010)

***

The idea of struggling to fit my extensive, complex and tangled family into a model focusing exclusively on two primary parents has always been absurd to me. My brother and I have always been confused by school assignments that required us to draw our family tree. How were we supposed to fit two moms and dad into the space for two parents? How was I supposed to organize the branches generationally when my moms were seventeen years apart and my aunt only eleven years older than me? Katie and I have both had more than two parental figures in our lives and know that many others around us have as well. Our families blur into communities, and we have benefited from many meaningful and supportive bonds that are not represented by either the conventional or the Marriage Equality movement's idea of marriage. In our first publication of this statement, we rejected the idea that any relationship based on love should have to register with the state to gain legitimacy.

Since our essay went out, however, I've heard a lot of smart and honest criticism from people who find it emotionally meaningful to be able to get state validation for their queer family structure. I had never considered the validation offered by the state meaningful, perhaps because I grew up in a queer family and community and have found support for my queer desires and identity from a young age regardless of state recognition. I now recognize the extent to which, for many queers (regardless of the environment in which they grew up and how queer friendly it was), the self-definition and emotional security offered by state recognition of a relationship can be important.

Many people responded to our essay defensively about their choice to get married. This confused me. Was our piece provocative? Offensive? How had we put people who should be our natural partners on the defense? I realized then, the extent to which our language could alienate people we wanted to convince. I realized that a great deal of what I wrote came from a place of anger: anger at the government for not recognizing my family, anger at my communities for fighting for gay marriage as though my family was invisible, and anger at the gay marriage movement for relentlessly inviting me to join without realizing they were leaving out my family structure. I know that writing from a place of anger stirs up anger and defensiveness in other people. I hope to move beyond the angry language in this statement towards open words that will encourage readers to identify rather than turn defensive. I choose the word "identify" with care. I actually think that everyone has a personal connection to the argument in our essay. Everyone has a messy family that extends beyond what the state can validate. Let's make space for all of our relationships to count.

In addition to realizing that a lot of our essay came from a place of anger, I've also realized that there is also some binary language in the essay that I am no longer comfortable with. Statements about what will "help" or "hurt" us, and who is on the "outside" or the "inside" fail to reflect the complex ways gay marriage both helps and hurts my family, how it simultaneously includes and excludes us.

Several months after we first wrote our essay, we were quoted in a *New York Times* article. The author quoted a number of younger queer-spawns who spoke out in favor of gay marriage. Reading the article, I was reminded suddenly of a press statement I gave at age fourteen, very much along the same lines as these younger queer-spawns. The more I consider this personal shift, the less I see my fourteen-year-old self or any of the younger queer-spawns in the article as standing in opposition to me. I see the impulse to ask the state to validate your family and the impulse to ask for a more expansive solution as two sides of the same coin: a challenge to the government for not understanding how families actually form.

While filling in family trees was difficult for my brother and me, I know it will only be more complicated for my baby sister who has two moms, two dads and a sister twenty years older than she is. After too many years of being asked to do this assignment, a few summers ago I finally revolted. Instead of a family tree, I created a family vine. I drew myself surrounded by all of the most important people in my life. Everyone was connected, but by winding branches instead of top-to-bottom limbs. It reflected a reality about every family I've ever en-countered: we are messy and complicated. I'm writing this now with the hope that we can move beyond a vision of marriage toward a world that recognizes that complexity and sustains and honors those of us who grow and thrive within it.

—MJ Kaufman (2010)

Why gay marriage IS the End of the World (or the queer world, at least)

MATTILDA BERNSTEIN SYCAMORE

THESE DAYS, LESBIAN SOCCER MOMS and gay military intelligence experts are all over the media, whether sermonizing in op-eds, befriending the liberal intelligentsia, or speaking softly to closeted cable news anchors: We. Are. Just. Like. You.

Supposedly gay people have made lots of progress, and that's why the only issues we hear about involve marriage, gays in the military, gay cops, adoption, ordination into the priesthood, hate crimes legislation, and unquestioning gentrification and consumerism—please, stop me before I choke on my own vomit! In honor of the *Maximum Rocknroll* queer issue, it's time to pull together a gang of queer troublemakers to tear this assimilationist agenda to shreds, okay?

Here's the cast of characters:

Hilary Goldberg is a San Francisco-based filmmaker currently in the finishing stages of *recLAmation*, the definitive movie about reclaiming

This piece was published in the October 2009 issue of Maximum Rockn-Roll *and online at* The Bilerico Project *(bilerico.com).*

Los Angeles from Los Angeles, and oh are we waiting! Yasmin Nair is a Chicago activist who delivers delicious rants about the war against single people, the tyranny of religion, fake immigration reform, and bachelorette parties with equal fervor and finesse. Gina Carducci throws Switch, New York City's only monthly "genderqueer / women / trans BDSM party"—she also fetishizes film, and is currently working on *All That Sheltering Emptiness*, a devastating short experimental film created in collaboration with your host for this splashy article.

***

MBS: I don't know about you, but have you noticed that freshly mined, blood-drenched South African diamonds are the new accessory for the gay elite, or they might as well be with how much the gaysbian "LGBT" agenda has become nothing but marriage marriage marriage—oh, and maybe a little bit of marriage with that marriage, thank you! Many of us grew up experiencing the lovely embrace of marriage or its aftermath, so we, and most queers, certainly know a lot about how marriage is, and has always been a central place for beating up, raping and abusing women, children, queers, and transpeople. And, even better—getting away with it! What are the other problems with marriage, and the gay marriage agenda in particular?

HG: I was at a protest against HIV budget cuts in California, but only four other people were there because the rest of the gaysbians had done their recommended yearly protest allowance for gay marriage a few months prior. And what is the point of marriage if everyone is sick or dead, how do you register for that—at cemeteries and Pottery Barn? Wow, that makes me think of health care—remember health care? Something universal-based, not privilege-shaped?

YN: Yeah, I don't get why a community of people who have historically been fucked over by their families and the state now consists of people who want those exact same institutions to validate their existence. I think marriage is the gay Prozac, the drug of choice for gaysbians today: It makes them forget that marriage isn't going to give everyone health care, it won't give us a subsistence wage, it won't end all these fucked up wars that are killing people everywhere else. I wish I could say that gay marriage is like Viagra, but alas it's actually making us forget about sex so that metaphor won't work.

MBS: Speaking of sex and metaphors, let's move on to gays in the military. It's time to forget about opposing all these bloody U.S. colonial wars, we just want to throw on those humpy battle fatigues so we can go abroad to kill people and get away with it, right? U-S-A! Can we say that again? U-S-A! Okay, so obviously the real answer is the end of the U.S. military, not rainbow Humvees. Anything to add?

HG: Let us not forget the Gay Bomb—much like the acid tests the CIA performed in the '50s and '60s, if that technology fell into savvy hands we could open some serious doors of perception to end the military in-dustrial complex with some good old fashioned loving.

GC: Oh, but military service is the best way to break down gay ste-reotypes and homophobia! The more we kill kill kill, the more respect we get from our country—we serve our country too! We are a valuable contribution! Show them you know how to be a man!

YN: It's time for us to call out the "gay patriots" as the enablers of U.S. imperialism. Has anyone else noticed that the public faces of Don't Ask Don't Tell tend to be relatively privileged and from the officer class? And that the stories go like this: "Oh, no, he was an educated Harvard graduate who spoke four languages in which to colonize other coun-tries, and we let him go!" One of the funniest photographs I ever saw was of a rally in downtown Chicago. A gay Army vet stood pontificat-ing about needing to be recognized by the U.S. military. Right behind him, his friends held up an anti-war slogan banner with the words, "US Out of Iraq." I wondered: Now, does that mean just the non-gay soldiers? Do the gay soldiers get to stay behind and kick the ass and blow the limbs off darkies?

MBS: Speaking of darkies, let's move on to adoption—if Madonna, Brad Pitt and Angelina, and any other jetsetter can run around the world in search of the cutest kids in the countries most devastated by transnational corporate violence, and then snatch those kids up and hold them in their arms, how will gay people compete? We all need kids, right? Kids are the next big thing! How do you feel about the issue of gay adoption, and child-rearing in general, as a central preoccupation of the so-called "movement?"

HG: Why don't Madonna and Angelina, in their gay wisdom, adopt some adult queer artists and activists instead? For a fraction of what they spend on a handful of appropriated transnational youths, they could adopt queer artists en masse, and foster a global queer trust fund for the movement. No need for nannies and we'd love them even more than their children, and could be just as dependent, if not more so. Average gay couples could do the same thing, direct their money towards something more expansive and useful than a handbag—I mean a gaybie. I'm thinking of a website that pairs queer artists with gay couples who have big hearts to share their love and help.

GC: Yeah, no need for pacifiers, no need to push us around in strollers, and you don't have to wait nine months for us. We're right here! Mommy!!!!

YN: If you're white, beautiful little blonde children are the best, because then you'll look like a normal and natural family. But adopting one can be next to impossible! Little brown babies make the best gay accessories. Although, like every gay fashion accessory, babies have shifted in trends. I think Mongolian babies are now much more hip. Central and South American countries were once popular, maybe NAFTA opened up free trade in cute Latin babies! Until they discovered that some of those babies were most likely kidnapped. Awkward. They may not have those pesky rules in Mongolia. Of course, if you can adopt an HIV+ African baby whose mother is still around to waste away in the last throes of the disease, so that you can show the world what you rescued the baby from, all the better. Why is it that lesbians generally give birth but gay men usually adopt?

MBS: It's because gay men are busy studying for the priesthood. I know you've been studying hard too! Of course, one of the central demands of early gay liberation was the end to organized religion and all of its layers of violence, but that's old news. What do you all think about the issue of "LGBT" people becoming powerbrokers within organized religion?

HG: It makes me cry blood. The only atonement gays should be thinking about is a nice bondage scene. And the last time I interacted with organized religion, a drag queen nun, in full make-up, yelled at me to get into a degrading gender-enforced line at a corporatized "pride" event colonized by so called do-gooders. Fuck her and the rest of organized religion.

MBS: Oh—and let's not forget the holy grail of the gay movement, hate crimes legislation! Because if you shoot those goddamn homophobes twice, that'll really teach them a lesson—the electric chair will end homophobia! Seriously, hate crimes legislation does nothing but put more money, energy, and resources into the hands of the notoriously racist, classist, misogynist, homophobic, and transphobic criminal so-called "justice" system. But then they trick us into thinking that hate crimes legislation will keep us safe. What is hate crimes legislation keeping us safe from?

HG: It keeps us safe from long-term solution-based healing. It's a real time saver, so we can focus on earning money instead of focusing on root causes of hatred. We can continue to own property and assimilate into larger society by avoiding any real discourse around the source of the hate, and perpetuate it instead, while upholding that pillar of community, the greatest benefactor of the hates crimes bills—oh-so-thriving, even in economic turmoil...Private Prison Business.

YN: Hate crimes legislation keeps us safe from the silly delusion that the justice system should actually work fairly for everybody, not just gays and defined "minorities." After all, a justice system that actually provides justice seems, well, just ever so 1970s and sweetly retrograde, darling. All bell bottoms and compassion. Hate crimes legislation keeps us from a world where people might actually have a chance to show that they have moved on from their mistakes, by locking them up for perpetuity. And it keeps us believing that letting people spend their lives in violent prisons where they're likely to be raped and beaten every day is somehow a way to... end anti-gay violence. Huh?

MBS: Speaking of anti-gay violence, let's move on to talking about the national institutions that drive this wonderful inclusive agenda. We'll start with everyone's favorite diamond merchant: HRC, the Human Rights Campaign. Also known as Helping Right-Wingers Cope, or Homogenous Ruling Class—what else are they good for?

GC: Harvesting Righteous Caucasians. Hiring Riot Cops.

YN: Press Releases. HRC can turn out a press release on a dime. Oh, and they're great at taking credit for every "gay agenda" item, through said press releases, whether or not they had anything to do with the action. So, yeah, cocktail parties and lobby days. HRC is really good at going to cocktail parties and hobnobbing with the rich and important.

MBS: Of course, HRC also likes to keep trans people out of so-called employment nondiscrimination legislation, and to make any hideous corporation look good, as long as they like HRC's press releases. Then there's NGLTF, the National Gay Lesbian Task Force. They're especially talented at recruiting well-meaning college students, and turning them into nonprofit office drones—Creating Change, their annual conference, is a great launching pad into the nonprofit industry, and a job at NGLTF is sure to get you more lucrative foundation work in the future—what else is NGLTF good for?

YN: For creating the illusion that the battle royale between Democrats and Republicans actually means anything. And for perpetuating the idea that there are no alternatives to either. For pretending that a few days of a conference filled with words like "organizing" and "social" and "progressive" actually changes much. For pretending that using the word "progressive" over and over again will a) actually make that stupid word mean anything b) make us believe that their support of marriage, hate crimes legislation, and repealing Don't Ask Don't Tell does not make them conservative.

GC: NGLTF is good for creating robots who are stuck repeating, "Do you have a moment for trans rights? Do you have a moment for trans rights?" And asking why why why why can you not come to our office for hours of volunteer calling calling calling and repeating what we tell you to think and say, "Why can't you make the time for trans rights? Why?" Two of these robots were harassing myself and a group of friends once and I was just waiting for my trans friend to say, "If you really want to know, I need a little time to recover from trying to overdose and kill myself last week." And for the robots to ask, "Why? It's trans rights."

MBS: Oh, and I love the Gay Lesbian Alliance Against Defamation, or GLAAD—I think they should be called SAAD, the Straight Alliance Against Defamation, since most of what they do involves giving awards to straight people for not saying "faggot" too much. What else are they good for?

YN: Being very confused, mostly. And whining. A lot. I think *Bruno* confused the hell out of them: "We object to this movie. We think. It's a set of offensive stereotypes. Although the lead character is so over the top, he couldn't even possibly be a stereotype. But wait, we live to be offended. Cohen's not gay. And he makes fun of gays. Even though he also makes fun of homophobes. Wait, are we offended? Or not? It's so hard to tell, because we have no sense of humor or logic. Even the gays are sick of us. Can we call that homophobia?"

MBS: Then there's the juicy Lambda Legal Defense Fund—fighting for our rights, one marriage at a time...

YN: Lambda might be scariest of the lot, because they're mostly lawyers who know how to twist any inane, conservative, retrograde idea like gay marriage into some kind of sterling social justice cause—and they do that by drowning us in legalese. I once watched Camilla Taylor, a Lambda power attorney in Chicago, spend an hour talking about the legal ins and outs of Prop 8. By the end of the hour, I was so stupefied by boredom that I was almost ready to sign on to gay marriage—just to get out of the room. There was, of course, not one word about whether marriage ought to be the way to gain any rights in the first place.

MBS: That's right—remember that the fight against anti-gay Proposition 8 in California that those marriage morons lost actually cost more than any other ballot measure in California history! Those maniacal marriage organizations spent $40 million on that shit—can you imagine what we would have if they took that $40 million and fought for single payer universal health care, or built an enormous queer youth shelter in San Francisco or Sacramento, Fresno or San Diego? With the leftovers, we could create a collectively run, all-ages, 24-hour sex club with free vegan food, knock-you-down music of all types, free massage, acupuncture, and health care for all needs, as well as a special area for training people in squatting and neighborhood redecoration projects—bricks, stencils, spray paint, you get the idea. Anything else you want to say about marriage marriage marriage, and what we need instead?

GC: Donate Donate Donate! Do you have a moment for Prop 8? Do you have a moment for Prop 8? But really—we need to be able to choose our own families and who visits us in the hospital and who shares our assets and who makes decisions for us, whether we are officially single or partnered. And gender is defined by us too, not by presentation but how we define our own identities. Sexual liberation and freedom and places to fuck without being policed. Housing. Health care. Social services. Protection for the environment.

HG: The last time I checked—the nuclear family model—was a disaster! Enough already. The gay rights movement needs to divorce marriage and pull it together. The system is broken, these institutions are failing, why are people so set on shoring them up? Let's focus on ending capitalism, abolishing prison, ending militarism, ensuring immigrant

94

rights, clean air, great food, love, equality, interdependence, independence, autonomy, non-hierarchical structures, and most importantly the universal reclamation of all land and water as public property.

YN: And, of course, the abolition of the prison industrial complex, the end of the illusion that more punishment and enhanced penalties in the form of hate crimes legislation will benefit anyone, safety for young queers who are beaten and/or raped by families and have nowhere to go, intergenerational sex that's not immediately stigmatized as pedophilia, an end to sex offender laws that do nothing to end the abuse of children but only add to the coffers of the prison industrial complex, an end to the death penalty, an end to the idea that life without parole is an acceptable alternative, queer sex in public without paying a fee in a bathhouse and without being harassed, jailed, or beaten for it, an immigration rights movement that acknowledges that it's a crisis of labor, not about "families" or spousal partners, an end to the disappearance and/or deportation of undocumented people, and oh, I could go on.

There's this popular line going around about how gay marriage is the rising tide that will lift all boats. But if we are to use a seafaring metaphor, it might be more apt to call it a Titanic, doomed to crash into an iceberg and take the rest of us down.

AGAINST EQUALITY:

DON'T ASK TO FIGHT THEIR WARS

EDITED BY
RYAN CONRAD

INTRODUCTION BY
MATTILDA BERNSTEIN SYCAMORE

"Community Spirit"
The New Gay Patriot and the Right to Fight in Unjust Wars

MATTILDA BERNSTEIN SYCAMORE

AN INTRODUCTION

I REMEMBER WHEN THE U.S. started bombing Iraq under the first President Bush. I was a senior in high school, studying for exams at the American University student center. For some reason, that's where disaffected outlaw kids at Washington, DC private schools went to study, maybe because you could smoke inside, and you could buy alcohol without ID, and I guess our schools were right nearby, but I had to drive a half hour to get there: I was trying really hard to fit in at not fitting in. I looked up at one of the TV screens flashing news updates, and the bombs were going off. That's how I remember it, anyway. My whole body went hot and then cold—I couldn't possibly study anymore; there was no point.

I went to the big antiwar demos in DC, enthralled by the possibilities of public protest, studying the pageantry and anger of the banners and costumes, designing my own handmade signs, taking pictures of my sister and a friend holding up their fingers to make peace in front of cops in riot gear. I watched the protests in other cities on the news, keeping track of the places with the most people out in the street. This was one of the first times that San Francisco entered my world view—there were as many people protesting there as in New York, even though I knew San Francisco was a tenth of the size.

Soon yellow ribbons appeared inside the avowedly liberal school in affluent Northwest DC that I had attended since second grade—I couldn't believe the hypocrisy. How could you support the troops if you opposed the war? To me, every soldier was a cold-blooded killer. Later, once I realized it was poor and working-class people, many of them people of color, sent around the world as cannon fodder, I would modify this stance to welcome deserters, those who came back from fighting to piece together their lives as antiwar activists, and anyone trying desperately to get out of the U.S. killing machine. Nevertheless, the pro-military antiwar agenda eagerly trumpeted in every left media outlet still leaves quite a bit to be desired: how will we ever end vicious wars of aggression if most of the experts we hear from aren't antiwar at all, but only speaking about why this particular war is unjust or badly organized?

I ended up in San Francisco sooner than I expected, after a year at the elite university I'd spent my whole life working towards, a place where everything I learned I discovered outside of class. I learned how to call myself queer, how to build a protest movement for racial and economic justice at a so-called liberal institution that still officially denied entrance to students based on their inability to pay. I helped to organize a building takeover that led to hundreds of arrests, months of protests, and national news. This was the culmination of years of student activism, but still it led to no tangible change because the administration didn't really care, and that's where I learned the most.

I left college to find what I really needed—radical queers, runaways, dropouts, anarchists, vegans, addicts, incest survivors, freaks, sluts, whores, and direct action activists trying desperately to piece together a culture of resistance. Soon after arriving in San Francisco, I went to an anti-Bush protest where I brought a sign that said "Break Down the American First Family," and maybe something using the word "assassinate," which didn't go over well with the Secret Service. I was detained for several hours in a Lincoln Town Car with tinted windows—hello

FBI file. This was the early '90s in San Francisco, and everywhere queers were dying of AIDS and drug addiction and suicide, but also there was an oppositional queer culture that I could finally grasp, become a part of, hold onto. For me that culture centered around ACT UP, the AIDS Coalition to Unleash Power. ACT UP meant fighting AIDS because everyone was dying, and it also meant making connections—between government neglect of people with AIDS and structural homophobia and racism; between the ever-increasing military budget and the lack of funding for health care; between misogyny and the absence of resources for women with AIDS; between the war on drugs and the abandonment of HIV-positive drug addicts and prisoners.

In 1993, I went with ACT UP to the March on Washington for Lesbian, Gay and Bisexual Rights (transgender inclusion was not yet on the table). ACT UP was planning a mass civil disobedience for universal health care at the Capitol, but, unlike at past national mobilizations, only several dozen people joined us in getting arrested. Our action took place on the same weekend as the largest gay march in history, which struck me as a sea of uniformity—white gays in white T-shirts applying for Community Spirit credit cards and rallying for the newly-elected President Clinton to follow through on his campaign promise to allow gays to openly serve in the U.S. military. I had never seen anything like it—a million gay people, on the streets of the city where I grew up feeling alone, broken, hopeless for any possibility of self-expression. A million gay people, gathered together to fight for inclusion in the most blatant institution of U.S. imperialism.

A day or two later, after the gay tide had subsided and no change was noticeable on DC streets except for piles of trash, I was making out with the person who would become my first boyfriend, outside the twenty-four-hour restaurant where I used to go late at night in high school. Two white frat types came right up to us and said: What are you doing? Kissing, I said, and went back to it. They sprayed something directly into my eyes from a few inches away, and all I could feel was a searing pain like my whole face was on fire—when I went inside the restaurant to splash cold water on my face it looked like my skin was covered in red spray paint. The manager or someone told me to take this outside. Eventually I got a cab to the hospital, where they said it was pepper spray, and they pumped saline into my eyes for close to an hour, to make sure that I didn't lose my vision. The next day I met my parents for dinner, who unwittingly echoed the gay movement when they asked: Why do you have to be so overt?

Getting bashed right after the March on Washington cemented my feelings that the assimilationist gay agenda would never make visible queers safer. In fact, by trumpeting a masculinist, pro-military agenda the gay establishment makes poor people all over the world more vulnerable to U.S. military aggression. It also creates value where there is none, rejecting decades of left opposition to the U.S. military in favor of the smiling, happy, proud, and pumped-up face of the new gay patriot.

It is no coincidence that the obsession with gay inclusion in the U.S. military emerged from the AIDS crisis. In the late-80s and early-90s, facing the deaths of lovers, friends, and sometimes entire social networks due not just to a new disease, but the old diseases of government neglect and structural homophobia, queers built systems of care that were breathtaking in their immediacy, shared vision, intimacy, and effectiveness. Out of rage and hopelessness came not just the brilliance of ACT UP, but a generation of incendiary art and brave visions for community-building.

As a nineteen-year-old queer activist surrounded by grieving, loneliness, desperation and visionary world-making in 1993, I'll admit that I held some hope that universal health care might become a central issue for queer struggle. What could have built more beautiful and far-reaching alliances, what could have held a greater impact not just for queers, but for everyone in this country? My hopes for a broad struggle based on universal needs were dashed at the March on Washington, which felt more like a circuit party than a protest: a circuit party with a military theme. Except that this wasn't just drug-fueled bacchanalia or straight-acting role play—brushing aside the ashes of dead lovers, the gay movement battled for the right to do its own killing.

The effects of this new gay militarism can be seen in all segments of the movement now pronounced "LGBT." As marriage entered the fray as the dominant gay issue, the stars and stripes began to eclipse even the empty symbolism of the sweatshop-produced nylon rainbow flag: gay (and "gay-friendly") people everywhere draped themselves in the U.S. flag at virtually every pro-marriage demonstration as the U.S. obliterated Iraq and Afghanistan, occupied Haiti, and funded the Israeli war on the Palestinians. Then there's the law-and-order message intrinsic to the fight for hate crimes legislation—that's right, the way to keep queer people safe is to put more power in the hands of a notoriously racist, classist, misogynist, homophobic, and transphobic system, right? Kill those criminals twice, and then they won't be around to engage in more violence.

But the effects of the pro-military gay agenda do not end there. Corporate-friendly, media-savvy gay lobbying groups have developed a stranglehold on popular representations of what it means to be queer, making sure that everyone knows that the only way to be "pro-LGBT" is to support marriage "equality," military inclusion, and hate crimes legislation. Maybe with the rest of our time we can fight for ordination into the priesthood while demanding gay and lesbian parental rights without talking about autonomy for children. Even when these gays in suits do talk about issues that matter, like nondiscrimination in housing or employment, the rhetoric prioritizes the most privileged while fucking over everyone else—sure, it's a great idea to protect people who already have housing or jobs, but what about the rest of us?

Unfortunately, the left is complicit in this silencing agenda. The left has never done its work to address structural homophobia, so now that the gays have Ellen (and Rachel Maddow!), left pundits are eager to prove themselves as gay-friendly as your average P-FLAG soccer mom. And so, ironically, what we see, over and over, are conservative gay media hacks, welcome in allegedly liberal, progressive, and even radical media venues, spouting off on the importance of gays in the military on antiwar programs, talking about marriage inclusion with straight radio hosts who are veterans of the '60s and made the conscious political choice never to get married, and foaming at the mouth about making anti-gay or anti-trans murderers pay for their crimes in the same pages where the injustices of the prison industrial complex are highlighted.

Occasionally a queer critique of the gay establishment appears on the left (including some of the pieces reprinted in this book). In 2010,

103

I had the rare opportunity to appear on *Democracy Now!*, a show I watch pretty much every day, to debate Lieutenant Dan Choi, a cover model for patriotic gays everywhere. On the show, he declared, with rare clarity: "War is a force that gives us meaning."

What, exactly, is the meaning of the U.S. obliterating Iraq, Afghanistan, and Pakistan? What is the meaning of soldiers pressing buttons in Nevada to destroy villages halfway around the world? What is the meaning of U.S. soldiers in Afghanistan establishing a "kill team" in order to murder innocent civilians, pose for photographs with the dead bodies, and cut off fingers as souvenirs? The U.S. is involved in overt and covert wars all over the world, in order to plunder indigenous resources for corporate profit. And the meaning of the fight for gays in the military is that the gay establishment will do anything to become part of the status quo. But nothing could be more hypocritical than a movement centering around the right to go abroad to kill people and get away with it. If that is a "civil rights" struggle, as we are led to believe, there is a problem with civil rights.

On September 20, 2011, the ban on gay soldiers serving openly in the U.S. military ended, and over a hundred celebrations were planned in cities across the U.S. and around the world. How many antiwar demonstrations were planned on the same day? What if eighteen years of fighting for gays in the military were spent fighting against the U.S. military?

This section of the anthology archives queer challenges to the militarization of gay identity, exposing the sad trajectory from gay liberation to gay assimilation. These essays spotlight the U.S. military's role in enforcing heterosexual norms and white supremacy, and ask what is lost when so much energy and attention, and so many financial resources are misdirected in the service of empire. Support for the U.S. military in this day and age always comes at the cost of social programs and social justice. A movement that should be about gender and sexual, social, political and cultural self-determination, not just for queers in this country, but for everyone in this country and around the world is instead centered around accessing dominant systems of oppression. As a queer teenager growing up in an abusive family and a homophobic world, I believed there were people like me but I didn't believe that I would ever find them. When I rejected the world that had made me—its homophobia, transphobia, racism, classism, misogyny, ableism, and all other forms of oppression and hierarchy, I never imagined there was a parallel violence on the other side of coming out, a gay establishment that believed in the right to fight in unjust wars. As long as war is a force that gives us meaning, there will never be hope for meaning anything else.

A Military Job is Not Economic Justice
QEJ Statement on DADT

KENYON FARROW FOR QEJ

IN JUST A FEW MOMENTS President Obama is scheduled to sign the repeal of the Don't Ask, Don't Tell (DADT) policy which, in theory, will allow for gay and lesbian members of the military to serve without being in the closet.

Queers for Economic Justice (QEJ) staff and constituents have all met people in the LGBT movement who have said to us that the DADT repeal is an economic justice victory, since many poor and working-class LGBT people join the military to have access to better jobs, and because the military is the nation's largest employer, QEJ should be joining in the victory dance.

But QEJ believes military service is not economic justice, and it is immoral that the military is the nation's de facto jobs program for poor and working-class people. Since QEJ organizes LGBTQ homeless people in New York City, we wanted to remind the LGBT

This piece originally appeared on Queers for Economic Justice's website (www.q4ej.org) on December 22, 2010, on the occasion of President Obama's repeal of DADT.

community and progressive anti-war allies that militarism and war profiteering do not serve the interests of LGBT people. Here's how:

1. The National Coalition for Homeless Veterans reports that about one-third of all homeless people in the U.S. are veterans, but about 1.5 million more veterans are at risk of homelessness "due to poverty, lack of support networks, and dismal living conditions in overcrowded or substandard housing." They also report that 56% of homeless veterans are Black or Latino.

2. Some studies also show that one in four veterans becomes disabled as a result of physical violence or the emotional trauma of war. There are currently 30,000 disabled veterans from the wars in Iraq and Afghanistan.

3. Rape and sexual violence are very common occurrences for women in the military, and the ACLU is currently suing the Pentagon to get the real numbers on reported incidences.

4. Half of the U.S. budget in 2009 was made up of military spending, including current expenditures, veterans' benefits and the portion of the national debt caused by military costs, according to the War Resisters' League. That is more than the U.S. spent on Health & Human Services, Social Security Administration, Housing and Urban Development and the Department of Education combined. Wouldn't more social safety net spending help the millions of queers who can barely make ends meet?

In short, military service is not economic justice.

Furthermore, QEJ understands that there are LGBTQ people in other parts of the world, particularly Iraq and Afghanistan, who have been killed, traumatized, or made disabled directly as a result of the recent U.S.-led wars, or who have become vulnerable targets by fundamentalist backlashes to U.S. imperialism. We stand in solidarity with other LGBTQ people around the globe, and do not condone violence against them or their home countries so that "our gays" have the "right" to serve openly in the military.

Don't Ask, Don't Tell, Don't Serve

CECILIA CISSELL LUCAS

"DON'T ASK, DON'T TELL" IS bad policy. It encourages deceit and, specifically, staying in the closet, which contributes to internalized as well as public homophobia, thus perpetuating discrimination and violence against LGBT people. Banning gay people from serving in the military, however, is something I support. Not because I'm anti-gay, nope, I'm one of those queer folks myself. I'm also a woman and would support a law against women serving in the military. Not because I think women are less capable. I would support laws against any group of people serving in the military: people of color, tall people, people between the ages of twenty-five and fifty-three, white men, poor people, people who have children, people who vote for Democrats—however you draw the boundaries of a group, I would support a law banning them from military service. Because I support outlawing the military. And until that has happened, I support downsizing it by any means necessary, including, in this one particular arena, sacrificing civil rights in the interest of human rights.

This piece originally appeared online on CounterPunch.org on February 10, 2010.

Civil rights would dictate that if a military exists, everyone, regardless of race, gender, sexuality, class, or religion, should have an equal opportunity to serve in it. But human rights dictate otherwise. Human rights do not support the equal right of everyone to kill. They support the right of everyone NOT to be killed, occupied, and exploited—another key function militaries carry out. As such, human rights are anti-military by nature.

I want to be clear that I'm not one of those knee-jerk anti-soldier types. I grew up in a military family, spent many years bagging groceries in an army commissary, and lots of time on military bases—the point is, as individuals, military personnel are as diverse a group of people as are academics or artists, the other two groups of people I've spent a lot of time around. Racism, sexism, homophobia, poverty-by-design—these problems are institutionalized throughout this country and you'll find people who accept the status quo as well as those fighting the long slow battle against injustice in all institutions, including the branches of the military. What makes the military unique is not the individuals in uniform but the fact that their job description, in the final instance, is to kill people. Legally and explicitly. Killing is not the exclusive or even the most frequent activity performed, but it is the ultimate threat, the ultimate purpose of having armed forces.

It's sad that advocating for the outlawing of the military is widely seen as naïve and utopian: after all, there are threats out there and without a military we would be defenseless. It's ironic that many who make that argument in support of the military also consider themselves Christians. Even though, to my understanding, being a Christian means "walking the Jesus path." And didn't Jesus refuse to use arms (or to let family or friends do so on his behalf) even in self-defense, even though that commitment resulted in his death? When it comes down to it, though, I'm not as principled as Jesus. I support the use of violence in slave uprisings and anti-colonial movements. I imagine that I would kill someone whom I witnessed in the act of attempting to kill, torture, or rape others or myself, if I had the means and if that were the only way to stop that act from happening. But what all of those situations have in common reflect a way in which the U.S. military is rarely used: to stop brutality as it is happening.

Queerness, broadly speaking, is a challenge to mainstream common sense. Why should we buy into the mantra of it being necessary to have a military? Or of American lives being so much more worthy than the lives of others that "collateral damage" in the course of preventing a possible attack on the U.S. is acceptable? Let's take the Orwellian factor out of the term "defense" and restore that word to its actual meaning: let's create a defense force that is ready to respond and is only utilized when actual attacks are in-progress. Not to enforce the unequal trade policies from which we benefit, not to enforce the installment or removal of politicians to better serve U.S. interests, not to prevent attacks on the U.S. And certainly not to attack people who are not actively killing, enslaving, colonizing, or torturing anyone. You can shoot down the plane as it is heading for the World Trade Center, but not bomb targets you suspect of harboring terrorists planning future attacks. Yes, that means risking the possible death of innocent Americans in a future attack. But the alternative is to guarantee the death of innocent non-Americans based on conjecture.

There is a lot of talk about the military "protecting" Americans. Frankly, a much better job of that will be done if the funds diverted from scaling back the military to an actual defense force are invested in universal health care, education, job creation, living wage legislation, cancer research, and the like. Eradicating poverty and ensuring health care will save far more lives every year than so-called "national security." There are far too many Americans who do, indeed, lead insecure lives. But terrorism is the least cause of their condition—the more significant threats are domestic policies that see their lives as acceptable collateral damage to an increasingly unregulated capitalism of every man for himself. In fact, the majority of young people who join the military do so out of their own sense of insecurity and a desire to make a difference in the world. They cite the military as the only option they see to afford college and/or to receive a steady paycheck, and as a source of meaningful work. Propaganda ensures that they can pursue this path without going insane, by being led to believe that they are heroes, nobly serving their country. But I believe that our country (not to mention many other places in the world) is actually being done a grave disservice by sacrificing such a large portion of our material and human resources to the military. And it is a tragedy that so many young people's desires to do good are preyed upon, manipulated through fear-mongering nationalist ideology, and diverted into the destruction of lives, the devastation of the planet, and the perpetuation of inequality.

Instead of fighting for the right to serve in the military, let's fight for the right of military service being prohibited. To increase our national security. And for the protection of all our human rights, globally.

AFTERTHOUGHT

It is tricky to write an essay that accepts discrimination as a means to an end. In what remains a homophobic, racist, sexist society, I fear enabling a slippery slope of arguments for identity-based discrimination. Although, of course, the entire notion of citizens who are "protected" by a military discriminates against people based on the identity factor of nationality. Hence my point about human rights trumping civil rights. My argument that we should be fighting against, not for, gay people's inclusion in the military is not actually about gay people at all. Nor is it about wanting others to do our dirty work for us. As I said, I think everyone should be banned from military service. But if the goal is demilitarization, fighting for even more people to have the right to join the military makes no sense. There are plenty of other civil rights denied gay people for which we still need to fight—civil rights that do not trample on others' human rights.

Rage, or the Lack Thereof

YASMIN NAIR

A MAN STANDS CHAINED TO a fence, his face carefully composed in a look that can only be described as telegenic martyrdom. He is wearing a camouflage military uniform, and a black beret. The fence, it turns out, is the one around the White House. The man's name is Dan Choi, it is March 2010, and he is set to become a symbol of all the contradictions of the new political rage in the United States.

What was Dan Choi so angry about in March—and again in April—of 2010? My leftist, anti-war heart beats more quickly at such a sight because I always imagine that the soldier in question is about to launch into a critique of the U.S. war machine: "With this act, I declare the end of my allegiance to the project of death and destruction carried out by our country." Or some such thing. You get the point.

So it was a disappointment to me to learn that Choi was protesting the fact that he, a gay soldier discharged under the U.S. military's "Don't Ask, Don't Tell" policy, was protesting his ouster and demanding to be let back in. Wait. "What was that again?" you ask. A man

---

This piece originally appeared in the November/December 2011 issue of the Montréal-based online magazine No More Potlucks *(nomorepotlucks.org).*

enters an institution, a man is unfairly ejected after it is discovered that he is gay, thus revealing, we must assume, said institution to be deeply flawed and even dangerous. And then the man demands to be let back in. If the definition of insanity is doing the same thing over and over again…is Dan Choi insane?

No, to the best of my knowledge, but he has frequently taken on the mantle of martyrdom, often comparing himself to historical figures like Martin Luther King and Mahatma Gandhi, as in an interview with *Newsweek* shortly after his first protest.[1] In the same interview, he spoke grandly against the stereotype of West Point graduates like him as a privileged people:[2] "We are tired of being stereotyped as privileged, bourgeois elites. Is someone willing to give up their career, their relationships with powerful people, their Rolodex, or their parents' love to stand up for who they are? I'm giving up my military rank, my unit—which to me is a family—my veterans' benefits, my health care, so what are you willing to sacrifice?"

One might be excused for being stunned into (temporary) silence at the sheer audacity of this statement. To date, over 50 million in the U.S. are without health insurance. Millions work without benefits or have seen a sizable cut in them. Medical costs constitute the leading cause of bankruptcy in the country. According to one report, citing a Harvard study, "62% of all personal bankruptcies in the U.S. in 2007 were caused by health problems—and 78% of those filers had insurance."[3] Given all this, it is hard to be admonished by a member of the ever-shrinking elite with benefits when one has none to sacrifice. As for his question about whether or not the rest of us are willing to give up "relationships with powerful people": he has, I think, a great many of us—who don't have such relationships in the first place—stumped.

As if his statement about who has privilege and who does not was not startling enough, Choi went on to speak of his experience in Iraq when the reporter asked him what it was like to be in jail: "I've detained people in Iraq, I've read them their rights, and I've applied handcuffs and zip ties. I've talked with people in Arabic who've just been arrested. I know what it means to arrest someone for my country's mission. But I've never been incarcerated, and for something that I thought was not my country's mission. I know my country's mission is not to make an entire group of people into second-class citizens."

This last sentence should give pause to anyone who knows anything of what goes on in Iraq and Afghanistan, or has even heard of the infamous Abu Ghraib photographs.

As expected, much of the gay press and community have held up Choi as their martyr. If there is dissension around him, it comes not from an examination of what his politics might mean but what they look like. While GetEqual, the group behind Choi, proclaims that it is "radical" for supposedly daring to engage in tactics like those used by Choi, the more conservative Human Rights Campaign (HRC), with a $35 million budget, focuses on expensive fundraisers and lobbying politicians in D.C., where the organization is based. Broadly speaking, the mainstream LGBT community in the U.S. advances an agenda whose ideology ranges from the right to the center of right. Issues like marriage, DADT, and hate crimes legislation take up the economic and political capital of the "community" while matters like the homelessness of queer youth or the drop in AIDS funding are routinely set aside with the explanation that the first three will take care of the rest. GetEqual, HRC, and GOProud simply want the status quo—in the form of marriage and the rest—to be expanded to gays and lesbians. None of their activism, in any form, challenges the hierarchy established by marriage, for instance.

Which is to say: conservative issues like marriage, DADT, and hate crimes legislation are the emphasis in the mainstream gay community, and the only differences between such groups lie in the styles of the advocacy they engage in, not the content. Yet a recent *Washington Post* article about the gay rights movement declared that HRC was on the left of the gay community and GOProud, the gay Republican group, was on the right. The fact that both groups are fighting for exactly the same thing did not seem to have occurred to the reporter.

But therein lies the fundamental problem with the left in the U.S.: its utter inability to separate itself from conservatives and liberals who, after all, merely want more of the same. When it comes to defining who is left and who is right, the distinctions come down to style, not ideology. Under these circumstances, it is no surprise that Choi should emerge as the brave and angry martyr who has had enough and will risk such things as "relationships to important people." And he is regarded as such even by those on the left, like Amy Goodman, the popular host of the progressive television and radio show *Democracy Now*, who should know better.

Amy Goodman is as popular as she is among lefties and liberals because she is often one of the few anti-war voices of reason on the radio. But Goodman has had Dan Choi on *Democracy Now* a few times and has never once criticized his fervent pro-war and pro-U.S. imperialist rhetoric. Not only that, she has gone so far as to pen not one but two op-eds, one of them titled "Lt. Choi Won't Lie for His Country," in which she repeated some of what he said to her during a 2009 interview:

> Choi got a message from an Iraqi doctor whose hospital Choi helped to rebuild while he was there. He said the doctor is "in South Baghdad right now. And he's seen some of the Internet, YouTube and CNN interviews and other appearances, and he said: 'Brother, I know that you're gay, but you're still my brother, and you're my friend. And if your country, that sent you to my country, if America, that sent you to Iraq, will discharge you such that you can't get medical benefits, you can come to my hospital any day. You can come in, and I will give you treatment.'"

More recently, Choi was on *Democracy Now*, in a debate with the queer radical anti-war activist Mattilda Bernstein Sycamore, and said, "...war is a force that gives us meaning. War is a force that teaches us lessons of humanity and allows us to realize something about our society and teaches us the lessons that we probably should have learned before we went to war." Neither Goodman nor Juan Gonzalez, her co-host, blinked an eye. Goodman has not simply featured Choi's views on her show, she has explicitly endorsed them in her op-eds outside her role as show co-host.

Within today's left, or what passes for the same, it is actually possible to have someone like Goodman, who has spent many hours among commentators critiquing the devastation caused to Iraq, listen to Choi talk about "rebuilding" a country that he is helping to bomb and destroy, without a single question about his politics. In this case, identity—and its efflorescence under a neoliberal war—becomes the excuse for war and it erases the possibility of a critique of Choi's ideology. Even further, the war on Iraq becomes a staging ground for Choi's personal dramas, a backdrop to the possibility of a doomed romance. As Mattilda Bernstein Sycamore puts it, "How many Iraqis died in order for him to express the 'truth of who I am?' What about the truth of the war?…Did you hear that? He's not worried about dying in an atrocious war, or killing innocent civilians, but about whether his boyfriend will be notified."[4]

Choi's anger at having been expelled from the military and his on-the-surface radical tactics are symptomatic of the failure of the left in the U.S. to mobilize for the things that matter, like health care, leaving the political arena wide open for the likes of gay soldiers to angrily demand that they should be allowed to fight unjust wars. Modern times have rarely been worse in the United States, and yet, all over, there is anger about maintaining the status quo instead of meaningful change. Hence the growth of the Tea Party and its deployment of anger, much of it foolish and misplaced, as in the signs that read, "Keep the government out of my Medicare" (the government's form of health care for the elderly).

In the wake of such struggles, what happens to the efforts of those who do fight for actual change?

Here in Chicago, I am a member of Gender JUST (GJ), a largely youth-led organization that has, for nearly two years, successfully fought for a Chicago Public Schools (CPS) to institute a grievance process that would make it easier for students to report harassment and bullying. The current CEO of CPS, Ron Huberman is an out gay man with a partner and an adopted infant. For nearly two years, Huberman stalled on meeting with GJ and acting upon his promise to help make schools safer for youth, particularly queer youth, despite public promises to do so. Finally, the group decided to enact the kind of tactics long employed by direct action groups: it showed up at Huberman's public appearances and even went to his house with a basket of cookies and testimonials from youth who had been harassed and bullied. Eventually, after a series of such escalations, Huberman agreed to institute a grievance process.

In the wake of the protest outside his house, we were told by some that they were troubled or even offended by the fact that GJ would actually show up at the house—where his child was. It was as if GJ had shown up and threatened to take away the infant, or had thrown stones at it. As Sam Finkelstein, one of the lead organizers, put it to me, "Why is no one thinking of the children and youth who suffer daily harassment and agony simply for going to school?" Implicit in the criticism of the actions was the idea that Huberman's private residence should be invulnerable and that GJ had committed a major social infraction by daring to go to his house. This kind of logic is typical of protests in the U.S. where dissent and protest have been nearly squelched by endlessly minute and refined bureaucratic efforts, via the process of having to ask for permits for every action or the constant admonition, during protests, to keep moving and stay on the sidewalk, instead of taking over the streets.

The students of Chicago's public schools study in the nation's most militarized school district; its largely minority and often poor population is constantly targeted by the U.S. army for recruitment. Over the years, there has been admirable resistance to such militarization from many local educators on the left and groups like Gender JUST which have consistently been critical of such developments. Those criticizing GJ for its tactics failed to make the connections between Huberman's supposed imperviousness to protest while inside his home, and the extreme vulnerability of students within school walls.

Our rage, the productive sort that might actually demand change, is constantly being curtailed either by convenient distinctions between private and public or by a public discourse that fails to see the contradictions in a gay soldier who considers himself a second-class citizen of the U.S. while handcuffing Iraqis. Rage appears in stylistic flourishes, as in the Tea Party protests where citizens rant and rave about policies about which they have little understanding or by soldiers demanding "fair" treatment in an institution that is fundamentally unfair to the rest of the world.

Rage has dissipated into conciliation and a call for the status quo.

NOTES

1 http://www.newsweek.com/2010/03/21/this-is-my-mission.
html

2 Choi was responding to criticisms that elite military personnel like him, who graduate from institutions like West Point
and choose to enter the military with specialized skills, are
different from the much poorer young Latino/a or African
American youth aggressively recruited by the army with the
explicit promise of social mobility. The U.S. military still boasts
of the G.I. Bill of 1944 as the best example of how it provides
college or vocational education for returning veterans, along
with various loans for homes and businesses. But today, with
military service being largely voluntary, the military must rely
on aggressive and even duplicitous forms of recruitment. In its
advertising, it shamelessly deploys narratives about troubled
youth of color within single-mother households who need the
discipline, targeting them as ideal candidates for "discipline" on
its visits to high schools (where it is allowed to enter for recruitment purposes); it even goes so far as to recruit undocumented
youth with the false promise of eventual citizenship. Today,
the military depends on a two-tier system for recruitment: elite
soldiers like Choi, who enter voluntarily, and the economically
and politically disenfranchised who join out of desperation.

3 http://www.businessweek.com/bwdaily/dnflash/content/
jun2009/db2009064_666715.htm?campaign_id=rss_daily

4 http://www.bilerico.com/2010/08/a_fine_romance_democracy
_nows_amy_goodman_and_lieu.php

Queer Eyes on What Prize?
Ending DADT

ERICA MEINERS AND THERESE QUINN

SO, WE'VE HEARD THAT BARACK OBAMA is going to repeal the Don't Ask, Don't Tell policy that prohibits gays and lesbians from serving openly in the military. As two queer teachers that have been working hard to arrest the militarism of education in Chicago—a public high school for every branch of the military, and two for the army (and not one of these with a Gay Straight Alliance for students), and over 10,000 youth from sixth to twelfth grade participating in some form of military program in their public schools—we are not leaping with joy at this rumor. Our reluctance has our allies scratching their heads:

"Isn't this what you want?"

"Equal right to fight!"

"What a success for the gay rights movement!"

"I guess this solves the discrimination problem in military public schools, then."

"Gay kids can join up!"

This piece was originally published on February 25, 2009 in the Chicago-based LGBT paper, Windy City Times.

Sure, we think uniforms are hot, but this—permitting out lesbians and gay men to enlist—was never the purpose of gay liberation, a movement aiming as tenaciously at peace as equal rights.

And for us, it's clear that overturning Don't Ask, Don't Tell (DADT) won't begin to address the public policy catastrophe of turning over our public schools, and some of our nation's poorest youth, to the military.

We argue that the system of public education should remain a civilian system. This statement rests on three proposals. First, adults may choose to enlist; youth cannot. Next, schools should educate students for the broadest possibilities and choices; the military narrowly aims to prepare recruits. And last, schools should protect young people and nurture peace; but the military is contagiously violent. From the ugly revelations of Abu Ghraib, and the rash of sexual assaults on military women by men in service, to many veterans' post-service violence turned both inward and outward—its legacy of brutality is so vast that the Department of Defense might more aptly be called the Department of Destruction.

This proposed repeal, far from any big win, offers queers an important opportunity to think about our strategies and goals. Let's not unfurl our victory banner too quickly; instead, we should keep our queer eyes, and organizing, focused on the real prize: social justice.

Yes, gays, lesbians and transgendered folks are discriminated against and excluded from full participation in our society and its institutions, including schools (read any report about rates of violence against gay students or employment discrimination for out queer or non-gendering conforming school staff), military (DADT—enough said?), families (remember the 57% majority that passed the 2008 gay adoption ban in Arkansas) and religion (many religious colleges and universities ban homosexual students, staff, and faculty—legally!).

Add to this list the ease with which otherwise smart people, including President Obama, reserve marriage and all its attendant privileges for "one man and one woman" while also claiming they are "ferocious" defenders of gay rights—that's a fairly self-serving stance, isn't it? Yes, gays and lesbians still have a long way to go toward achieving... let's just call it "fully human status" in the United States.

The push to repeal DADT is, on the one hand, a no-brainer—all people should have all rights, right?

But this proposal can also be understood, and it is by us, as an attempt to remap what our social justice goals, as queers, should be—not the right to privacy and the right to public life, and certainly not the right to live lives free from our nation's ever-present militarism and never-ending war. Instead, lesbians, gays, transgendered, and bisexuals are encouraged to forget our historical places at the helm of social justice thinking and labor (to mention just a few, Jane Addams, Bayard Rustin, Barbara Jordan, and of course, Harvey Milk), constrict our vision and dreams, and just be happy for an opportunity to participate in a military that depends on poverty and permanent war to keep enlistment high.

Let's forget repealing DADT and cut right to the chase: Repeal the Department of Defense. What about establishing a Department of Peace, as Dennis Kucinich has already proposed? Let's pair that with bear brigades tossing pink batons (and, of course, an annual teddy bear picnic). Or, we can take up the mermaid parade as an organizing celebration, with its dress-up and float creation. Either of these fanciful, and very queer, forms would allow us all to play and create together, and each seems a better activity for a school to take up than pretend soldiering.

Then let's organize for some real social justice goals.

For starters, let's demand universal health care, affordable housing, and meaningful living wage employment that supports flourishing, not merely subsisting, lives, for all.

We know we don't need sixth or twelfth graders wearing military uniforms, marching with wooden guns on public school grounds. We don't need twelve-year-olds parsing military ranks or plotting battles. However, we could use more teens painting murals, stitching gowns, and writing code and lyrics. In short, we don't need child soldiers, but we could use more young artists.

A public school system that teaches peace and art, with fiercely equal opportunities for all students. We can see it now: painting classes, soccer clubs, computer gaming classes, drum-kits, comprehensive sexuality education, and musical theatre in every school. That's so excellently queer, and so very just.

Why I Oppose Repealing DADT & Passage of the DREAM Act

TAMARA K. NOPPER

ONE OF THE FIRST BOOKS I read about Asian American feminism was the anthology *Dragon Ladies: Asian American Feminists Breathe Fire*. In one of the essays, author Juliana Pegues describes scenes from a "radical Asian women's movement." One such scene involves lesbian and bisexual Asian and Pacific Islanders marching at Gay Pride with signs reading "Gay white soldiers in Asia? Not my liberation!" and "ends with the absence of all soldiers, gay and straight, from any imperialist army."

Although it has been over a decade since I read this passage, I return to this "scene" as I watch far too many liberals and progressives praise the possible repeal of Don't Ask, Don't Tell (DADT) as well as the possible passage of the DREAM Act (Development, Relief, and Education for Alien Minors Act).

In some ways, I understand why people are supportive of such gestures. The idea that certain identities and status categories, such as gay

---

This piece originally appeared on Tamara K. Nopper's blog (bandung1955. wordpress.com) on September 19, 2010.

or lesbian or (undocumented) immigrants are either outlawed or treated as social problems has rightfully generated a great deal of sympathy. And the very real ways that people experience marginalization or discrimination—ranging from a lack of certain rights to violence, including death—certainly indicates that solutions are needed. Further, far too many non-whites have experienced disproportionate disadvantages, surveillance, and discipline from both DADT and anti-immigrant legislation. For example, Black women, some of whom are not lesbians, have been disproportionately discharged from the U.S. military under DADT. And anti-immigrant legislation, policing measures, and vigilante xenophobic racism is motivated by and reinforces white supremacy and white nationalism.

Yet both the repeal of DADT and the passage of the DREAM Act will increase the size and power of the U.S. military and the Department of Defense, which is already the largest U.S. employer. Repealing DADT will make it easier for gays and lesbians to openly serve and the Dream Act in its present incarnation may provide a pathway to legal residency and possibly citizenship for some undocumented immigrant young people if they serve two years in the U.S. military or spend an equal amount of time in college.

Unsurprisingly, the latter, being pushed by Democrats, is getting support from "many with close ties to the military and higher education." As the *Wall Street Journal* reports:

> Pentagon officials support the Dream Act. In its strategic plan for fiscal years 2010–2012, the Office of the Under Secretary of Defense for Personnel and Readiness cited the Dream Act as a "smart" way to attract quality recruits to the all-volunteer force...

> "Passage of the Dream Act would be extremely beneficial to the U.S. military and the country as a whole," said Margaret Stock, a retired West Point professor who studies immigrants in the military. She said it made "perfect" sense to attach it to the defense-authorization bill.

> Louis Caldera, secretary of the Army under President Bill Clinton, said that as they struggled to meet recruiting goals,

"recruiters at stations were telling me it would be extremely valuable for these patriotic people to be allowed to serve our country."

Additionally, in a 2009 Department of Defense strategic plan report, the second strategic goal, "Shape and maintain a mission-ready All Volunteer Force," lists the DREAM Act as a possible recruitment tool under one of the "performance objectives":

> Recruit the All-Volunteer Force by finding smart ways to sustain quality assurance even as we expand markets to fill manning at controlled costs as demonstrated by achieving quarterly recruiting quality and quantity goals, and through expansion of the Military Accessions Vital to the National Interest (MAVNI) program and the once-medically restricted populations, as well as the DREAM initiative.

What concerns me is that far too many liberals and progressives, including those who serve as professional commentators on cable news and/or progressive publications (and some with a seemingly deep affinity for the Democratic Party) have been praising the passage of the DREAM Act. Unsurprising is that many of the same people support the repeal of DADT. While a sincere concern about discrimination may unite both gestures, so too does a lack of critical perspective regarding the U.S. military as one of the main vehicles in the expansion and enforcement of U.S. imperialism, heterosexuality, white supremacy, capitalism, patriarchy, and repression against political dissent and people's movements in the United States and abroad. Far too many liberals and progressives, including those critical of policies or the squashing of political dissent, take an ambivalent stance on the U.S. military. It is unclear what makes some of these folks unwilling to openly oppose the military state. Perhaps it's easier than dealing with the backlash from a variety of people, including the many people of color and/or women who are now building long-term careers in the military. Or maybe it's more amenable to building careers as pundits in both corporate and progressive media, both of which may be critical of some defense spending or "wasted" (read unsuccessful) military efforts but not necessarily of U.S. militarism.

Whatever the case, the inclusion of more gays and lesbians and/or undocumented immigrant youth in the U.S. military is not an ethical project given that both gestures are willing to have our communities serve as mercenaries in exchange for certain rights, some of which are never fully guaranteed in a homophobic and white supremacist country. Nor is it pragmatic. By supporting the diversification of the U.S. military we undermine radical democratic possibilities by giving the military state more people, many of whom will ultimately die in combat or develop PTSD and health issues and/or continue nurturing long-term relationships with the U.S. military, including a political affinity with its culture and goals. We will also have a more difficult time challenging projects of privatization, the incurring of huge amounts of debt, and the erosion of rights and protections in other countries— efforts buttressed by the threat of military action—which ultimately affects people in the United States.

Of course I am not the first person to raise these concerns. There are gay, lesbian, bisexual, and transgender folks, many of them non-white and non-middle class, who promote a queer politic that challenges the heteronormative desires of mainstream movements, including that pushed by some LGBT organizations and their purported "allies" within the Democratic party and heteronormative people of color organizations. Some of these folks organize for better economic opportunities, access to housing, and safer existences in the civilian sector for poor and working-class LGBTs. And some also openly oppose military recruitment or challenge the push for gays and lesbians to (openly) serve in the military by countering with "Don't serve" as a slogan. For example, Cecilia Lucas, who grew up in a military family, writes in a 2010 *CounterPunch* article:

> Don't Ask, Don't Tell is bad policy. It encourages deceit and, specifically, staying in the closet, which contributes to internalized as well as public homophobia, thus perpetuating discrimination and violence against LGBT people. Banning gay people from serving in the military, however, is something I support. Not because I'm anti-gay, nope, I'm one of those queer folks myself. I'm also a woman and would support a law

against women serving in the military. Not because I think women are less capable. I would support laws against any group of people serving in the military: people of color, tall people, people between the ages of 25 and 53, white men, poor people, people who have children, people who vote for Democrats—however you draw the boundaries of a group, I would support a law banning them from military service. Because I support outlawing the military. And until that has happened, I support downsizing it by any means necessary, including, in this one particular arena, sacrificing civil rights in the interest of human rights...

It is tricky to write an essay that accepts discrimination as a means to an end. In what remains a homophobic, racist, sexist society, I fear enabling a slippery slope of arguments for identity-based discrimination. Although, of course, the entire notion of citizens who are "protected" by a military discriminates against people based on the identity factor of nationality. Hence my point about human rights trumping civil rights. My argument that we should be fighting against, not for, gay people's inclusion in the military is not actually about gay people at all. Nor is it about wanting others to do our dirty work for us. As I said, I think everyone should be banned from military service. But if the goal is demilitarization, fighting for even more people to have the right to join the military makes no sense. There are plenty of other civil rights denied gay people for which we still need to fight—civil rights that do not trample on others' human rights.

As Lucas's comments reveal, opposing LGBT folks from serving openly in the military is not to condone the harassment and unfair surveillance that they experience; nor is it meant to support a culture that suggests they should stay in the closet in the name of military stability and national security. Rather, it is to discourage the attractiveness of military enlistment as well as martial citizenship, a process that provides marginalized groups a "pathway to citizenship" via military service. More, opposition to people serving in the military is also grounded in an understanding that the military negatively impacts practically everyone in the world (including those in the United States), and in particular people of color and/or women and/or gays and lesbians, and not just those who are discriminated against while serving or who are expected to serve as pathways to citizenship or access to education.

Along with folks like Lucas, there are immigrants and their allies challenging us to rethink the possible passage of the DREAM Act because of its pro-military provision and for basically "making a pool of young, bilingual, U.S.-educated, high-achieving students available to the recruiters." Some have withdrawn their support for the current version of the act in objection to its terms. For example, a letter from one such person, Raúl Al-qaraz Ochoa, states:

> Passage of the DREAM Act would definitely be a step forward in the struggle for Migrant Justice. Yet the politicians in Washington have hijacked this struggle from its original essence and turned dreams into ugly political nightmares. I refuse to be a part of anything that turns us into political pawns of dirty Washington politics. I want my people to be "legalized" but at what cost? We all want it bad. I hear it. I've lived it. But I think it's a matter of how much we're willing to compromise in order to win victories or crumbs...So if I support the DREAM Act, does this mean I am okay with our people being used as political pawns? Does this mean that my hands will be smeared with the same bloodshed the U.S. spills all over the world? Does this mean I am okay with blaming my mother and my father for migrating "illegally" to the U.S.? Am I willing to surrender to all that in exchange for a benefit? Maybe it's easier for me to say that "I can" because I have papers, right? I'd like to think that it's because my political principles will not allow me to do so, regardless of my citizenship status or personal benefit at stake. Strong movements that achieve greater victories are those that stand in solidarity with all oppressed people of the world and never gain access to rights at the expense of other oppressed groups.

> I have come to a deeply painful decision: I can no longer in good political conscience support the DREAM Act because the essence of a beautiful dream has been detained by a colonial nightmare seeking to fund and fuel the U.S. empire machine.

Unfortunately, the willingness of folks like Lucas and Al-qaraz Ochoa as well as others to critically engage military diversification or the passage of the DREAM Act given its military provisions have gotten less air time or attention among liberal and progressives actively pushing for both measures. In terms of repealing DADT, it is unfortunately not surprising that the rejection of military inclusion by LGBT folks has gotten minimal attention from professional progressives, some of whom are straight. Too many straight people who profess to be LGBT allies tend to align themselves with the liberal professional wings of LGBT politics given shared bourgeois notions of "respectable" (i.e., not offensive to straight people) gay politics that also promotes a middle-class notion of democracy—and supports the Democratic Party. Additionally, it's more time efficient to find out what professional LGBT organizations think, since they are more likely to have resources to make it easier to learn their agendas without as much effort as learning from those who politically labor in the margins of the margins, given their critical stances toward the political mainstream. Yet given the tendency for many professional progressives to be on the Internet and social media sites, it is a bit telling that many have supported DADT without addressing the critical stances of some LGBT folks against the military state that are easily available on the Internet. This noticeable lack of engagement raises some questions: Why is it that the straight progressives are more willing to have gays and lesbians serve in the U.S. military (or get married) than, let's say, breaking bread with and seriously considering the political views of LGBT folks who take radical political stances against the military state (as well as engage in non-middle-class aesthetics)? And why do many straight progressives fight for LGBT folks to openly serve in the military—one of the most dangerous employment sites that requires its laborers to kill and control others, including non-whites and/or LGBTs, in the name of empire—but rarely discuss how working-class, poor, and/or of color LGBTs are treated and politically organize for opportunities in the civilian sector job market where they are also expected to remain closeted, subject to homophobic harassment and surveillance, or excluded altogether?

Also concerning is the willingness of many progressives to support the DREAM Act, despite it possibly being tied up to a defense-authorization bill and having support from a diverse group of people united by a commitment to military recruitment. While some support is due to a righteous critique of white supremacy that shapes pathways to citizenship, some (also) support the DREAM Act because it serves as a form of "reparations" for foreign policies and colonialism toward third world or developing countries once called home to many of the immigrant youth or their families targeted by the legislation That is, the famous quote "We're here because you were there" seems to be the underlying mantra of some pushing for the act's passage. Yet if "being there" involved the U.S. military, it is unclear how a resolution to this issue, ethically or pragmatically, calls for immigrant youth to serve for the same U.S. military that devastated, disrupted, undermined, and still controls many of the policies and everyday life of the immigrants' homelands.

Partially to blame for the uncritical support of the DREAM Act are different factions of the immigrant rights movement, as well as funders and some progressive media, that have pushed for an uncritical embrace of the immigrant rights movement among progressives. It is difficult to raise critical views of the (diverse) immigrant rights movement, even when making it clear that one rejects the white supremacy and white nationalism of the right wing (as well as white-run progressive media and progressive institutions, such as some labor unions) without experiencing some backlash from other progressives, particularly people of color. In turn, critical questions about how immigrant rights movements may support, rather than undermine U.S. hegemony or white supremacy, have been taken off the table at most progressive gatherings, large and small. Subsequently, while some may express concern about the DREAM Act being part of a defense-authorization bill, there are probably fewer who will openly take stands against the bill, given the threat of being labeled xenophobic by some progressives unwilling to reject the U.S. military state or interrogate the politics of immigration from an anti-racist and anti-capitalist perspective. In the process, the military may end up getting easier access to immigrant youth who may have difficulty going to college.

As the passage from *Dragon Ladies* shows, some take into account the complexity of identities and political realities as well as maintain oppositional stances against those apparatuses that are largely responsible for the limited choices far too many people have. Many of us are looking for ways to mediate the very real vulnerabilities and lack of job security, as well as forms of social rejection that causes the stress, fear, and physical consequences experienced before and especially during this recession. And given the recent upsurge in explicit gestures of white supremacy and white nationalism as demonstrated by the growing strength of the Tea Party, it may be the most expedient to play up on the shared support of the U.S. military among a broad spectrum of people in order to secure, at least on paper, some basic rights to which straight and/or white people have gotten access. But progressives who support the repeal of DADT and passage of the DREAM Act might instead consider other political possibilities explored by some of those who are the subjects of such policy debates; these folks, some of whom are desperately in need of protection, job security, and safety, encourage us to resist the urge for quick resolutions that ultimately serve to stabilize the military state and instead explore more humane options— for those targeted by DADT and the DREAM Act as well as the rest of the world.

Bradley Manning
Rich Man's War, Poor (Gay) Man's Fight

LARRY GOLDSMITH

A POOR, YOUNG GAY MAN from the rural South joins the U.S. Army under pressure from his father, and because it's the only way left to pay for a college education. He is sent to Iraq, where he is tormented by fellow soldiers who entertain themselves watching "war porn" videos of drone and helicopter attacks on civilians. He is accused of leaking documents to Wikileaks and placed in solitary confinement, where he has been held for more than a year awaiting a military trial. The President of the United States, a former Constitutional law professor lately suffering amnesia about the presumption of innocence, declares publicly that "he broke the law." The United Nations Special Rapporteur on Torture, Amnesty International, and the American Civil Liberties Union express grave concern about the conditions of his imprisonment, and the spokesman for the U.S.

This piece originally appeared online at CommonDreams.org on June 7, 2011. As an archival editorial collective, Against Equality is committed to preserving and presenting work in its original form, so that we may consider issues and events in their original contexts. This article was written in 2011, when Chelsea Manning was still publicly known as Bradley.

State Department is forced to resign after calling it "ridiculous and counterproductive and stupid." A letter signed by 295 noted legal scholars charges that his imprisonment violates the Eighth Amendment prohibition of cruel and unusual punishment and the Fifth Amendment guarantee against punishment without trial, and that procedures used on Manning "calculated to disrupt profoundly the senses or the personality" amount to torture.

The National Gay and Lesbian Task Force, the Lambda Legal Defense and Education Fund, and the Human Rights Campaign, having invested millions lobbying for "gays in the military," have no comment. Of course not. Bradley Manning is not that butch patriotic homosexual, so central to the gays-in-the-military campaign, who Defends Democracy and Fights Terrorism with a virility indistinguishable from that of his straight buddies. He is not that pillar of social and economic stability, only incidentally homosexual, who returns home from the front to a respectable profession and a faithful spouse and children.

No, Bradley Manning is a poor, physically slight computer geek with an Oklahoma accent. He is, let us use the word, and not in a negative way, a sissy. Having grown up in a dysfunctional family in a small town in the South, he is that lonely, maladjusted outsider many gay people have been, or are, or recognize, whether we wish to admit it or not. He broke the law, the president says. And he did so—the liberal press implies, trying terribly hard to temper severity with compassion—because he wasn't man enough to deal with the pressure. He did so because he's a sissy and he couldn't put up with the manly rough-and-tumble that is so important to unit cohesion, like that time three of his buddies assaulted him and instead of taking it like a good soldier he peed in his pants. And then of course he was so embarrassed he threw a hissy fit and sent Wikileaks our nation's most closely guarded secrets, like some petulant teenage girl who gets her revenge by spreading gossip. This is, of course, the classic argument about gays and national security—they'll get beat up or blackmailed and reveal our secrets. And NGLTF, Lambda, and HRC, with their impeccably professional media and lobbying campaign, based on the best branding and polls and focus groups that money could buy, have effectively demolished that insidious stereotype.

They have demolished it by abandoning Bradley Manning.

Why was Bradley Manning in the U.S. Army in the first place? Why does anyone join the U.S. Army nowadays? Perhaps a few join out of a sincere if misguided idealism that they are truly going to defend freedom and democracy. But if that were commonly the case, one would expect to see a certain number of the more affluent classes, those who never stop preaching the need to defend democracy and freedom by military means, eager to enlist. There would be at least a few Bush and Cheney children fighting on the bloody ground of Iraq and Afghanistan.

Dick Cheney, of course, famously explained that he declined to fight in Vietnam—and invoked the privilege of the student deferment five times to avoid being drafted—because he "had better things to do." The draft is now a thing of the past, and the vast majority of those in the U.S. military are there precisely because they do not have better things to do. That is to say, there are few other opportunities available. The official national unemployment rate, now at 9.1 percent, masks a rate more than twice that figure for young people generally and more than three times that rate among young black men. Decent jobs are difficult to get, of course, without a college education. The U.S. manages, in the midst of an international economic crisis, to spend half a billion dollars every day on the wars in Iraq, Afghanistan, and Libya, but the federal and state governments have drastically cut funding for education, and public as well as private universities have reacted to funding cuts with astronomical increases in tuition and fees. Publicly-funded financial assistance to poor students is a thing of the past—except as part of a military recruitment package.

Bradley Manning wanted an education. He also wanted to get away from his family and out of his small town. Military recruiters do not spend much time in middle-class neighborhoods. They seek out those like Bradley Manning: poor, isolated teenagers dazzled by the slick brochures, the cool technology, the lofty rhetoric of duty and honor, and the generous promises—or who see right through the hype but know they have no other option. The military does not discriminate solely on the basis of sexual preference. In its recruitment it has always observed the time-honored and deeply discriminatory precept of "Rich man's war, poor man's fight."

This is the club that NGLTF, Lambda, and HRC would have gay people join. Let us leave aside for the moment the question of whether the club is a defender of freedom and democracy or an imperialist killing machine. It is in either case an institution that sends the Bradley Mannings of the world, and not the Dick Cheneys, to be killed or maimed—killing or maiming the Bradley Mannings, and not the Dick Cheneys, on the other side. Whatever collective psychosexual hang-ups or perverse ideological interests have prevented it from openly accepting homosexuals (or, not so long ago, women, or African Americans in integrated units), it is an institution whose fundamental design is to send poor people to die defending the interests of the affluent.

We did not need Bradley Manning to tell us that the military is an institution in defense of a class society. But his case does uniquely reveal a seldom-acknowledged disjuncture between modern LGBT politics, based as it is on the individualizing concepts of "gay identity" and "equal rights," and the way in which political power continues to be exercised through social relationships of class. It was a complex combination of factors—a lack of economic and educational opportunities, and the absence of a community and culture where he could be himself as a gay man—that led Bradley Manning to where he is now. These factors cannot be separated into the neat, discrete categories of single-issue politics. Organizations like NGLTF, Lambda Legal, and HRC would like to pretend that Bradley Manning's case is not a "gay issue," or worse, remain silent because they know that it is indeed a gay issue, one that threatens to undermine their carefully-crafted plea for admittance to the military. Addressing it as a gay issue would mean looking critically not only at the specific discriminatory policy of the military, but also at the very purpose of the military. It would mean taking a good close look at the patriotic rhetoric of "equal rights" to serve in an "all-volunteer" military, whose purpose is to defend "freedom" and "democracy," where LGBT people can be just as "virile" in carrying out organized killing as their heterosexual counterparts. It would mean considering how such rhetoric hides unpleasant truths about economic domination in our world, understanding how such domination relies on structures of power embedded in social relations of class, race, and gender, and recognizing that these structures cannot be addressed individually, but must be attacked simultaneously. Organizations like NGLTF, Lambda Legal, and HRC that define "LGBT rights" as a single issue divorced from such considerations abandon the Bradley Mannings of the world not just to psychological torture by Presidential edict, but at the entrances to universities barred to those without money, at the military recruiting stations that have replaced the financial aid offices, and at the bases where soldiers, when not engaged in killing the declared enemy, learn to entertain themselves by bullying each other and watching war porn.

Why I Won't Be Celebrating the Repeal of DADT
Queer Soldiers are Still Agents of Genocide

JAMAL RASHAD JONES

SO "DON'T ASK DON'T TELL" is looking like it will be repealed and there will be a party in the Castro. I, for one, am not going to be one of the many queens marching throughout the streets of the Castro with my American flag, fatigues, and pink helmet shining.

It seems almost ironic that the Queer liberation movement (now more aptly called the Gay Rights movement) has done a 180 since its radical inception. If anyone were to look into the rich history of Queer struggle they would, no doubt, come into close contact with the Gay Liberation Front (GLF). This group of radical queer groups, which crystallized around the time of the Stonewall Riots, took its name from the Vietnamese Liberation Front. This show of solidarity, through name, was symbolic of the fact that the GLA took a stance against capitalism, racism, and patriarchy in all their forms.

This piece first appeared on Jamal Rashad Jones's personal blog (ordoesitex-plode.wordpress.com) on December 22, 2010.

Gay Rights activists now find themselves crying out for marriage equality and inclusion in the military as if these issues are at the core of what it means to be a Queer oppressed in our current society and as if the rash of media-covered teen suicides would not happen if these two barriers could be overcome. They clearly have forgotten or didn't get the memo about the U.S. army being the symbol of Western imperialism and marriage being the backbone of patriarchy. Other issues, such as decent housing, medical treatment, and resistance to police brutality have become things associated with people of color and other groups. Gays have obviously come to a place where these are non-issues in their minds. Queer assimilation is the sinister nature of the State and Capitalism at its finest.

"The most dangerous creation of any society is the man who has nothing to lose."
—James A. Baldwin

The Queer population, in addition to others in the 60s and 70s, fought against the State and Capitalism, in large part because they had no material connection to the State. Queers found themselves outside of the nuclear family structure and the light of mainstream acceptance. This is why you see the great flight to San Francisco happen; this is why you see San Francisco become a Mecca of all things Gay. A home was needed and a home was found. This home, ironically, is the most symbolic of the radical change that has happened in the Queer population in the last 40–50 years.

The Castro district in San Francisco now stands as the most alienating piece of land to anyone that finds himself or herself not a rich, white, gay male. It is a destination for global tourism and one of the city's biggest moneymakers. Commodities line the windows of almost every store and you'd be lucky to find a flat here that is under 4,000 dollars. A few years back, the residents of the Castro district refused to have a youth center be built in the neighborhood because it would "bring down property value," in their words. The Castro is the perfect symbol of the complete bankruptcy and co-optation of the Queer

Rights movement. Tourism and profit stand over the lives and safety of youth who desperately need to escape from their abusive families. This is what happens when the Queers desire to become mainstream. It becomes an issue of "who can comfortably assimilate and who can't." And you can see what happens to those who can't.

My problem with the hype and pressure around DADT is that it distracts from the very things that the Queer Liberation movement was founded on: Anti-imperialism, anti-racism, equal access to housing and health care, and struggles against patriarchy. It seems almost irrelevant to me whether or not gay soldiers can "come out" in the military when the U.S. military is not only carrying out two genocidal campaigns for U.S. imperialism and corporate profit, but also when the war budget is draining the funds needed for almost every other service we so desperately need in this country. When I see the situation as such, not only does it become apparent to me that the Queer Movement must be anti-war, but also that the movement, as is, has been hijacked by a few high-powered assimilationists dragging everyone along through corporate propaganda.

So no, I will not be getting my tens in the Castro when DADT is struck down.

Pictures at an Execution

BILL ANDRIETTE

SOMETIMES PHOTOS PACK SUCH A punch that they're not just pictures of something, but also give off X-rays. Such photos yield secondary images—the shadows cast as the X-rays pass through the body-politic, revealing perhaps fractures, tumors, and clots otherwise unseen.

The bootleg snapshots from Abu Ghraib beamed such X-rays widely. The photos, you remember, depicted U.S. soldiers tormenting Iraqis held at Baghdad's infamous prison—piling them up naked, siccing dogs on them, mocking their corpses. But the corresponding X-ray image revealed as well a hidden abscess of brutality at U.S. prisons—day jobs at which a number of the reservist ring-leaders had just departed to fight in Iraq. In passing through the angry Muslim street, the X-rays revealed an intestinal blockage in Arab politics—for many Middle East rulers, sometimes not at the behest of American sponsors, had committed far more deadly atrocities against their people without thereby losing legitimacy. The X-rays as well showed a strange disconnect between the hemispheres in the Bush brain, which had ordered

This piece was originally printed as a feature article in the October 2005 edition of The Guide, *a gay travel magazine owned by Pink Triangle Press.*

careful juridical defenses of torture on one hand, and yet expressed shock—shock!—that American soldiers might force conquered Iraqis to simulate cocksucking.

The photos taken July 19 of Iranian teenagers Mahmoud Asgari, 16, and Ayaz Marhoni, 18, about to be hanged for sodomy, also radiated X-rays. The images made only a brief appearance in the mainstream media. But for gay people, even a glance was liable to catch the eye, as if on a hook. The two youths were executed in Mashad, a city in northeast Iran, and had each been in custody fourteen months. They confessed also to drinking, disturbing the peace, and theft. The youths had been tortured, at least by the 228 lashes they received before they were killed.

The photos produced various reactions—from calls to smash Iranian "Islamo-Fascism," to denunciations of executions of underage lawbreakers, to demands for an official U.S. investigation.

Yet the X-ray cast by the photos from Mashad also reveal contradictions in the Western gay body-politic and the human-rights groups that, by default, often serve as its foreign ministry.

WHAT HAPPENED?

The fate of Mahmoud Asgari and Ayaz Marhoni is clear, but what led up to their hangings isn't. There are two versions—that their crimes consisted mainly of consensual sex, either together, or with another teenager, 13; or that the two assaulted the younger boy.

The photos accompanied a report in Farsi from the Iranian Student News Agency on July 19. OutRage!, a British gay group, noticed ISNA's dispatch on the web, and says it had the article translated by a native speaker. OutRage! says the ISNA account said the youths were executed for sodomy, claims repeated in English on two other Iranian websites, one tied to an armed insurgent group fighting the Iranian state. On July 21, OutRage! issued a release: "Iran executes gay teenagers." Citing ISNA's interview with the youths as they were taken to the gallows, OutRage! noted that "They admitted (probably under torture) to having gay sex but claimed in their defense that most young boys had sex with each other and that they were not aware that homosexuality was punishable by death."

OutRage!'s report—and the shock of the photos—surged through the Internet, and caught the notice of U.S. gay groups that normally don't look much beyond American shores. Log Cabin Republicans and blogger Andrew Sullivan joined in expressing horror at the execution of the "gay teenagers." On Sullivan's blog, an unidentified soldier wrote that "Your post on the Islamo-fascist hanging/murder of the two gay men confirmed for me that my recent decision to join the U.S. military was correct. I have to stuff myself back in the closet... but our war on terror trumps my personal comfort at this point. Whenever my friends and family criticize—I'll show 'em that link." The Human Rights Campaign, along with some congressmen—Tom Lantos and openly-gay Barney Frank among them—called on the U.S. to investigate.

OutRage! contends that only subsequent news reports made other claims—that the two executed teenagers (when they were presumably aged 15 and 17) forced the other boy into sex. These allegations are not reliable, the group argues, but were likely concocted as a cover to blunt Western criticism. "It could be that the 13-year-old was a willing participant but that Iranian law (like the laws of many Western nations) deems that no person aged 13 is capable of sexual consent," says OutRage!'s Brett Lock, "and that therefore even consensual sexual contact is automatically deemed in law to be statutory rape."

Human Rights Watch (HRW) disputes key parts of OutRage!'s account. The original ISNA report uses an archaic term that suggests forced sodomy, says HRW's Scott Long, director of the group's GLBT rights project. And details about an assault appeared in a Mashad newspaper on the morning of the execution, before any Western protests. That report quotes the father of the alleged victim at length describing how his son was, he says, led from a shopping area in Mashad to a deserted alley where five other boys were waiting (they also face execution, but apparently have not been caught), and forced him to have sex at knife-point. Passersby, also quoted, say that when they tried to intervene, they and their cars were attacked.

By the time the pictures hit the mainstream Western media, the story was about executions for rape—and official interest dampened. The Human Rights Campaign briefly removed mention of the case from its website, and spokesman Steven Fisher told *The Nation*, "We would be relieved to learn that the charges of homosexual sex were wrong, and that this turned out to be a case of assault." The U.S. State Department issued a statement criticizing the Iranian judiciary for its mingling of prosecutorial and judicial functions, among other alleged shortcomings, mentioning nothing about its oppression of homosexuals.

Mainline human-rights groups, including Amnesty International and the International Gay and Lesbian Human Rights Commission (IGLHRC), agreed with the U.S. line that the Mashad executions were not gay-related. But they should be condemned, these groups said, on the grounds that the youths were minors when put to death or when they committed the crimes for which they were convicted.

Paula Ettelbrick, IGLHRC's director, cites a litany of cases—including Iran's execution of a 16-year-old girl, Atefeh Rajabi, last August for "acts incompatible with chastity"—as showing that Iran is capable of hanging and stoning people simply for consensual sex, so recourse to made-up tales of coercion wasn't necessary.

However, Ettelbrick also expressed concern at what she felt was "language having the potential to be racially/religiously charged" that OutRage! spokespeople and others were using to characterize Iran.

"Skepticism about official accounts in any country with a record of rights violations—be it Iran or the U.S.—is merited," writes HRW's Long, "and no one under these circumstances would claim total certainty that consensual sex was not involved. But the basis for believing that the boys were convicted of consensual sex is essentially a web of speculation."

"Rights aren't for saints, and if we only defend them for people onto whom we can project our own qualities, our own identities, we aren't activists but narcissists with attitude," Long goes on. "If these kids aren't 'gay,' or 'innocent,' but are 'straight' or 'guilty,' does it make their fear less horrible, their suffering less real? Does it make them less dead?"

OutRage! still insists the hangings were, whatever else, also anti-gay, and emanations of what it regards as a hateful regime. Threat of severe punishment hung over all the boys involved—including the one characterized as the victim. Reports from witnesses and the teenager's father about assault at knife-point could stem as much as anything from a desire to save his son's life or reputation. Sex among young Iranian males is, on many accounts, commonplace—sometimes through trickery or bullying that falls along a spectrum from the gameful to the cruel. Authorities might have concocted an account of coercion not because they needed it to prosecute or execute, but because otherwise, the scenario of boys having sex together would have seemed too ordinary. The statement by the doomed youths on the way to their execution that they didn't know what they did could lead to execution makes less sense if they were involved in a gang rape at knife-point, and more plausible if it was mere homosex, or some kind of sex-tinged hazing.

In addition, the executed youths were ethnic Arabs from Khuzestan, one of Iran's ethnic minorities in longstanding conflict with Iran's Persian Shiite majority. Khuzestan abuts the Iraqi border, and many Arabs had been forced to migrate during the Iran-Iraq war, the families of the executed teenagers among them. Iranian authorities—as elsewhere— have smeared members of ethnic minorities whom they've targeted with sexual innuendo. In a report on the killing by security forces July 9 of a Kurdish activist, Shivan Qaderi, HRW's website notes that authorities accused him of "moral and financial violations."

Certainly in another recent case, the commingling of sodomy and rape charges has the ring of implausibility. In Arak, 150 miles south of Tehran, at the end of August, two men—Farad Mostar and Ahmed Choka, both 27—were reportedly set to be executed for what was alleged as the sequestering and rape of another man, 22.

Back in Mashad, Asgari and Marhoni may indeed have coerced another teenager into sex—HRW says they are "90 percent" sure. But there were also plenty of hooks by which highly interested parties might have transformed a fairly innocent act into a seemingly more monstrous one.

If Western media interest in the youths' case faltered once it was characterized as assault, the images of the hangings could not be erased from the gay imagination. The Dutch gay group COC collected almost 30,000 signatures on an on-line petition, and protests were held, among other places, in London, Moscow, Paris, and Vancouver.

AMERICA = IRAN?

So in the aftermath of the hangings, everything went about as well as could be expected, right? Newspapers reported, bloggers blogged, protests broke out, and politicians queried. Militant gay activists ventured further out on their thicker limbs with bold speculation, while human-rights groups stuck cautiously, as they should, to the main trunk of proof and principle. Even the potshots each sometimes took at the other were just signs of healthy debate.

Yet a closer look shows abounding contradictions and blind spots. Everyone who responded arguably got key points seriously wrong, so that the cumulative effect wasn't to erase the errors but amplify them.

Asgari and Marhoni were terribly unlucky to have done what they did in Iran, but even on the most benign reading of their actions, they would have fared only a little better in America. Under the toxic bloom of anti-sex laws in the last generation—but especially the last decade, intimately connected to the mainstreaming of vanilla LGBT—the youths would have faced years in prison, and in some ways effectively guaranteed life sentences. They would have fallen into a separate-and-unequal legal netherworld that has developed around sex law that bears comparison to that created to control African Americans in the post-Civil-War South.

Authorities have not yet figured out a way to dye sex-offenders' skin permanently scarlet—but Asgari and Marhoni, as residents of Memphis instead of Mashad—would have been labeled as "predators" for the rest of their lives—and depending on the precise jurisdiction (though all are now racing to the bottom) their pictures and addresses of home and workplace (assuming they had either) would be forever posted on the Internet, shown regularly on TV, and plastered on posters around their neighborhoods. The electronic tags they'd be forced to wear—or on scenarios now being worked out, the chips that would be implanted in their bodies—would track their location constantly—so that police could always find them. Or outraged citizens—as happened August 27, when a man posing as an FBI agent came to the home where three registered sex-offenders lived in Bellingham, Washington, and shot two of them dead, one of them a gay man, 49-year-old Hank Eisses, convicted in 1997 of sex with a teenage boy. Eisses did not exactly become the next Matthew Shepard: the murders were barely noticed by the media.

But more and more, the impulse is to keep people convicted of illegal sex in the West forever in prison. In 1997, five years before Guantanamo Bay, the U.S. Supreme Court established that persons, convicted or not, can be imprisoned indefinitely for illegal sex they might have in the future—a provision that was only later applied to those labeled terrorists. If sex-offenders do get out of prison, they take the ball and chain with them. Lifetime parole—which gradually most U.S. states are adopting, as a natural extension of the registries—gives probation officers a level of complete personal control over their charges not seen since serfdom. Authorities can send their charges back to prison for failing a lie-detector test, possessing a copy of *The Best Gay Short Stories of 1995* (a case in York City), having too much candy in the cupboard (one in California), or passing too close to a school (Baltimore, Maryland).

You don't have to be a sociopathic rapist to feel the brunt of the repression. Gay men whose erotic profile bears resemblance to Oscar Wilde, Walt Whitman, André Gide, or Alan Turing are in danger. Anyone who has a 1960's physique magazine with teenage models in posing straps, or who gropes a bearded 17-year-old who's cruising at a rest stop is at risk. Indeed, the range of people affected is even bigger, because sex-offenders in the West have become guinea pigs for technologies of biometric and electronic surveillance-and-tracking that increasingly, under the guise of fighting terror, are rolled out for everyone.

A CHILD LEADS THEM?

Rather than confronting these realities—which in any case they've completely ignored—human rights groups responding to the Iranian hangings, in a sense, gave in to them. Killing Asgari and Marhoni was wrong, Human Rights Watch and IGLHRC said, because they were executions of "children," or, in Marhon's case, someone who offended when he was a "child." In other words, the executions were wrong for the same reason the two criminals were, in the eyes of most Westerners today, deserving of utmost punishment. Thus was indulged one of the West's great current conceits—the child as the central category of moral discourse and a primary justification of repression. The concept of the "child" absurdly lumps 2-year-olds, 8-year-olds, and 17-year-olds—and increasingly twenty-somethings—into the same essential category of sub-person. This is a conceit to which Iran—which grants the vote to 15-year-olds even as it allows their execution—is far less in thrall.

Human-rights groups understandably played the child-card in service to their principled opposition to the death penalty. Iran is a party to the Convention on the Rights of the Child, which commits it not to execute juvenile offenders, so this was a chance to make an argument that might have practical effect. But even here, the approach was something of a cop-out. While the execution of young lawbreakers may be a wedge into the main point—against states executing anybody—it is also a distraction from it. In the same way, a campaign to spare the lives of puppies at the dog-pound may serve as entrée to increasing people's concern about the web of bacteria, insects, plants, and animals that sustains an ecosystem. Or it may just impart the lesson that only adorable life-forms have reason to exist.

DOING GOOD, DOING WELL

Which raises the question of how much human-rights groups focus on "what's sexy" rather than what's principled. In their principles, in their equal regard for all persons, the human rights movement enjoys enormous global prestige—akin to the status of Catholicism in medieval Europe, or socialism before the taint of Stalin and Mao. Human rights is the successor to the best of what, in their heyday, these universalist projects stood for. In the post-'60s West, perhaps the only more-successful movements are those centered around various identities—such as race, sex, and sexuality. The two tendencies are different—sometimes diametrically—and each is tempted to draw on the unique strengths of the other. Hence, perhaps, Human Rights Watch's elevation, as shown on its website, of same-sex marriage to a basic human right—while ignoring, say, any right to polygamy, or other matrimonial arrangements to which people might freely contract.

Certainly mainline gay groups fail to protest civil-commitment laws, kiddie-porn statutes the likes of Canada's just-passed Bill C-2—a law that, in removing the "artistic merit" provision, makes possessing a book of, say, 16th-century Persian Safavid boy-love poems punishable by up to ten years in prison. Human Rights Watch, in a nod to the identity movements whose success it must envy, joins in the silence.

To be sure, groups such as Amnesty International and Human Rights Watch do vital work, and mostly hew to their principles, avoiding the short-termist excitability that goes with the territory of identity-politics. The prestige of these groups is largely deserved. However, it's just this prestige the U.S. aims to cash in on when it claims that its smart bombs and bunker-busters are the greatest force ever assembled for promotion of, as is continually intoned, "democracy and human rights." But as well, the human-rights cause risks death-by-a-thousand-cuts when special interests wrap themselves in its mantle.

A classic instance is America's Human Rights Campaign, which puts the magic phrase into its name (even if only to avoid saying "gay"), but "doesn't have a position" on what is one of human rights most basic planks—against execution. Being a pure-play lesbigay organization has helped make HRC the biggest and richest in America. The really fat donors don't want tearoom cruisers and drag queens (let alone the class of folk stuck last month in the Superdome) spoiling their high-Episcopal gay weddings.

Ettelbrick expresses surprise that HRC would issue public statements about the Iranian hangings without consulting the human-rights groups that have some depth in that part of the world. But that misses the successful political arbitrage HRC pulled off—selling the photo from Mashad long when it had huge political value as depicting "Brutal Islamic Execution of Gay Teens" and buying it short when the caption was "Pedo Rapists Get Just Desserts."

It was the same trick played by Rep. Tom Lantos, who demanded a U.S. investigation into the hangings and lambasted Iran's treatment of gays, but voted for the 2003 PROTECT Act, under which an American Asgari or Marhoni could face years in federal prison—not for raping a teenager, not for having consensual sex with him, but merely calling him on a cell phone (think "interstate commerce") with the intention of arranging to "hook up." (Barney Frank, to his credit, voted nay.)

But if identity politics often conflicts with the demands of human rights, it was the militant identistas of UK's OutRage! who demonstrated the best grasp of the human dynamics of the case. Yet OutRage!'s portrayal of Asgari and Marhoni as "gay teenagers" is off-the-mark. They evidently, like many young Iranian males, enjoyed same-sex activity, but "Did the hanged kids claim 'gay' identity?" asks journalist Doug Ireland. "Most probably not—since the concept is virtually unknown among the uneducated classes in Iran."

Yet Ireland is wrong, as well, to make gayness an ID every same-sexer would embrace if only he had cash and a diploma. Most Islamic societies allow ample space for unspoken and private homoeroticism. Amnesty International and IGLHRC have waged campaigns protesting crackdowns on gay Egyptian hookup sites—which serve only the tiny and westernized elite who have net access. But one effect is to increase scrutiny on the unmarked homosexual spaces on which most Egyptians with same-sex desires depend.

Which leads Joseph Massad, historian at Columbia and author of the forthcoming *Desiring Arabs*, to wonder whether gay and human-rights groups really care about same-sex love and affection, in its diverse forms, around the world. Because with such campaigns, Massad declares, "the 'Gay International' is destroying social and sexual configurations of desire in the interest of reproducing a world in its own image, one wherein its sexual categories and desires are safe from being questioned."

REFORMING ISLAM

If protesting anti-gay crackdowns from afar has perverse effects for Islamic homosociality, all the more so when Westerners actually invade. Which makes the pride Andrew Sullivan's gay soldier feels bitterly ironic. In post-Saddam Iraq, power lies with the majority Shiites, who have forged warm ties to Tehran. Iran's victory in Iraq was delivered by its arch-enemies America and Iraq's Sunni Arabs—the first by deposing the secularist Saddam, the second in resisting the Americans, bogging them down, and preventing Stage Two of the neo-con agenda: a march to Tehran.

But step back further and the irony of Western intervention is even more bitter and hugely sadder. Time after time, Islamic modernizers were deposed by Western powers, starting with the British in India, and continuing in Iran with the CIA's overthrow of the democratically-elected Mohammad Mosaddeq in 1953, with the subsequent imposition of the Shah Pahlevi. Islamic fundamentalism may seem today immensely potent, but—from Afghanistan to Gaza—it's usually been a politics of last resort.

In Iran, gayness can't avoid some odor of colonial occupation. "Not all the accusations leveled against the Pahlevi family and their wealthy supporters stemmed from political and economic grievances," notes Ireland, citing Iranian scholar Janet Afary. "A significant portion of the public anger was aimed at their 'immoral' lifestyle. There were rumors that a gay lifestyle was rampant at the court. The Shah himself was rumored to be bisexual. There were reports that a close male friend of the Shah from Switzerland, a man who knew him from their student days in that country, routinely visited him."

Post-revolutionary Iran, for all its bloody repression, had also shown signs of thaw—there was a reformist president and an emerging gay-activist underground. "The GLBT situation in Iran has changed over the past 26 years," says an unnamed activist interviewed on www.gayrussia.ru/en after the executions. "The regime does not systematically persecute gays anymore. There are still some gay websites, there are some parks and cinemas that everyone knows are meeting places for gays. Furthermore, it is legal in Iran that a transsexual applies for sex-change, and it is fully accepted by the government. Having said that, Islamic law, according to which gays face punishment by death, is still in force, but it is thought not much followed by the regime nowadays."

That may be changing, with a right-wing resurgence, egged on by U.S. threats, and exemplified by the election this summer of Mahmoud Ahmadinejad—whose authoritarian puritanism may be linked to the uptick in sodomy executions.

And Iran's nuclear ambitions, the rationale for the U.S. saber-rattling, are relevant as well. Iran chose its nuclear course, argues Joost Hilterman, after what happened in its eight-year-long war with then-U.S.-sponsored Iraq, when Iranian troops were bombarded with Saddam's chemical weapons. When Iran protested and invoked international agreements on their illegality, the U.S. balked, and cooked up phony evidence showing Iran—not client-state Iraq—as the chemical-weapons perp. "The young and inexperienced Islamic Republic learned from its experience [that] when you are facing the world's superpower, multilateral treaties and conventions are worthless," notes Hilterman in *Middle East Report*. Only military self-sufficiency could guard its independence. And indeed, all that Iran has aimed at so far—mastery of the nuclear fuel-cycle—is within its rights under the UN's anti-proliferation treaty. But still the country faces a U.S. attack—possibly a nuclear one—under rules that America has unilaterally changed mid-course.

So Iranians are alive to imperial self-interest and bigotry masked in the flowery language of universal principle. They also know that on sexual perversion—in the different ways each defines it—America and Iran see eye-to-eye.

Seeing the photograph of Mahmoud Asgari and Ayaz Marhoni in tears before they died on the scaffold gives many of us a terrible urge to do something. Yet that image yields another—cast by the X-rays it shines upon the organs and metabolic pathways of the Western body-politic. The X-ray offers an inner-view of the organizations, principles, and conceptual categories that we have at-hand to act on that urge to "do something." And that's where we find ourselves at a further loss, facing an organism that is artery-clogged, cataract-ridden, and palsied. Like a doddering old man trying to drink tea but spilling it everywhere, the gap between cup and lip seems for now insurmountable.

Illustrating Against Militarism

MR. FISH

THREE OF MR. FISH'S SASSY and incisive cartoons, focused on militarism and sexuality, appear on these pages. We've spread them out so that you can easily rip out the pages with images, enlarge them on a photocopier or scanner, and disseminate in your own community without losing any pages of text!

The following cartoons have appeared in numerous places online and in print. They are archived on Truthdig.com and Mr. Fish's own website, clowncrack.com.

Serve Your Country!
Be
GAY
and
SAY
FUCK
YOU
to
the
ARMED
FORCES
"The PEACE MOVEMENT needs
YOU"
MR. FISH

DON'T ASK ME TO SUBMIT TO VIGOROUS TRAINING THAT SUBVERTS MY NATURAL INCLINATIONS TOWARDS COMPASSION, HOPE, OPTIMISM AND COMMON SENSE SO THAT I AM ENTHUSIASTIC ABOUT TERRORIZING OTHER NATIONS BY INVADING AND OCCUPYING THEM DAY IN AND DAY OUT, YEAR AFTER YEAR AFTER YEAR, AND THEN BY ABDUCTING AND TORTURING THEIR INNOCENT DAY IN AND DAY OUT, YEAR AFTER YEAR AFTER YEAR, AND THEN BY SLAUGHTERING MASSIVE AMOUNTS OF THEIR DEFENSELESS CIVILIANS DAY IN AND DAY OUT, YEAR AFTER YEAR AFTER YEAR, AND I WON'T GIVE A SHIT ABOUT HOW THE IDEA OF TWO MEN HUGGING AND KISSING MIGHT TURN YOUR STOMACH.

MR.FISH

AGAINST EQUALITY
PRISONS WILL NOT PROTECT YOU

EDITED BY RYAN CONRAD
INTRODUCTION BY DEAN SPADE

Their Laws Will Never Make Us Safer

DEAN SPADE

AN INTRODUCTION

AT MANY TRANSGENDER DAY OF Remembrance events, a familiar community anecdote surfaces. The story goes that convicted murderers of trans people have been sentenced to less punishment than is meted out to those convicted of killing a dog. In Istanbul, where trans sex workers have been resisting and surviving severe violence, criminalization, and displacement caused by gentrification, recent advocacy for a trans-inclusive hate crime law has included sharing stories of trans women being raped by attackers who threaten them with death and openly cite the fact that they would only go to prison for three years even if they were convicted of the murder. These stories expose the desperate conditions faced by populations cast as disposable, who struggle against the erasure of their lives and deaths.

The murder of Trayvon Martin in 2012 raised related dialogues across the U.S. The possibility that Martin's murderer would not be prosecuted, and the awareness that anti-black violence consistently goes uninvestigated and unpunished by racist police and prosecutors, led to a loud call for the prosecution of George Zimmerman. In the weeks after Martin's murder, I heard and read many conversations and commentaries where people who are critical of the racism and violence of the criminal punishment system struggled to figure out whether it made sense to call on that system to make Martin's murderer accountable for his actions.

On the one hand, the failure to prosecute and punish Zimmerman to the full extent of the law would be a slap in the face to Martin's family and everyone else impacted by racial profiling and anti-black violence. It would be a continuation of the long-term collaboration between police and perpetrators of anti-black violence, where the police exist to protect the interests of white people and to protect white life and operate both to directly attack and kill black people and to permit individuals and hate groups to do so.

On the other hand, given the severe anti-black racism of the criminal punishment system, what does it mean to call on that system for justice and accountability? Many people working to dismantle racism identify the criminal punishment system as one of the primary apparatuses of racist violence and probably the most significant threat to black people in the U.S. Opposing that system includes both opposing its literal growth (the hiring of more cops, the building of more jails and prisons, the criminalization of more behaviors, the increasing of sentences) and disrupting the cultural myths about it being a "justice" system and about the police "protecting and serving" everyone. For many activists who are working to dismantle that system, it felt uncomfortable to call for Zimmerman's prosecution, since the idea that any justice can emerge from prosecution and imprisonment has been exposed as a racist lie.

The tensions inside this debate are very significant ones for queer and trans politics right now. Increasingly, queer and trans people are asked to measure our citizenship status on whether hate crime legislation that includes sexual orientation and gender identity exists in the jurisdictions in which we live. We are told by gay and lesbian rights organizations that passing this legislation is the best way to respond to the ongoing violence we face—that we need to make the state and the public care about our victimization and show they care by increasing surveillance of and punishment for homophobic and transphobic attacks.

Hate crime laws are part of the larger promise of criminal punishment systems to keep us safe and resolve our conflicts. This is an appealing promise in a society wracked by gun violence and sexual violence.[1] In a heavily armed, militaristic, misogynist, and racist society, people are justifiably scared of violence, and that fear is cultivated by a constant feed of television shows portraying horrifying violence and brave police and prosecutors who put serial rapists and murderers in prison. The idea that we are in danger rings true, and the message that law enforcement will deliver safety is appealing in the face of fear. The problem is that these promises are false, and are grounded in some key myths and lies about violence and criminal punishment.

Five realities about violence and criminal punishment are helpful for analyzing the limitations of hate crime legislation (or any enhancement of criminalization) to prevent violence or bring justice and accountability after it has happened:

1. *Jails and prisons are not full of dangerous people, they are full of people of color, poor people, and people with disabilities.* More than 60% of people in U.S. prisons are people of color. Every stage and aspect of the criminal punishment and immigration enforcement systems is racist—racism impacts who gets stopped by cops, who gets arrested, what bail gets set, which workplaces and homes are raided by Immigration and Customs Enforcement (ICE), what charges are brought, who will be on the jury, what conditions people face while locked up, and who will be deported. Most people in the U.S. violate laws (like traffic laws and drug laws) all the time, but people of color, homeless people, and people with disabilities are profiled and harassed and are the ones who get locked up and stay locked up or get deported. Ending up in prison or jail or deportation proceedings is not a matter of dangerousness or lawlessness, it's about whether you are part of a group targeted for enforcement.

2. *Most violence does not happen on the street between strangers, like on TV, but between people who know each other, in our homes, schools, and familiar spaces.* Images of out-of-control serial killers and rapists who attack strangers feed the cultural thirst

for retribution and the idea that it is acceptable to lock people away for life in unimaginably abusive conditions. In reality, the people who hurt us are usually people we know, and usually are also struggling under desperate conditions and/or victims of violence. Violence, especially sexual violence, is so common that it is not realistic to lock away every person who engages in it. Most violence is never reported to police because people have complex relationships with those who have hurt them, and the whole framing of criminalization where "bad guys" get "put away" does not work for most survivors of violence. If we deal with the complexity of how common violence is, and let go of a system built on a fantasy of monstrous strangers, we might actually begin to focus on how to prevent violence and heal from it. Banishment and exile—the tools offered by the criminal punishment and immigration enforcement systems—only make sense when we maintain the fantasy that there are evil perpetrators committing harm, rather than facing the reality that people we love are harming us and each other and that we need to change fundamental conditions to stop it.

3. *The most dangerous people, the people who violently destroy and end the most lives, are still on the outside—they are the people running banks, governments, and courtrooms and they are the people wearing military and police uniforms.* Fear is an effective method of social control. Prison and war profiteers fuel racist and xenophobic fears by circulating images of "terrorists" and "criminals."[2] In reality, the greatest risks to our survival are worsening poverty and lack of access to health care, adequate housing, and food. This shortens the lives of millions of people in the U.S. every day, along with the violence of police and ICE attacks, imprisonment and warfare that the U.S. government unleashes every day domestically and internationally, and the destruction of our climate, water, and food supplies by relentlessly greedy elites. If we really want to increase well-being and reduce violence, our resources should not be focused on locking up people who possess drugs or

get in a fight at school or sleep on a sidewalk—we should be focusing on dismantling the structures that give a tiny set of elites decision-making power over most resources, land, and people in the world.

4. *Prisons aren't places to put serial rapists and murderers, prisons are the serial rapists and murderers.* If we acknowledge that the vast majority of people in prisons and jails are there because of poverty and racism, not because they are "dangerous" or violent, and if we acknowledge that prisons and jail utterly fail to make anyone who spends time in them healthier or less likely to engage in violence, and if we recognize that prisons and jail are spaces of extreme violence,[3] and that kidnapping and caging people, not to mention exposing them to nutritional deprivation, health care deprivation, and physical attack is violence, it becomes clear that criminalization and immigration enforcement increase rather than decrease violence overall.

5. *Increasing criminalization does not make us safer, it just feeds the voracious law enforcement systems that devour our communities.* The U.S. criminal punishment and immigration enforcement systems are the largest prison systems that have ever existed on Earth. The U.S. imprisons more people than any other society that has ever existed—we have 5% of the world's population and 25% of the world's prisoners. Our immigration prisons quadrupled in size in the decade after 2001. This hasn't made us safer from violence, it is violence.

The fundamental message of hate crime legislation is that if we lock more bad people up, we will be safer. Everything about our current law enforcement systems indicates that this is a false promise, and it's a false promise that targets people of color and poor people for caging and death while delivering large profits to white elites. Many might hope that queer and trans people would be unlikely to fall for this trick, since we have deep community histories and contemporary realities of experiencing police violence and violence in prisons and jails, and we know something about not trusting the cops. However, this same ongoing experience of marginalization makes some of us deeply crave recognition from systems and people we see as powerful or important. This desperate craving for recognition, healing and safety can cause us to invest hope in the only methods most of us have ever heard of for responding to violence: caging and exile. Many of us want to escape the stigmas of homophobia and transphobia and be recast as "good" in the public eye. In contemporary politics, being a "crime victim" is much more sympathetic than being a "criminal." By desiring recognition within this system's terms, we are enticed to fight for criminalizing legislation that will in no way reduce our experiences of marginalization and violence.

In recent years, these concerns about hate crime legislation have gotten somewhat louder, though they are still entirely marginalized by the corporate-sponsored white gay and lesbian rights organizations and mainstream media outlets from which many queer and trans people get their information about our issues and our resistance. More and more people in the U.S. are questioning the drastic expansion of criminalization and immigration enforcement, and noticing that building more prisons and jails and deporting more people does not seem to make our lives any safer or better. Many queer and trans people are increasingly critical of criminalization and immigration enforcement, and are unsatisfied by the idea that the answer to the violence we experience is harsher criminal laws or more police.

Three kinds of strategies are being taken up by queer and trans activists who refuse to believe the lies of law enforcement systems, and want to stop transphobic and homophobic violence. First, many people are working to directly support the survival of queer and trans people who are vulnerable to violence. Projects that connect queer and trans people outside of prisons to people currently imprisoned for friendship and support and projects that provide direct advocacy to queer and trans people facing homelessness, immigration enforcement, criminalization and other dire circumstances are under way in many places. Many people are providing direct support to people coming out of prison, or opening their homes to one another, or collaborating to make sex work safer in their communities. This kind of work is vital because we cannot build strong movements if our people are not surviving. Directly helping each other during our moments of crisis is essential—especially when we do it in ways that are politically engaged, that build shared analysis of the systems that produce these dangers. This is not a social service or charity model that provides people with minimal survival needs in a moralizing framework that separates "deserving" from "undeserving" and gives professionals the power to determine who is compliant enough, clean enough, hard-working enough, or quiet enough to get into the housing, job training, or public benefits programs. This is a model of mutual aid that values all of us, especially people facing the most dire manifestations of poverty and state violence, as social movement participants who deserve to survive and to get together with others facing similar conditions to fight back.

The second kind of work is dismantling work. Many people are working to dismantle the systems that put queer and trans people into such dangerous and violent situations. They are trying to stop new jails and immigration prisons from being built, they are trying to decriminalize sex work and drugs, they are trying to stop the expansion of surveillance systems. Identifying what pathways and apparatuses funnel our people into danger and fighting against these systems that are devouring us is vital work.

The third kind of work is building alternatives. Violent systems are sold to us with false promises—we're told the prison systems will keep us safe or that the immigration system will improve our economic well-being, yet we know these systems only offer violence. So we have to build the world we want to live in—build ways of being safer, of having food and shelter, of having health care and of breaking isolation. Lots of activists are working on projects to do this, for example, on alternative ways to deal with violence in our communities and families that don't involve calling the police, since the police are the most significant danger to many of us. Many people are engaged in experimental work to do what the criminal and immigration systems utterly fail to do. Those systems have grown massive, built on promises of safety. But they have utterly failed to reduce rape, child sexual abuse, poverty, police violence, racism, ableism, and the other things that are killing us. Their growth has increased all of those things. So, we have to look with fresh eyes at what actually does make us safer. Some people are building projects that try to directly respond when something violent or harmful happens. Others are building projects that try to prevent violence by looking at what things tend to keep us safe—things like having strong friendship circles, safe housing, transportation, not being economically dependent for survival on another person so you can leave them if you want to, and having shared analysis and practices for resisting dangerous systems of meaning and control like racism and the romance myth.

Some people who are identifying prisons and borders as some of the most significant forms of violence that need to be opposed and resisted by queer and trans politics, are calling for an end to all prisons. For me, prison abolition means recognizing prisons and borders as structures that cannot be redeemed, that have no place in the world I want to be part of building. It means deciding that inventing and believing in enemies, creating ways of banishing and exiling and throwing away people, has no role in building that world. This is a very big deal for people raised in a highly militaristic prison society that feeds us a constant diet of fear, that encourages us from early childhood to sort the world into "bad guys" and "good guys." Our indoctrination into this prison culture deprives us of skills for recognizing any complexity, including the complexity of our own lives as people who both experience harm and do harm to others. Working to develop the capacity to even imagine that harm can be prevented and addressed without throwing people away or putting anyone in cages is a big process for us.

In the growing debate about whether hate crime legislation is something that will improve the lives of queer and trans people, and whether it is something we should be fighting for, we can see queer and trans activists working to develop important capacities to discern and analyze together. This form of discernment is familiar to prison abolitionists, and it is also visible in other areas of queer and trans politics. It is an ability to analyze the nature of an institution or system, rather than just to seek to reform it to include or recognize a group it targets or harms. Abolitionists have long critiqued prison reform, observing that prison expansion usually occurs under the guise of prison reform. Important complaints about prison conditions, for example, often lead to prison profiteers and government employees proposing building newer, cleaner, better prisons that inevitably will result in more people getting locked up.[4] Queer activists have engaged this kind of discernment about reforming violent state apparatuses in our work to oppose the fights for same-sex marriage and the ability to serve in the U.S. military. In this work, we have questioned the assumption that inclusion in such institutions is desirable, naming the existence of marriage as a form of racialized-gendered social control and the ongoing imperial and genocidal practices of the U.S. military. This work is complex, because so many queer and trans people, conditioned by shaming and exclusion, believe that getting the U.S. government to say "good" things about us in its laws and policies, no matter what those laws and policies actually exist to do, is progress. This framing asks gay and lesbian people to be the new face of the purported fairness and liberalism of the United States, to get excited about fighting its wars, shaping our lives around its family formation norms, and having its criminal codes expanded in our names. The ability to recognize that an enticing invitation to inclusion is not actually going to address the worst forms of violence affecting us, and is actually going to expand the apparatuses that perpetrate them—whether in Abu Ghraib, Pelican Bay, or the juvenile hall in your town—is one that requires collective analysis for queer politics to grasp.

The Against Equality book projects, of which this section makes up the third and final, offer us a bundle of tools for building that analysis and sharing it in our networks, for trading in the dangerous ideas that the Human Rights Campaign and the other organizations that purport to represent our best interests are not likely to disseminate. This section, in particular, focuses on how criminalization and imprisonment target and harm queer and trans people, and why expanding criminalization by passing hate crime laws will not address the urgent survival issues in our lives. The most well-funded and widely broadcast lesbian and gay rights narratives tell us that the state is our protector, that its institutions are not centers of racist, homophobic, transphobic, and ableist violence, but are sites for our liberation. We know that is not true. We are naming names—even if you wrap it in a rainbow flag, a cop is a cop, a wall is a wall, an occupation is an occupation, a marriage license is a tool of regulation. We are building ways of thinking about this together, and ways of enacting these politics in daily work to support one another and transform the material conditions of our lives.

NOTES

1   A 2011 study published in the *Journal of Trauma-Injury Infection & Critical Care* reported that "[t]he U.S. homicide rates were 6.9 times higher than rates in the other high-income countries, driven by firearm homicide rates that were 19.5 times higher. For 15-year olds to 24-year olds, firearm homicide rates in the United States were 42.7 times higher than in the other countries."

Richardson, Erin G. S.M.; Hemenway, David PhD, "Homicide, Suicide, and Unintentional Firearm Fatality: Comparing the United States With Other High-Income Countries," 2003, *Journal of Trauma-Injury Infection & Critical Care*, January 2011 - Volume 70 - Issue 1 - pp 238-243. http://journals.lww.com/jtrauma/Abstract/2011/01000/Homicide,Suicide,_and_Unintentional_Firearm.35.aspx.

Every year, approximately 100,000 people in the U.S. are victims of gun violence, and about 85 people per day die from gun violence in the U.S. "Gun Violence Statistics," Law Center to Prevent Gun Violence, http://smartgunlaws.org/category/gun-studies-statistics/ gun-violence-statistics/. An average of 207,754 people age 12 or older experience sexual assault every year in the U.S. Approximately every two minutes, someone is sexually assaulted. 54% of assaults are not reported to the police, and 97% of rapists do not serve any jail time. "Statistics," Rape, Abuse & Incest National Network, http://www.rainn.org/statistics/. According to the Colorado Coalition Against Sexual Assault, in the U.S. one out of every six women and one out of thirty three men have experienced an attempted or completed rape. Citing National Violence Against Women Survey, "Prevalence, Incidence, and Consequences of Violence Against Women," November 1998. The Colorado Coalition Against Sexual

Assault also reports that "the United States has the world's highest rape rate of the countries that publish such statistics—4 times higher than Germany, 13 times higher than England, and 20 times higher than Japan" citing NWS, "Rape in America: A Report to the Nation," 1992). See, http://web.archive.org/web/20100822123802/http://www.ccasa.org/statistics.cfm.

2 It is helpful to remember that people in the U.S. are eight times more likely to be killed by a police officer than a terrorist. "Fear of Terror Makes People Stupid," Washington's Blog, http://www.washingtonsblog.com/ 2011/06/fear-of-terror-makes-people-stupid.html citing National Safety Council, "The Odds of Dying From…" http://web.archive.org/web/20080508135851/http://nsc.org/research/odds.aspx.

3 By conservative estimates, 21% of people in men's prisons are estimated to experience forced sex while imprisoned. Cindy Struckman-Johnson & David Struckman-Johnson (2000). "Sexual Coercion Rates in Seven Midwestern Prisons for Men" (PDF). *The Prison Journal* 80 (4): 379–390.

4 Angela Davis lays out this argument succinctly and effectively in *Are Prisons Obsolete?* Angela Y. Davis, *Are Prisons Obsolete?* (New York: Seven Stories Press, 2003). In 2012, these dynamics were visible when anti-prison activists in Seattle started a campaign to stop the building of a new youth jail that the local government was promoting as a way of resolving long-term complaints about horrible conditions of confinement in the existing youth jail. The anti-prison activists argued that the old jail should be closed, but not replaced. The campaign is ongoing. See, http://nonewyouthjail.wordpress.com.

A Compilation of Critiques on Hate Crime Legislation

COMPILED BY JASON LYDON FOR BLACK AND PINK

MANY LIBERAL, AND EVEN SELF-PROCLAIMED progressive, organizations are fighting for "hate crime" legislation nationally and state-by-state. The Senate just voted in favor of the "Matthew Shepard Bill." Challenges and critiques are made over and over again by queer/trans/gender non-conforming folks, people of color, low-income/poor folks, and others most impacted by the many tentacles of the prison industrial complex, yet the campaigns continue on. This document is intended to be a bullet point compilation of materials put out by the following organizations (in no particular order): Sylvia Rivera Law Project, Audre Lorde Project, FIERCE, Queers for Economic Justice, Peter Cicchino Youth Project, Denver Chapter of INCITE! Women of Color Against Violence, Denver on Fire, and the article "Sanesha Stewart, Lawrence King, and why hate crime legislation won't help" by Jack Aponte. The intention behind this document is to present a somewhat simplified critique that can inspire a desire for more information.

This compilation originally appeared in 2009 on the website of Black and Pink (blackandpink.org), an LGBTQ group that works towards the abolition of the prison industrial complex.

If a particular crime is deemed a hate crime by the state, the supposed perpetrator is automatically subject to a higher mandatory minimum sentence. For example, a crime that would carry a sentence of five years can be "enhanced" to eight years.

Plain and simple, hate crime legislation increases the power and strength of the prison system by detaining more people for longer periods of time.

Trans people, people of color, and other marginalized groups are disproportionately incarcerated to an overwhelming degree. Trans and gender non-conforming people, particularly trans women of color, are regularly profiled and falsely arrested for doing nothing more than walking down the street.

If we are incarcerating those who commit violence against marginalized individuals/communities, we then place them behind walls where they can continue to target these same people. It is not in the best interest of marginalized communities to depend on a system that already commits such great violence to then protect them.

Hate crime laws do not distinguish between oppressed groups and groups with social and institutional power.

This reality of the state makes it so that white people can accuse people of color of anti-white hate crimes, straight people accuse queers, and so on. Such a reality opens the door for marginalized people to be prosecuted for simply defending themselves against oppressive violence. This type of precedent-setting also legitimizes ideologies of reverse racism that continuously deny the institutionalization of oppression.

Hate crime laws are an easy way for the government to act like it is on our communities' side while continuing to discriminate against us. Liberal politicians and institutions can claim "anti-oppression" legitimacy and win points with communities affected by prejudice, while simultaneously using "sentencing enhancement" to justify building more prisons to lock us up in.

Hate crime legislation is a liberal way of being "tough on crime" while building the power of the police, prosecutors, and prison guards. Rather than address systems of violence like health care disparities, economic exploitation, housing crisis, or police brutality, these politicians use hate crime legislation as their stamp of approval on "social issues."

Hate crime laws focus on punishing the "perpetrator" and have no emphasis on providing support for the survivor or families and friends of those killed during an act of interpersonal hate violence.

We will only strengthen our communities if we take time to care for those who have experienced or been witness to violence. We have to survive systems of violence all the time and are incredibly resilient. We must focus on building our capacity to respond and support survivors and create transformative justice practices that can also heal the perpetrator (though focusing first and foremost on survivors).

Hate crime law sets up the State as protector, intending to deflect our attention from the violence it perpetrates, deploys, and sanctions. The government, its agents, and their institutions perpetuate systemic violence and set themselves up as the only avenue in which justice can be allocated; they will never be charged with hate crimes.

The state, which polices gender, race, sexuality, and other aspects of identity, is able to dismiss the ways it creates the systems that build a culture of violence against marginalized communities as it pays prosecutors to go after individuals who commit particular types of interpersonal violence. Hate crime legislation puts marginalized communities in the place of asking the state to play the savior while it continues to perpetuate violence.

Hate crimes don't occur because there aren't enough laws against them, and hate crimes won't stop when those laws are in place. Hate crimes occur because, time and time again, our society demonstrates that certain people are worth less than others, that certain people are wrong, are perverse, are immoral in their very being.

Creating more laws will not help our communities. Organizing for the passage of these kind of laws simply takes the time and energy out of communities that could instead spend the time creating alternative systems and building communities capable of starting transformative justice processes. Hate crime bills are a distraction from the vital work necessary for community safety.

Passing hate crime legislation will not bring back those who have been killed by hateful violence, it will not heal the wounds of the body or spirit, it will not give power to communities who have felt powerless after episodes of violence.

Organizations like the Human Rights Campaign, National Gay and Lesbian Task Force, and others take advantage of our pain and suffering to garner support for these pieces of legislation. Advocates in the campaigns for hate crime legislation tokenize individuals like Sanesha Stewart [murdered trans woman of color from New York City in 2008] and Angie Zapata [murdered trans woman from Colorado in 2008] while still pushing forward the white, class privileged, gay and lesbian agenda. To truly honor those we have lost and to honestly heal ourselves we must resist the inclination to turn to the state for legitimacy or paternalistic protection; let us use the time to build our communities and care for ourselves.

SRLP opposes the Matthew Shepard and James Byrd, Jr. Hate Crimes Prevention Act

SYLVIA RIVERA LAW PROJECT

IN OCTOBER 2009, PRESIDENT OBAMA signed the Matthew Shepard and James Byrd, Jr. Hate Crimes Prevention Act into law. This law makes it a federal hate crime to assault people based on sexual orientation, gender and gender identity by expanding the scope of a 1968 law that applies to people attacked because of their race, religion or national origin. In support of this goal, it expands the authority of the U.S. Department of Justice to prosecute such crimes instead of or in collaboration with local authorities. The law also provides major increases in funding for the U.S. Department of Justice and local law enforcement to use in prosecuting these crimes—including special additional resources to go toward prosecution of youth for hate crimes.

The recent expansion of the federal hates crime legislation has received extensive praise and celebration by mainstream lesbian, gay,

This statement first appeared on the website of the Sylvia Rivera Law Project (srlp.org) in 2009.

bisexual and transgender organizations because it purports to "protect" LGBT people from attacks on the basis of their expressed and/or perceived identities for the first time ever on a federal level. The Sylvia Rivera Law Project does not see this as a victory. As an organization that centers racial and economic justice in our work and that understands mass imprisonment as a primary vector of violence in the lives of our constituents, we believe that hate crime legislation is a counterproductive response to the violence faced by LGBT people.

Already, the U.S. incarcerates more people per capita than any other nation in the world. One out of every thirty-two people in the U.S. lives under criminal punishment system supervision. African-American people are six times more likely to be incarcerated than white people; Latin@ people are twice as likely to be incarcerated as white people. LGBTs and queer people, transgender people, and poor people are also at greatly increased risk for interaction with the criminal justice system. It is clear that this monstrous system of laws and enforcement specifically targets marginalized communities, particularly people of color.

What hate crime laws do is expand and increase the power of the same unjust and corrupt criminal punishment system. Evidence demonstrates that hate crime legislation, like other criminal punishment legislation, is used unequally and improperly against communities that are already marginalized in our society. These laws increase the already staggering incarceration rates of people of color, poor people, queer people and transgender people based on a system that is inherently and deeply corrupt.

The evidence also shows that hate crime laws and other "get tough on crime" measures do not deter or prevent violence. Increased incarceration does not deter others from committing violent acts motivated by hate, does not rehabilitate those who have committed past acts of hate, and does not make anyone safer. As we see trans people profiled by police, disproportionately arrested and detained, caught in systems of poverty and detention, and facing extreme violence in prisons, jails and detention centers, we believe that this system itself is a main perpetrator of violence against our communities.

We are also dismayed by the joining of a law that is supposedly about "preventing" violence with the funding for continued extreme violence and colonialism abroad. This particular bill was attached to a $680 billion measure for the Pentagon's budget, which includes $130 billion for ongoing military operations in Iraq and Afghanistan. Killing people in Iraq and Afghanistan protects no one, inside or outside of U.S. borders.

We continue to work in solidarity with many organizations and individuals to support people in prison, to reduce incarceration, to end the wars on Iraq and Afghanistan, and to create systems of accountability that do not rely on prisons or policing and that meaningfully improve the health and safety of our communities—especially redistribution of wealth, health care, and housing. A few of the many other organizations doing radical and transformative work to increase the health and safety of our communities include:

- The Audre Lorde Project
- FIERCE
- Incite! Women of Color Against Violence
- Queers for Economic Justice
- Right Rides
- TGI Justice Project
- The Transformative Justice Law Project of Illinois

For these reasons, we believe that a law that links our community's experiences of violence and death to a demand for increased criminal punishment, as well as further funding for imperialist war, is a strategic mistake of significant proportions.

Do Hate Crime Laws Do Any Good?

LILIANA SEGURA

"We have seen a man dragged to death in Texas simply because he was black. A young man murdered in Wyoming simply because he was gay. In the last year alone, we've seen the shootings of African-Americans, Asian Americans, and Jewish children simply because of who they were. This is not the American way. We must draw the line."
    —President Bill Clinton, final State of the Union Address, January 27, 2000.

IT WAS A YEAR-AND-A-HALF after the horrific torture-murder of James Byrd Jr., the African-American man who was assaulted, chained to a pickup truck and dragged for three miles by three white men in Jasper, Texas, a crime that the *New York Times* called "one of the grisliest racial killings in recent American history."

A few months later came the similarly brutal killing of Matthew Shepard, a twenty-one-year-old gay man who was savagely beaten and left to die in Laramie, Wyoming.

This piece first appeared on alternet.org on August 3rd, 2009.

The perpetrators in both cases were slapped with severe punishments—life sentences for Shepard's killers, and two death sentences and one life sentence for Byrd's. Nonetheless, in the emotional public upheaval that followed, both cases became rallying cries for the passage of state laws to toughen the sentences for hate-motivated crimes.

On the federal level, laws were already on the books defining race-motivated violence as hate crimes, but the same was not true of crimes against the LGBT community. The Matthew Shepard case would set the stage for a ten-year fight to pass federal hate crime legislation to protect LGBT people. Leading the charge were such influential groups as the Human Rights Campaign, the country's largest gay-rights organization.

Despite the fact that when it came to other issues—"Don't Ask, Don't Tell" or marriage equality—the Clinton administration was no friend of gay rights, the White House and congressional Democrats threw their weight behind hate crime legislation. And no wonder: with Clinton presiding over some of the most expansive criminal justice reforms in U.S. history, anyone lobbying for tougher sentencing in the 1990s was in good company. In Congress, supporting hate-crime laws gave Democrats a chance to look tough on crime while also throwing a bone to the LGBT community.

"We hope Congress will heed this call and put aside politics to protect our nation's citizens from the brutal hate crimes that claimed the lives of Matthew Shepard and James Byrd Jr.," Elizabeth Birch, executive director of the Human Rights Campaign, said in November 1999.

Almost ten years later, on July 16, 2009, the U.S. Senate finally passed the Local Law Enforcement Hate Crimes Prevention Act, otherwise known as the Matthew Shepard Act, as an amendment to the 2010 National Defense Authorization bill, by a strong bipartisan vote of 63–28. The amendment extends federal hate crime laws to include crimes that target a victim based on his or her "actual or perceived" gender, sexual orientation, gender identity, or disability.

The Matthew Shepard Act is likely to be signed by President Obama, marking a major victory for HRC and other groups that have fought hard for it over the past ten years. But even as many see this is a cause for celebration, nearly a decade after Clinton's final state-of-the-union address urged Congress to "draw the line" on hate crimes, the practical value of hate crime legislation remains dubious.

Despite supporters' contention that they will make vulnerable communities safer, there is little proof that the tougher sentencing that comes with hate crime legislation prevents violent crimes against minority groups. Meanwhile, the U.S. prison system continues to swallow up more and more Americans at a record pace. With 1 in 100 Americans behind bars, is a fight for tougher sentencing really a fight worth waging?

WILL TOUGHER SENTENCES DETER HATE CRIMES?

In 2007, the *Dallas Morning News* ran an editorial titled "The Myth of Deterrence," which took on the canard that maximum penalties would protect people from violent crime.

In theory, the death penalty saves lives by staying the hand of would-be killers. The idea is simple cost-benefit analysis: if a man tempted by homicide knew that he would face death if caught, he would reconsider.

But that's not the real world. The South executes far more convicted murderers than any other region, yet has a homicide rate far above the national average. Texas's murder rate is slightly above average, despite the state's peerless deployment of the death penalty. If capital punishment were an effective deterrent to homicide, shouldn't we expect the opposite result? What's going on here?

"The devil really is in the lack of details," the paper concluded. "At best, evidence for a deterrent effect is inconclusive, and shouldn't officials be able to prove that the taking of one life will undoubtedly save others? They simply have not met that burden of proof, and it's difficult to see how they could."

The arguments for enhanced sentencing in hate crime legislation takes a similar tack, arguing that tougher sentencing will protect LGBT communities by putting "would-be perpetrators on notice," in the words of the HRC.

But will a white supremacist really refrain from harming another person whom he or she believes to be fundamentally inferior over the distant chance it might mean more jail time? Would Byrd's or Shepard's killers have stopped to rethink their violent, hate-fueled crimes?

"Even as national lesbian-and-gay organizations pursue hate crime laws with single-minded fervor, concentrating precious resources and energy on these campaigns, there is no evidence that such laws actually prevent hate crimes," Richard Kim wrote in *The Nation* in 1999. Ten years later, there still doesn't seem to be a lot of data to support this claim.

In 1999, some twenty-one states and the District of Columbia had hate crime laws on the books. Today, forty-five states have enacted hate-crime laws in some form or other. Yet the trend has not been a lowering of hate crimes. In 2006, 7,722 hate-crime incidents were reported to the Federal Bureau of Investigation—an 8 percent increase from 2005.

The data: 2,640 were anti-black (up from 2,630 in 2005); 967 were anti-Jewish (up from 848 in 2005); 890 were anti-white (up from 828 in 2005); 747 were anti-male homosexual (up from 621 in 2005); 576 were anti-Hispanic (up from 522 in 2005); 156 were anti-Islamic (up from 128 in 2005).

Hate groups also appear to be on the rise. According to the Alabama-based Southern Poverty Law Center, the number of hate groups has increased by 54 percent since 2000.

Speaking before the Senate vote on July 16, Sen. Patrick Leahy, D-Vt., declared, "this legislation will help to address the serious and growing problem of hate crimes." But as one *San Francisco Chronicle* columnist recently asked, bluntly: "If hate crime laws prevent hate crimes, shouldn't hate crimes be shrinking, not growing?"

Whether hate crimes are on the rise because more crimes are being classified as such is another question. But the data leave the question of deterrence unanswered.

Regardless, the deterrence argument has been embraced by Democratic politicians. Speaking in favor of the Matthew Shepard Act, Rep. Jan Schakowsky, D-Ill., cited the crimes of Benjamin Nathaniel Smith, a white supremacist who killed two people and wounded nine others in a violent "spree" in 1999, apparently targeting Jews and African Americans. California Democrat Rep. Mike Honda cited the case of Angie Zapata, an eighteen-year-old transgender woman who was beaten to death in Greeley, Colorado, last year [2008].

But, as with the Clinton administration, the real political value of this recent round of votes was that it gave politicians a chance to appear tough on crime while also appearing to support gay rights. A number of those Democrats who supported the Matthew Shepard Act have been slow to back measures that would actually bestow equal rights on LGBT people. Sens. Max Baucus of Montana, Kent Conrad of North Dakota, and Herb Kohl of Wisconsin, to name a few, all oppose same-sex marriage, yet voted in favor of the Shepard Act.

What's more, a number of Democratic senators who voted for the Shepard Act voted in favor of the Defense of Marriage Act in 1996. Even Nebraska Democrat Ben Nelson, who in 2004 was one of two Democrats to vote in favor of amending the Constitution to limit marriage to heterosexual couples—along with then-Georgia Democrat, and certifiable lunatic, Zell Miller—voted for the Matthew Shepard Act.

Given the years of ad campaigns and political lobbying it has taken to get this legislation through Congress, it seems worth considering whether this is the best use of resources by influential LGBT groups, especially given that, as the Shepard case demonstrated, it is already possible to fully prosecute brutal crimes driven by hate or bigotry.

One expert on hate crimes and deterrence, James B. Jacobs, wrote as far back as 1993: "The horrendous crimes that provide the imagery and emotion for the passage of hate-crime legislation are already so heavily punished under American law that any talk of 'sentence enhancement' must be primarily symbolic."

Many LGBT activists agree. As one blogger argued on *Feministing* recently: "Putting our energy toward promoting harsher sentencing takes it away from the more difficult and more important work of changing our culture so that no one wants to kill another person because of their perceived membership in a marginalized identity group."

TOUGH ON CRIME FOR PROGRESSIVES?

In a country that leads the world in incarceration—2.3 million people are lodged in the nation's prisons or jails, a 500 percent increase over the past thirty years—the U.S. criminal justice system most brutally affects those very communities that hate-crime laws, historically, have ostensibly sought to protect.

An example: this summer, a new study found that 1 in 11 prisoners are serving life sentences in this country, 6,807 of whom were juveniles at the time of their crimes. According to the Sentencing Project, its findings "reveal overwhelming racial and ethnic disparities in the allocation of life sentences: 66 percent of all persons sentenced to life are nonwhite, and 77 percent of juveniles serving life sentences are nonwhite."

When it comes to LGBT communities, it is only recently that the "homosexual lifestyle" didn't itself amount to criminal activity in the eyes of the law. (The Supreme Court only overturned laws banning sodomy in 2003.) And the history of police brutality against gays, lesbians, and transgender people is hardly history.

Just this month, a gay couple was detained by police in Salt Lake City merely for kissing. A similar incident in El Paso, Texas led to five gay men being kicked out of a restaurant because the restaurant did not tolerate "the faggot stuff." "Particularly troubling for the El Paso case is that the security officers actually tried to cite laws against sodomy that were thrown out by the U.S. Supreme Court more than five years ago," pointed out one blogger at Change.org.

The criminal justice system has proved to be particularly brutal when it comes to those who are already behind bars, with violence and segregation regularly targeting gays, lesbians, and transgender people.

This summer, news broke that prisoners in a Virginia women's prison were being segregated for not looking "feminine" enough, being thrown into a "butch wing" by prison guards. According to the *Washington Blade*, the Bureau of Justice Statistics "has identified sexual orientation to be the single-highest risk factor for becoming the victim of sexual assault in men's facilities."

Although well-established groups like the HRC, the National Gay and Lesbian Task Force, and Parents, Families and Friends of Lesbians and Gays have poured much energy into hate crime legislation, other, smaller LGBT organizations have opposed them on the grounds that toughening the criminal justice system will do little to further tolerance or equality for LGBT people, particularly given the fact that they continue to be targeted by the very same system.

Many more radical LGBT groups reject hate crime legislation on the grounds that the any further expansion of the criminal justice system is at odds with their fight for human rights.

In a letter this spring to supporters of New York's Gender Employment Non-Discrimination Act (GENDA)—which includes a provision that would enhance sentences for existing hate crimes—a coalition of local advocacy groups wrote: "It pains us that we cannot support the current GENDA bill, because we cannot, and will not, support hate crime legislation."

Rather than serving as protection for oppressed people, the hate crime portion of this law may expose our communities to more danger—from prejudiced institutions far more powerful and pervasive than individual bigots. Trans people, people of color, and other marginalized groups are disproportionately incarcerated to an overwhelming degree.

Trans and gender non-conforming people, particularly transwomen of color, are regularly profiled and falsely arrested for doing nothing more than walking down the street. Almost 95 percent of the people locked up on Riker's Island are black or Latino/a. Many of us have been arrested ourselves or seen our friends, members, clients, colleagues, and lovers arrested, often when they themselves were the victims of a violent attack.

Once arrested, the degree of violence, abuse, humiliation, rape, and denial of needed medical care that our communities confront behind bars is truly shocking, and at times fatal.

The Human Rights Campaign argued that passage of the Shepard Act would "put would-be perpetrators on notice that our society does not tolerate bias-motivated, violent crime." But what happens when the perpetrators are those whose duty it is to supposedly enforce the law?

WHEN TOUGH ON CRIME MEETS HUMAN RIGHTS

Just before the vote on the Shepard Act on July 16, Alabama Republican Senator Jeff Sessions—an opponent of the legislation who could hardly be less tolerant of LGBT rights—pulled a cynical maneuver: he introduced three last-minute additions to the amendment, which was widely decried as a transparent ploy to derail the legislation.

One of them would make the federal death penalty available for prosecutions of hate crimes, an idea that alarmed the legislation's supporters. "This amendment is unnecessary and is a poison pill designed to kill the bill," reported *HRC Backstory* (the blog of the Human Rights Campaign).

There's no question Sessions has zero interest in bolstering the hate crime bill. But nor does it seem particularly likely that his maneuver would "kill the bill." After all, as previously discussed, it has been a long time since Democrats had a problem supporting tough-on-crime legislation.

Regardless of its actual strategic value, many of the groups that fought hard for the hate crime bill have sent messages asking Congress to oppose the Sessions amendment.

"The death penalty is irreversible and highly controversial—with significant doubts about its deterrent effect and clear evidence of disproportionate application against poor people," read a letter signed by a long list of advocacy groups, from the Anti-Defamation League to the HRC to the NAACP, which reminded legislators that "no version of the bill has ever included the death penalty."

The National Gay and Lesbian Task Force, for example, called the death penalty a "state-sponsored brutality that perpetuates violence rather than ending it," saying, "It is long past time to send a clear and unequivocal message that hate violence against lesbian, gay, bisexual and transgender people will no longer be tolerated—but it must be done in a way that saves lives, not ends them."

But in a country with the largest prison system in the world and the toughest sentences on the books, this discomfiting run-in between supporters of tougher hate crime legislation and the "ultimate punishment" seemed almost inevitable.

Indeed, it is emblematic of a fundamental flaw at the heart of hate crime legislation: human rights groups that lobby for tougher sentencing may believe that, despite all its ugly dimensions, the criminal justice system can be used for more noble ends, to force bigoted elements within society to change and to protect vulnerable communities. But at the end of the day, it amounts to the same classic "tough on crime" canard, just tailored to more liberal sensibilities.

Sanesha Stewart, Lawrence King, and Why Hate Crime Legislation Won't Help

JACK APONTE

I'VE BEEN OUT OF TOWN and subsequently out of touch for a while now, visiting El Paso with my partner to meet her incomprehensibly adorable two-week-old nephew. But in the midst of the happiness that babies and family and vacation bring, two pieces of tragic news have weighed heavily on my mind. Both of them demonstrate how dangerous and hostile a world this is for people who are trans and gender non-conforming.

On February 10, Sanesha Stewart, a young trans woman of color, was brutally murdered in her apartment in the Bronx. This is tragic and deeply saddening in and of itself, and part of a frightening and enduring pattern of violence against trans people. But because of this woman's identities—trans, woman, person of color, low income—the tragedy doesn't end with her death and the grief of those who knew

This piece first appeared online at angrybrownbutch.com on February 20, 2008.

and loved her. Instead, the mainstream media, specifically the *Daily News*, has managed to add to the tragedy with grossly disrespectful and transphobic journalism—if such garbage can even be called journalism. This, too, is part of a pattern, one that I've written about before. And yet, every time I read another disgustingly transphobic article, I'm still shocked and appalled that some media sources will stoop so low. Even in death, even after having been murdered, trans people are given no respect and are treated as less than human.

In an eloquent and resonating post on *Feministe.us*, Holly posits a world in which Sanesha Stewart's murder would be treated with respect for the victim and a cold eye for the killer, then contrasts that with the lurid reality:

> There was no respect and no cold eye, none at all. I must be imagining some completely different universe where young trans women of color aren't automatically treated like human trash. Where we all live, business as usual is to make a lot of comments about what the murder victim dressed like and looked like, reveal what her name was before she changed it, automatically assume she's getting paid for sex, and to make excuses for the alleged killer.

Only days after Sanesha was murdered, Lawrence King, a fifteen-year-old, openly gay, gender non-conforming junior high schooler was shot in the head and killed by Brandon McInerney, a fellow classmate, a fourteen-year-old boy. McInerney has been charged with first-degree murder and a hate crime, for which he could face a sentence of twenty-four years to life with an additional three years because of the hate crime status.

It's mind-boggling. Mind-boggling that someone so young could be so severely punished for simply being himself; mind-boggling that someone so young could have so much hatred or anger inside of him that he could kill another kid. Or, as Holly suggests in another post, that perhaps McInerney was not acting out of simple hatred:

> I fear the worst—and the worst would not just be that some homophobic asshole killed a child. There's an even worse worst: that a child is dead, and the other child who pulled the

trigger did so because he couldn't deal with his own feelings. And now that second child will be tried as an adult, and another life destroyed.

When crimes like the murders of Lawrence King and Sanesha Stewart occur, I often hear queer and trans advocates call for strong hate crime legislation. In a statement from the Human Rights Campaign about King's murder (mind you, I doubt the HRC would ever release any statement about Stewart's murder), Joe Solmonese reiterated this demand:

> While California's residents are fortunate to have state laws that provide some protection against hate crimes and school bullying, this pattern of violence against gay, lesbian, bisexual and transgender students is repeated too often in schools and communities across America each day. This tragedy illustrates the need to pass a federal hate crime law to ensure everyone is protected against violent, bias-motivated crimes, wherever they reside.

I disagree with this response. I cannot see how hate crime legislation can do anything to protect anyone—queer and trans people, people of color, women, and other victims of hate crimes. Hate crime legislation only works after the fact, after someone has been victimized, hurt, or killed. Hate crime legislation cannot undo what has been done. Nor can it undo what has been done to our society and to the individuals within it: the inscription of hatred, of intolerance, of prejudice upon our psyches. Hate crimes don't occur because there aren't enough laws against them, and hate crimes won't stop when those laws are in place. Hate crimes occur because, time and time again, our society demonstrates that certain people are worth less than others; that certain people are wrong, are perverse, are immoral in their very being; that certain people deserve discrimination, derision, and disrespect.

Perhaps advocates of hate crime legislation believe that such laws would send a message to people that homophobia, transphobia, and other forms of prejudice and hatred are wrong. I don't think it will. How could such laws counteract the prejudices that permeate our society? I seriously doubt that hate crime legislation that is only brought up after someone is hurt or killed can make a dent in the ubiquitous flood of messages that we receive from politicians, religious leaders, the media and pop culture stating that queers and trans people are less deserving of respect and rights than straight and non-trans people. In this country, all signs point to queer people being second-class citizens, and trans and gender non-conforming people being maybe third or fourth-class citizens. That is what sets up a situation where someone is targeted because of their sexuality or their gender identity, just as such dehumanization is what has fueled racist and sexist violence for centuries. And that's simply not going to be undone by hate crime legislation. Attacking a few of the symptoms of hatred while leaving others unhindered and the root causes untouched is never going to change much of anything.

Moreover, hate crime legislation is far too tied up with our unjust judicial system and prison industry. How can we rely on systems that continuously target and abuse people of color, queer folks, and trans folks to protect us from targeting and abuse? Can we really trust the police, the courts, and prisons to protect us when much of the time they're violating our rights, tearing apart our families, and ravaging our communities? Is it likely that hate crime legislation will be applied fairly across the board in a system that consistently fails to treat all people equally? I think not. For communities that often find themselves being victimized by the judicial and prison systems, there can be little to gain in bolstering those systems and giving them more power to imprison, possibly unjustly. For my part, I'm invested in prison abolition, so "protections" that serve primarily to send more people to jail for longer periods of time are counter-intuitive.

In fact, because hate crime legislation involves no analysis of power—it's not legislation against homophobic or transphobic or racist acts, but rather against general hatred in any direction—such laws can even be applied against oppressed people. Now, I'm not defending or condoning acts of violence or hatred perpetuated by oppressed people, nor am I saying that one form of violence is better than the other. But the lack of a power analysis built into such legislation reminds me of accusations of "reverse racism" in that they both completely miss the point. Queer folks, trans folks, people of color aren't disproportionately victimized simply because some individuals hate them: that hatred is backed up, reinforced, and executed by an entire system of institutionalized power that allows and in fact encourages such acts of violence. The lack of acknowledgment of these systems of power in hate crime legislation only reinforces my belief that such legislation is relatively useless in doing anything to stop homophobia, transphobia, racism and other forms of oppression, and therefore won't do much to stop the violence that stems from said oppression.

Hate crime legislation won't bring Sanesha Stewart or Lawrence King back, nor will it protect other trans and gender non-conforming folks and people of color from violence fueled by hate. Instead of reacting to hatred with disapproval after the fact, we need to instill a pro-active condemnation of hatred, prejudice and discrimination into our society. Sure, that's a much more difficult job to do, but it can be done, slowly but surely, and it's the only way we're truly going to protect those who need protection most.

Why Hate Crime Legislation is Still Not a Solution

YASMIN NAIR

THE MATTHEW SHEPARD AND JAMES Byrd Act (H.R. 1592) expands the 1969 United States federal hate crime law to include crimes motivated by a victim's actual or perceived gender, sexual orientation, gender identity, or disability. The bill also requires "the FBI to track statistics on hate crimes" against transgender people.

When I first began writing against hate crime legislation (HCL) in the early 2000s, public opinion appeared to be overwhelmingly in favor of it. It was largely determined, in public discourse, that those against HCL were ogres who hated minorities and that those for it were saviors of the same.

Yet, even with the battle lines drawn so carefully, there have been several ruptures in the public's general attitude towards hate crime legislation, the most significant of which was around the trial of Dharun Ravi for the 2010 suicide of Tyler Clementi. Clementi's suicide prompted the

---

This piece originally appeared online at The Bilerico Project *(bilerico. com) as two separate articles in 2009 and 2011, which have been edited and updated into one.*

gay community to engage in its usual orgy of demonizing and hatred. It set about portraying Dharun Ravi as a cold-blooded killer who committed a "hate crime" against a gay student.

Lost in the quest to declare this a classic case of "bullying" was a more complex and nuanced understanding of how such a thing had come to be, and lost also were the complicated intersections of class and ethnicity that surrounded the case. As reported by the *The New Yorker*'s Ian Parker, Ravi faced charges that could have increase his sentencing: "...shortly before Molly Wei [co-defendant] made a deal with prosecutors, Ravi was indicted on charges of invasion of privacy (sex crimes), bias intimidation (hate crimes), witness tampering, and evidence tampering. Bias intimidation is a sentence-booster that attaches itself to an underlying crime—usually, a violent one."

HCL is a panacea embraced by the left, which seeks easy solutions to the complicated problems facing societies broken by the violence of neoliberalism. Several pieces in this anthology have pointed out the problems with HCL and its furthering of the prison industrial complex. HCL can seem to be the only solution when racial and ethnic minorities and the transgender community confront cases of harassment and/or murder. Yet in reducing deaths to the result of "hatred," we tend to forget that vulnerable communities are not vulnerable solely on account of their perceived identity, but because of a host of intersecting factors, including economic vulnerability. In Chicago, Sex Workers Outreach Project has shown that sex workers on the street have to worry more about harassment and violence from cops than from clients, and they are likely to be targeted precisely because they are seen as undeserving of protection. In other words, they are seen as people whose lives simply don't matter. No amount of sentence-enhancement, like the kind advocated for in the trial of Ravi, is going to help with the multiple vulnerabilities faced by so many. All it does is funnel more people into the prison industrial complex.

In the end, Ravi was sentenced to thirty days, on charges of "invasion of privacy, bias intimidation, witness tampering and hindering arrest, stemming from his role in activating the webcam to peek at Clementi's date with a man in the dorm room on Sept. 19, 2010" and of "encouraging others to spy during a second date, on Sept. 21, 2010, and intimidating Clementi for being gay," as reported by ABC news at the time.

Without the spurious attachment of "invasion of privacy" and "bias intimidation," there would have been no conviction at all. Even several gay commentators wrote against the push for sentencing Ravi, pointing out that this would allow everyone to forget about, for instance, what Clementi had already discussed as his parents' discomfort with his sexuality. In other words, what emerged from the Ravi trial was a disruption in the causality model evoked by HCL, and an evoking of the larger contexts and nuances of the harm done to queers.

No one can deny that particular groups are in fact treated with discrimination and even violence. But rather than ask how about how to combat such discrimination and violence, we've taken the easy route out and decided to hand over the solution to a prison industrial complex that already benefits massively from the incarceration of mostly poor people and mostly people of color. It's also worth considering the class dynamics of hate crime legislation, given that the system of law and order is already skewed against those without the resources to combat unfair and overly punitive punishment and incarceration.

Let's be honest: we already think that bigots and "haters" are just "low-class punks and thugs" anyway. It's easy to put a twenty-year-old Latino from Chicago's Pilsen neighborhood in jail for six to ten years because he yelled "fag" while stealing a gay man's wallet. Does that solve the problem of homophobia and bigotry in the boardroom? Do we even have ways to discern and address the latter?

What do we do when the violence is committed by the system itself? What do we do with the case of Victoria Arellano, a transgender undocumented immigrant who died shackled to her bed in Immigration and Customs Enforcement detention in 2007 after being denied her AIDS medication? Does the system that brought about her death have a way of accounting for its own "hate crime?"

Hate crime legislation has a murky history already detailed by other writers. But it's worth remembering that one reason it's so popular today is that it's often the only way for some marginalized groups to claim recognition as groups, and to seek redress for the very real violence their members experience in everyday life.

At this point, for instance, the issue of violence against the transgender community is seen as a real threat. Indeed, the only way for trangender people to gain recourse from the criminal legal system is to invoke the language of HCL; in effect, transgender identities are brought into being only through narratives of their erasure. But do we address that violence by helping the state to perpetrate more violence against the most marginal who already fill our jails? Or do we think of better ways to address the consequences of bigotry and prejudice? How do those of us struggling to make sense of what often seems like the overwhelming violence surrounding queer and trans bodies in particular work with the seeming contradictions of wanting that violence to end while faced with the criminal legal system as the only option?

Eric A. Stanley writes, in "Near Life, Queer Death: Overkill and Ontological Capture" in the journal *Social Text*, about the conceptual and material ruptures that occur when queer bodies are mutilated and dismembered far beyond the point of death. Yet, even while noting that such deaths are often not entered into the litany of "hate crimes," Stanley points out that HCL is itself a function of the same liberal democratic principles that claim to provide redress:

> "Reports" on antiqueer violence, such as the "Hate Crime Statistics," reproduce the same kinds of rhetorical loss along with the actual loss of people that *cannot be counted*. The quantitative limits of what gets to count as anti-queer violence cannot begin to apprehend the numbers of trans and queer bodies that are collected off cold pavement and highway underpasses, nameless flesh whose stories of brutality never find their way into an official account beyond a few scant notes in a police report of a body of a "man in a dress" discovered.

Herein lies our dilemma: our dead are uncounted and unmourned and the only system that exists to help us comprehend the extent of their numbers is the one that exerts that violence upon us in the first place. But surely there is a way out of all this. As Stanley goes on to write, "What I am after then is not a new set of data or a more complete set of numbers. What I hope to do here is to re-situate the ways we conceptualize the very categories of 'queer' and 'violence' as to remake them both."

That is exactly what we must do as we are met with new reports of violence against trans and queer bodies. As I write, the newspapers report yet another murder of a gender-variant person, this one of a Chicago nineteen-year-old who went by "Tiffany," and who was also identified as Donta Gooden. Immediate responses already echo the same narratives and language: that Tiffany was killed because of her desire to live an "authentic" life and for "who she was." Already, several organizations are calling for this to be classified as a "hate crime."

But as with so many other such murders, we have no proof that Tiffany was actually killed for exercising a "right" to be an "authentic self." Even if gender presentation had been a reason, Tiffany was made far more vulnerable by a system that refused him or her [at this point, it's unclear whether Tiffany actually preferred female pronouns] resources to the most basic needs, like health care.

This will be the easy route out: claim without ever having to prove that Tiffany was murdered because she was being herself, and you get to ignore the vast complexity of the issues that put him or her in danger in the first place.

To be trans usually means being shut out of housing and employment opportunities, and to be denied medical resources. When we decide, erroneously and on a gut level, that someone was killed for their identity, we are ignoring the greater systemic problems that put trans people in danger in the first place. When we place the burden on an individual's identity, we are in effect personalizing greater systemic and societal problems.

In making the claim that people are killed because they are targeted as transgender, the entire HCL industrial complex, including several trans organizations, is reproducing the erasure of the state's violence towards them.

The violence against queers and trans people is comprised of hateful, vicious, and brutal crimes for which there can be no excuse. But there are already legal remedies in place for such crimes: there are punishments for brutality and for murder.

It makes more sense to come to terms with a difficult fact: that the hatred against queer and gender-non-conforming people which incites such brutality is about a deep-seated hatred of the overturning of codes and performances to which people are strangely and deeply cathected, and it's a hatred that flares up without meaning or the comfort of narrative and deep-seated intention. It's true that kind of hatred sometimes becomes an excuse for violence: "I was so deeply disturbed that I couldn't help but beat/kill him/her."

But HCL only presents a way for us to forget that the senseless violence of which we are constantly made aware is exactly that: senseless and brutal. In the end, HCL grants us nothing more than the cold comfort of extended prison sentences or death—in effect, extending the very violence that we claim to abhor.

Is jailing people for their prejudice really going to curtail bigotry and ignorance? Or will it just end up policing thought and filling the coffers of the prison industrial complex?

Lesbians Sentenced for Self-Defense
All-White Jury Convicts Black Women

IMANI KEITH HENRY

ON JUNE 14, FOUR AFRICAN-AMERICAN women—Venice Brown (19), Terrain Dandridge (20), Patreese Johnson (20) and Renata Hill (24)—received sentences ranging from three-and-a-half to eleven years in prison. None of them had previous criminal records. Two of them are parents of small children.

Their crime? Defending themselves from a physical attack by a man who held them down and choked them, ripped hair from their scalps, spat on them, and threatened to sexually assault them—all because they are lesbians.

The mere fact that any victim of a bigoted attack would be arrested, jailed, and then convicted for self-defense is an outrage. But the length of prison time given further demonstrates the highly political nature of this case and just how racist, misogynistic, anti-gay, anti-youth, and anti-worker the so-called U.S. justice system truly is.

This piece was first published Jun 21, 2007 in the Worker's World Paper *(workers.org) and was subsequently reprinted by the Bay Area NJ4 Solidarity Committee.*

The description of the events, reported below, is based on written statements by Fabulous Independent Educated Radicals for Community Empowerment (FIERCE), a community organization that has made a call to action to defend the four women, verbal accounts from court observers, and evidence from a surveillance camera.

THE ATTACK

On Aug. 16, 2006, seven young, African-American, lesbian-identified friends were walking in the West Village. The Village is a historic center for lesbian, gay, bi, and trans (LGBT) communities, and is seen as a safe haven for working-class LGBT youth, especially youth of color.

As they passed the Independent Film Cinema, twenty-nine-year-old Dwayne Buckle, an African-American vendor selling DVDs, sexually propositioned one of the women. They rebuffed his advances and kept walking.

"I'll f— you straight, sweetheart!" Buckle shouted. A video camera from a nearby store shows the women walking away. He followed them, all the while hurling anti-lesbian slurs, grabbing his genitals, and making explicitly obscene remarks. The women finally stopped and confronted him. A heated argument ensued. Buckle spat in the face of one of the women and threw his lit cigarette at them, escalating the verbal attack into a physical one.

Buckle is seen on the video grabbing and pulling out large patches of hair from one of the young women. When Buckle ended up on top of one of the women, choking her, Johnson pulled a small steak knife out of her purse. She aimed for his arm to stop him from killing her friend.

The video captures two men finally running over to help the women and beating Buckle. At some point he was stabbed in the abdomen. The women were already walking away across the street by the time the police arrived.

Buckle was hospitalized for five days after surgery for a lacerated liver and stomach. When asked at the hospital, he responded at least twice that men had attacked him.

There was no evidence that Johnson's kitchen knife was the weapon that penetrated his abdomen, nor was there any blood visible on it. In fact, there was never any forensics testing done on her knife. On the night they were arrested, the police told the women that there would be a search by the New York Police Department for the two men—which to date has not happened.

After almost a year of trial, four of the seven were convicted in April. Johnson was sentenced to eleven years on June 14.

Even with Buckle's admission and the video footage proving that he instigated this anti-gay attack, the women were relentlessly demonized in the press, had trumped-up felony charges levied against them, and were subsequently given long sentences in order to send a clear resounding message—that self-defense is a crime and no one should dare to fight back.

POLITICAL BACKDROP OF THE CASE

Why were these young women used as an example? At stake are the billions of dollars in tourism and real estate development involved in the continued gentrification of the West Village. This particular incident happened near the Washington Square area—home of New York University, one of the most expensive private colleges in the country and one of the biggest employers and landlords in New York City. On June 17th, *The New York Times* reported that Justice Edward J. McLaughlin used his sentencing speech to comment on "how New York welcomes tourists."

The Village is also the home of the Stonewall Rebellion, the three-day street battle against the NYPD that, along with the Compton Cafeteria "Riots" in California, helped launch the modern-day LGBT liberation movement in 1969. The Manhattan LGBT Pride march, one of the biggest demonstrations of LGBT peoples in the world, ends near the Christopher Street Piers in the Village, which have been the historical "hangout" and home for working-class trans and LGBT youth in New York City for decades.

Because of growing gentrification in recent years, young people of color, homeless and transgender communities, LGBT and straight, have faced curfews and brutality by police sanctioned by the West Village community board and politicians. On Oct. 31, 2006, police officers from the NYPD's 6th Precinct indiscriminately beat and arrested several people of color in sweeps on Christopher Street after the Halloween parade.

Since the 1980s there has been a steady increase in anti-LGBT violence in the area, with bashers going there with that purpose in mind.

For trans people and LGBT youth of color, who statistically experience higher amounts of bigoted violence, the impact of the gentrification has been severe. As their once-safe haven is encroached on by real estate developers, the new white and majority heterosexual residents of the West Village then call in the state to brutalize them.

For the last six years, FIERCE has been at the forefront of mobilizing young people "to counter the displacement and criminalization of LGBTSTQ [lesbian, gay, bi, two spirit, trans, and queer] youth of color and homeless youth at the Christopher Street Pier and in Manhattan's West Village." (www.fiercenyc.org) FIERCE has also been the lead organization supporting the Jersey Seven and their families.

THE TRIAL AND THE MEDIA

Deemed a so-called "hate crime" against a straight man, every possible racist, anti-woman, anti-LGBT and anti-youth tactic was used by the entire state apparatus and media. Everything from the fact that they lived outside of New York, in the working-class majority Black city of Newark, N.J., to their gender expressions and body structures were twisted and dehumanized in the public eye and to the jury.

According to court observers, McLaughlin stated throughout the trial that he had no sympathy for these women. The jury, although they were all women, were all white. All witnesses for the district attorney were white men, except for one Black male who had several felony charges.

Court observers report that the defense attorneys had to put enormous effort into simply convincing the jury that they were "average women" who had planned to just hang out together that night. Some jurists asked why they were in the Village if they were from New Jersey. The DA brought up whether they could afford to hang out there—raising the issue of who has the right to be there in the first place.

The *Daily News*'s reporting was relentless in its racist anti-lesbian misogyny, portraying Buckle as a "filmmaker" and "sound engineer" preyed upon by a "lesbian wolf pack" (April 19) and a "gang of angry lesbians." (April 13)

Everyone has been socialized by cultural archetypes of what it means to be a "man" or "masculine" and "woman" or "feminine." Gender identity/expression is the way each individual chooses or not to express gender in their everyday lives, including how they dress, walk, talk, etc. Transgender people and other gender non-conforming people face oppression based on their gender expression/identity.

The only pictures shown in the *Daily News* were of the more masculine-appearing women. On April 13th one of the most despicable headlines in the *Daily News*, "'I'm a man!' lesbian growled during fight," was targeted against Renata Hill, who was taunted by Buckle because of her masculinity.

Ironically, Johnson, who was singled out by the judge as the "ringleader," is the more feminine of the four. According to the June 15th *New York Times*, in his sentencing remarks, "Justice McLaughlin scoffed at the assertion made by…Johnson, that she carried a knife because she was just 4-foot-11 and 95 pounds, worked nights and lived in a dangerous neighborhood." He quoted the nursery rhyme, "Sticks and stones will break my bones, but names will never hurt me."

All of the seven women knew and went to school with Sakia Gunn, a nineteen-year-old butch lesbian who was stabbed to death in Newark, N.J., in May 2003. Paralleling the present case, Gunn was out with three of her friends when a man made sexual advances to one of the women. When she replied that she was a lesbian and not interested, he attacked them. Gunn fought back and was stabbed to death.

"You can't help but wonder that if Sakia Gunn had a weapon, would she be in jail right now?" Bran Fenner, a founding member and co-executive director of FIERCE, told *Workers World*. "If we don't have the right to self-defense, how are we supposed to survive?"

NATIONAL CALL TO ACTION

While racist killer cops continue to go without indictment and anti-immigrant paramilitary groups like the Minutemen are on the rise in the U.S., The Jersey Four sit behind bars for simply defending themselves against a bigot who attacked them in the Village.

Capitalism at its very core is a racist, sexist, anti-LGBT system, sanctioning state violence through cops, courts, and its so-called laws. The case of the Jersey Four gives more legal precedence for bigoted violence to go unchallenged. The ruling class saw this case as a political one; FIERCE and other groups believe the entire progressive movement should as well.

Fenner said, "We are organizing in the hope that this wakes up all oppressed people and sparks a huge, broad campaign to demand freedom for the Jersey Four."

First Coffins, Now Prison?

SÉBASTIEN BARRAUD FOR POLITIQ-QUEERS SOLIDAIRES!

TO MARK DECEMBER 1, 2009, PolitiQ-queers solidaires! is denouncing the criminalization of nondisclosure, exposure to, and sexual transmission of HIV. This repressive approach is ineffective, discriminatory, and stigmatizing. We want to live in a society of solidarity where HIV is prevented rather than punished. We will never defeat HIV/AIDS by hiding it behind bars!

In Quebec and Canada, as in all countries with universal access to antiretroviral (ARV) treatment, HIV has become a chronic disease that can be effectively controlled when it is detected in time. Provided they have equal life conditions, people with HIV can have a life expectancy practically equal to HIV-negative people.

We now know that ARV treatments considerably diminish or even eliminate the level of infectiousness in HIV-positive people.[1] Accordingly, if a large majority of HIV-positive people were treated now, the virus could be eradicated in the medium to long term,[2] since if one is no longer infectious, one cannot transmit the virus to partners, despite

This text originally appeared in French on a 2009 World AIDS Day broadsheet produced by PolitiQ-queers solidaires (http://politiq.wix.com/politiq) in Montréal, Canada. The text was peer reviewed by Bruno Laprade and Maxime De L'Isle.

difficulties in consistently using condoms. The remainder of transmissions would be the result of not knowing one's HIV status. In fact, it appears that people who do not know whether they are HIV-positive show less consistent and realistic preventive behaviors than those who know they are HIV-positive.[3] This is why the key to HIV/AIDS prevention, now more than ever, is detection. The maximum possible number of HIV-positive people must be diagnosed. The growing availability of rapid tests is encouraging, and PolitiQ supports this.[4] However, from our point of view, the lives that HIV-positive people face do not at all encourage these means of protection. The ostracism and violence that people who know they are HIV-positive face—in particular, criminalization—makes these measures ineffective. How can we hope for people to take responsibility by being tested when they will clearly face prejudice and discrimination if they test positive?

This being the case, PolitiQ-queers solidaires! calls for concrete work in coalition to ensure the social and economic conditions needed to ensure that nobody has to be afraid of the consequences a positive result.

1. *Providing accurate and up-to-date information on the biomedical and day-to-day consequences of being HIV-positive.* Everyone needs to understand that it is possible to live normally with HIV and that an HIV-positive person is not just a dangerous infectious agent allowed to walk around free. This logically means informing young people as soon as possible, i.e. before they begin their sexual lives. Since in our opinion education is fundamental to a struggle against HIV and against discrimination against HIV-positive people, PolitiQ denounces the abolition of sexual education and sexual health classes in high schools and demands their immediate reinstatement.

2. *Fighting still harder against prejudice against HIV-positive people.* This prejudice, like all irrational discriminations, stigmatizes and isolates people. This damages self-esteem and eliminates the drive to care for oneself and others. Why be socially responsible when society discriminates against you and rejects you socially and sexually? Living in a society that discriminates against HIV-positive people is a major obstacle towards

revealing one's HIV status, an absolute necessity for negotiating safer-sex practices. Even though the overwhelming majority of HIV-positive people are responsible (a 2006 U.S. study found that 95% of HIV-positive people have not transmitted the virus),[5] it is logical that numerous people prefer not to know their HIV status rather than live with the stigma of being HIV-positive.

3. *Fighting against the criminalization of exposure to and transmission of HIV.* Why would someone be tested if the consequence is to become a potential criminal? This legal pressure is a terrible obstacle to prevention and is therefore grossly counterproductive in the struggle against HIV. It clearly works against our public health and reinforces social HIV discrimination more than ever.[6]

But even beyond the negative impact on the fight against HIV that brings us together today, PolitiQ also wants to raise the other harmful consequences of the criminalization of nondisclosure, exposure to and sexual transmission of HIV.

What about other transmissible diseases? Will transmitting the human papilloma virus (HPV), with which 75% of Canadians are estimated to be infected during their lifetime,[7] and responsible for many cervical, uterine, and colorectal cancers, be criminalized? What about hepatitis B and C, or even herpes? Will people be able to sue their co-worker if they don't get vaccinated against a (H1N1) flu?

Does it make any sense, under the Charter of Rights, to legally require a person to consistently reveal their HIV status? Isn't medical privacy a fundamental value of our society and an equality guarantee for all citizens, ill or not? We are concerned about universal access to diagnosis, care, and health care being called into question.

Since certain ethnic and sexual minorities who are particularly affected by HIV/AIDS (Haitians, Africans (especially women), migrants, sex workers, prisoners, trans women and men who have sex with men) are already afflicted by discrimination due to their identity, does it make sense to add another source of stigmatization to those members of these groups who are HIV-positive? Sex workers are under extreme pressure from their clients not to use condoms, and their work and lives are already criminalized more than enough! This is not meant to dismiss the suffering of people infected with HIV in clearly fraudulent situations (false HIV testing, hiding treatments, etc.). People in these situations have a legitimate right to compensation for the moral and possibly physical harm they have undergone. But why in criminal court? Aren't there other means of redress available, as there were for contaminated blood? Remember that 1,200 Canadians became HIV-positive and 12,000 contracted hepatitis C in the tainted blood scandal—but nobody was ever criminally convicted![8] Why should all HIV-positive people be punished while only a small minority have ever transmitted HIV at all, and only a tiny handful have ever transmitted it truly intentionally? Why place all the responsibility for preventing sexual transmission of HIV on HIV-positive people alone, eliminating shared responsibility—"protect yourself, protect your partner"—which has been the chief preventive principle since the beginning of the pandemic?

Love, ignorance, and law have never protected anyone from any virus or disease. But information, equality, and solidarity have always improved people's well-being and ability to care for themselves and others. With the limits of prevention and the need to diversify to reach all forms of sexuality, penalization will not solve anything: courts cannot do the work of schools!

NOTES

1   Vernazza P, Hirschel B, Bernasconi E, Flepp M. (2008). Les personnes séropositives ne souffrant d'aucune autre MST et suivant un traitement antirétroviral efficace ne transmettent pas le VIH par voie sexuelle. Commission fédérale pour les problèmes liés au sida (CFS), Commission d'experts clinique et thérapie VIH et sida de l'Office fédéral de la santé publique (OFSP): http:// www.saez.ch/pdf_f/2008/2008-05/2008-05-089. pdf. In 2012, treatment as prevention (TasP) is now one of the tools with condoms (combinated prevention) to fight against HIV transmission within sero-discordant couples, especially those who want to have babies naturally.

2   Lima VD, Johnston K, Hogg RS, Levy AR, Harrigan PR, Anema A, Montaner JS. (2008). "Expanded access to highly active antiretroviral therapy: a potentially powerful strategy to curb the growth of the HIV epidemic." *Journal of Infectious Diseases*, July 1, 198(1), p.59–67.

3   Burman W, Grund B, Neuhaus J, Douglas J, Friedland G, Telzak E, Colebunders E, Paton N, Fisher M, Rietmeijer C. (2008). "Episodic Antiretroviral Therapy Increases HIV Transmission Risk Compared With Continuous Therapy: Results of a Randomized Controlled Trial," *Journal of Acquired Immune Deficiency Syndrome*, 49, p.142–150.

4   In 2012, even home testing is in development, since the FDA has just approved Oraquick test: http://www.fda.gov/News Events/Newsroom/PressAnnouncements/ucm310542.htm.

5   Holtgrave DR, Irene Hall H, Rhodes PH, Wolitski RJ. (2008). Updated Annual HIV Transmission Rates in the United States, 1977–2006. *Journal of Acquired Immune Deficiency Syndrome* and Center for Disease Control and Prevention.

6   In 2012, we know from two studies that HIV criminalization may discourage testing.

    O'Byrne P, Bryan A, Woodyatt C, Nondisclosure prosecution and HIV prevention: results from an Ottawa-based gay men's sex survey: https://dl.dropbox.com/ u/1576514/O%27Byrne, %20nondisclosure%20prosecutions,%20JANAC,%202012. pdf.

    The Sero Project: National criminalization survey preliminary results, July 25, 2012: http://seroproject.com/wp-content/ uploads/2012/07/ Sero-Preliminary-Data-Report_Final.pdf.

7   http://www.hpvinfo.ca/hpvinfo/professionals/ overview-normal3 .afpx.

8   http://www.dentist-dentiste.com/canada5.htm.

The Devil in Gay Inc.

How the Gay Establishment Ignored a Sex Panic Fueled by Homophobia

JAMES D'ENTREMONT

WHILE STRIVING TO ENHANCE PENALTIES for homophobic thought-crimes, the gay mainstream has been tossing people harmed by some of the worst excesses of homophobia overboard. In the 1980s and '90s, a wave of baroque child-molestation trials steeped in bias against sexual minorities swept the U.S. In response, LGBTQ organizations sometimes joined in virtual lynchings. More often, they maintained a silence interrupted only by the mantra, "We are not child molesters."

Scores of day-care workers, nursery school teachers, baby-sitters, and others imprisoned on false sex-abuse charges during the height of the child-protection panic have been exonerated and freed, but a number of almost certainly innocent people convicted of sex crimes against children remain under lock and key. Among them are four women from San Antonio, Texas, now in their second decade of incarceration.

This piece first appeared online at Friends of Justice *(bobchatelle.net) in the summer of 2012.*

The women's ordeal began in September, 1994, when Serafina Limon caught her granddaughters, Stephanie and Vanessa, in apparently sexualized play with naked Barbie dolls. When Serafina reported this scene to her son Javier, the girls' father, he concluded the girls, aged seven and nine, had been exposed to lesbian sex at the home of their aunt. Police were informed. The girls were brought to the Alamo Children's Advocacy Center for evaluation. Following an investigation, Javier's estranged partner's younger sister, Elizabeth Ramirez, 19, and three of her friends were charged with multiple counts of aggravated sexual assault.

In July, Liz Ramirez's nieces had spent a week at her San Antonio apartment. During that period, a Latina lesbian couple, Anna Vasquez and Cassandra "Cassie" Rivera, had visited, bringing with them Cassie's children. Liz's roommate, Kristie Mayhugh, was also present. Neighbors' children ran in and out of the apartment. Days passed without incident. When the girls returned home, they showed no signs of trauma.

The chief investigator was a homicide detective, Thomas Matjeka, who had never previously interviewed children thought to have been sexually abused. He made no recordings of his sessions with Stephanie and Vanessa, who had already been grilled by others including their father. Interrogating Liz Ramirez, Matjeka told her that although she currently had a boyfriend, he knew about her sexual history of involvement with women, implying that homosexuality made her a menace to children.

The case took a long time to go to trial. Elizabeth Ramirez was tried separately and convicted in February, 1997. Having previously been offered ten years' probation in exchange for a guilty plea, she received a prison term of thirty-seven years and six months. A year later, Anna, Cassie, and Kristie were tried together, found guilty, and given fifteen-year sentences. At both trials, prosecutors repeatedly alluded to the defendants' sexual orientation, implying it was a short step from lesbianism to child rape. There was minimal evidence except the uncorroborated testimony of Liz Ramirez's nieces, who recited carefully prepped claims that the women had pinned them down and inserted objects and substances including a tampon and a strange white powder into their vaginas.

The women, who have come to be known as the "San Antonio Four" or the "Texas Four," have gained a growing number of supporters convinced they are innocent. Few of those advocates belong to the gay community of San Antonio, a city that ironically, according to the 2010 U.S. census, has the highest concentration in the U.S. of lesbian parents raising children under eighteen.

In scores of trumped-up cases dating back to the early '80s, police claimed to have apprehended groups of care-givers conspiring to have sex with children entrusted to their care. The abuse scenarios, often confabulated through coercive questioning of child witnesses, were given a diabolical spin. Investigative journalist Debbie Nathan, co-author of *Satan's Silence: Ritual Abuse and the Making of a Modern American Witch Hunt*, has called the San Antonio Four debacle "probably the last gasp of the Satanic ritual abuse panic."

Somewhere in the long, rich pageant of American brutality, there may indeed have been instances of devil-worshippers sexually abusing children. But the Satanic ritual abuse (SRA) pandemic was made of thin air. Rigorous investigations, some by law enforcement officials eager to unearth a vast Satanic underground, have shown that no such network exists. As historian Philip Jenkins states in *Moral Panic: Changing Concepts of the Child Molester in Modern America*, "The SRA movement represents an eerily postmodern dominance of created illusion over supposedly objective reality—what Baudrillard would term the stage of pure simulation."

The nonexistence of SRA in the real world didn't prevent it from becoming a staple of junk journalism and daytime talk shows. The implausibilities of self-proclaimed SRA survivors' narratives didn't lessen the fervor with which belief in SRA was promoted by such "experts" as New York psychiatrist Judianne Densen-Gerber, founder of the Odyssey House drug-rehabilitation chain, and such public personalities as Geraldo Rivera, Oprah Winfrey, and Gloria Steinem. "Believe It!" trumpeted *Ms. Magazine*. "Cult Ritual Abuse Exists!"

The phenomenon owed a great deal to the 1980 publication of *Michelle Remembers*, in which Michelle Smith, a patient of Canadian psychiatrist Lawrence Pazder, described how she had, through treatment, overcome traumatic amnesia to access awareness of childhood abuse by the ubiquitous, powerful "Church of Satan." Michelle remembered being raped, locked in a cage, forced to witness human sacrifice, and smeared with fresh blood.

The book was a bestseller. Eventually exposed as fraudulent, *Michelle Remembers* followed such '70s pulp-psych blockbusters as the multiple personality/recovered memory saga *Sybil* into popular consciousness. The pseudo-memoir validated rumors that thousands of cultists were subjecting thousands of children to outré sexual assault. Both the Smith/Pazder book and *Sybil* helped popularize the idea that although countless people had, as children, been subjected to ritualistic kinky sex, most required therapeutic intervention to recall such horrors. That notion gave rise to a huge, lucrative, now compellingly debunked therapy movement centered on repressed memory.

SRA allegations were excluded from evidence presented to both juries at the trials of the San Antonio Four, but belief in that phenomenon shaped pre-trial investigations. Examining pediatrician Nancy Kellogg, respected co-founder of the Alamo Children's Advocacy Center, was a true believer in SRA. In her medical reports on Stephanie and Vanessa, Kellogg stated that she had notified the police that the abuse, which she was convinced took place, might well have been "Satanic-related."

The principal mass sex-abuse scares of the SRA era involved "sex rings" and imagined predation at child-care facilities. Many of the alleged abusers were said to be manufacturing child pornography, although no child porn linked to SRA cases was ever found and used as evidence. Most of the sex-abuse trials flouted standards requiring presumption of innocence and determination of guilt beyond a reasonable doubt.

In *Sex Panic and the Punitive State* (2011), Roger N. Lancaster asks, "Do overblown fears of pedophile predators represent new ways of conjuring up and institutionally using homophobia, even while disavowing it as motive?" Typically, late 20th-century witch hunts began with allegations tinged with homophobia even when the principals were straight. A man, perceived as gay, with children directly in his care—or working in close proximity to children—would be suspected of having preyed upon at least one boy. There was a widespread assumption that any man who sought work with very young children *must* be gay.

The panic was launched in 1982 when a volley of accusations echoed through Kern County, California, where fabricated evidence pointed to half a dozen active sex rings in and around the city of Bakersfield. Thirty-six people were arrested and convicted of child rape. One of the harshest sentences, forty years, went to gas plant foreman John Stoll, convicted of seventeen counts of molesting five boys.

In 1983, as the Bakersfield sex-abuse frenzy wore on, the hysteria spread southeast to the L.A. suburb of Manhattan Beach, site of the McMartin Pre-School. The McMartin case, which morphed into the longest, costliest criminal process in U.S. history—a marathon ending in no convictions—started with a schizophrenic's fantasy that Ray Buckey, the founder's grandson, had sodomized her two-and-a-half-year-old son. Seven McMartin employees were implicated in a host of imaginary crimes including kiddie-porn photo shoots and dark, perverted rites in nonexistent tunnels. Michelle Smith and Lawrence Pazder appeared on the scene to advise prosecutors and comfort parents.

Lurid publicity sparked fresh accusations. In late September 1983, about three weeks after the McMartin case began to snowball, authorities in Jordan, Minnesota, began delving into allegations that twenty-four adults and one teenager held orgies involving over thirty children, including infants. By 1984, the contagion had reached Massachusetts. Gerald Amirault, whose mother ran the Fells Acres Day Care Center near Boston, was accused of raping a four-year-old boy; he and his mother and sister were imprisoned for a host of crimes against children, including production of never-located child pornography. As the Amirault investigation came to a boil, a nineteen-year-old gay child care worker, Bernard Baran, was arrested in Pittsfield at the opposite end of the state.

The child-molestation panic that spread across the U.S. in the 1980s had gay-specific antecedents. These included two high-profile witch hunts targeting largely imaginary cabals of gay men. One tore through Boise, Idaho, in 1955; the other hit the Boston area in 1977–78.

In Boston, anti-gay dread was incited and amplified by Christian citrus-industry shill Anita Bryant's "Save Our Children" campaign, a Florida-based propaganda blitz against gay rights ordinances. Bryant's chief message was that gay men and lesbians target children for conversion to the "homosexual lifestyle." As John Mitzel notes in *The Boston Sex Scandal* (1980), the Save-Our-Children panic was given respectable secular underpinnings by Dr. Judianne Densen-Gerber of Odyssey House, who proclaimed that child pornography was rampant and mainly the work of rapacious queers. In California, meanwhile, State Senator John Briggs railed against gay teachers, accusing them of "seducing young boys in toilets."

At the heart of the Massachusetts furor was a man in Revere, a Boston suburb, who had been letting friends and acquaintances use his apartment as a discreet place to bring male hustlers for sex. Suffolk County's paleo-Catholic District Attorney, Garrett Byrne, 80, learned of the arrangement and ordered a crackdown. Local rent boys were rounded up and ordered to name their johns. Thirteen cooperated. Little more than the depositions of two fifteen-year-old hustlers were finally used to indict two dozen men for over one hundred sexual felonies. The lives of the accused adults were shattered, although only one—Dr. Donald Allen—went to trial. Allen received five years' probation; only the man who supplied the apartment did prison time. Most of the streetwise young men corralled by Garrett Byrne were above the state's legal age of consent, 16, though at a time when sodomy laws could be enforced at the whim of the enforcer, age of consent was almost beside the point.

The scandal owed much of its heat to the input of Boston-based pediatric nurse Ann Burgess, who created a diagnostic sex-ring model widely applied in the '80s and '90s, from the Bakersfield circus to the 1994–95 panic in Wenatchee, Washington, where forty-three adults, including parents and Sunday school teachers, were held on 29,726 false charges of sexual abuse. Burgess asserted that international gay sex rings were flying boys to secret locations where they could be ravished. Although most of the child-protection books she wrote or edited, such as *Child Pornography and Sex Rings* (1984) and *Children Traumatized in Sex Rings* (1988), have dated badly, Burgess now teaches victimology and forensics at Jesuit-run Boston College. She remains influential. One of her pupils, Susan Kelley, played a key role in the Amirault case, interviewing children by means of leading questions and "anatomically correct" dolls, refusing to take no for an answer.

In 1978, Boston activists formed the Boston/Boise Committee, out of which grew two organizations that survive. One was the North American Man-Boy Love Association (NAMBLA), originally focused on relationships between adult men and adolescents, now demonized out of all proportion to the varied predilections of its minuscule membership. The other was Gay and Lesbian Advocates and Defenders (GLAD, not to be confused with the anti-defamation group GLAAD). Created as a legal resource for gay people accused of sex crimes, GLAD long ago ceased to deal with criminal cases, choosing instead to work usefully on HIV/AIDS and gender identity issues, and less usefully on marriage rights and hate-crime legislation.

No gay organization of any kind acknowledged the existence of Bernard Baran. The first day-care worker to be convicted of mass molestation, Baran went to trial before the McMartin staff and the Amirault family. He was an openly gay teacher's aide at the Early Childhood Development Center (ECDC) in Pittsfield, Massachusetts. His original accuser was a woman who had just removed her four-year-old son from ECDC, complaining about the facility's willingness to let a homosexual work with children. The woman and her boyfriend had a history of violence and substance abuse. The investigation, however, yielded tidier accusers. The case took on a measure of *gravitas* when a middle-class mother who taught ceramics at Pittsfield's posh Miss Hall's School for Girls claimed Baran had attacked her three-year-old daughter.

A grand jury was shown edited videotapes of child interviews, omitting extensive footage showing the children being coached, prodded, and offered rewards while they denied everything. Baran's attorney, hired out of the phone book on a $500 retainer, did not object. By the time Baran's trial began in January, 1985, he had been indicted on five counts of rape and five counts of indecent assault and battery against two boys and three girls aged three to five. A third boy was added at trial. The courtroom was closed for children's testimony which, when not incoherent, echoed prompting from prosecutor Daniel Ford. Ironically, the "index child"—Paul Heath, 4, the boy whose mother made the first accusation—was dropped from the case after when he refused to cooperate in court, denying abuse and responding to questions with "Fuck you!"

The prosecution exploited jurors' fears of homosexuality. At a time when the specter of AIDS was everywhere, the Berkshire County D.A. adopted a diseased-pariah strategy. Because Paul Heath had tested positive for gonorrhea—according to a test now known to produce a high rate of false positives—Ford brought in a physician to testify to the prevalence of gonorrhea among prostitutes and homosexuals. It didn't matter that Baran's gonorrhea tests came back negative. Paul Heath had, in fact, recently made a more credible disclosure of abuse by one of his mother's boyfriends, a likelier source of STD. Word that this allegation was being investigated never reached Baran's lawyer.

In his closing argument, Ford described Baran's "primitive urge to satisfy his sexual appetite." Given access to children, he continued, Baran acted "like a chocoholic in a candy factory." Found guilty on all counts, Baran received three concurrent life sentences. Sent to the maximum-security state prison at Cedar Junction, he was savagely raped on arrival. He had repeatedly been offered—and refused—five years of low-security incarceration in exchange for a guilty plea.

Similar cases with homophobic overtones kept finding their way into court. Prosecution of lesbians for ritualistic sex abuse was rare, but hardly unknown before the arrest of the San Antonio Four. Women enmeshed in sex-ring hysteria were often accused of assaulting young girls. At the 1988 trial of Margaret Kelly Michaels, prosecutors devoted two days to exploiting a same-sex relationship in her personal history, implying that lesbianism had impelled her to force toddlers of both sexes to lick peanut butter off her crotch at the Wee Care Nursery School in Maplewood, New Jersey.

Some abuse trials may have been impacted by anti-gay propaganda swirling around seemingly unrelated issues. In February 1998, at the time of the second San Antonio Four trial, a local funding controversy was still raging.

In 1997, San Antonio talk-radio host Adam McManus and a Christian horde campaigned to end city funding of the Esperanza Center for Peace and Justice. The effort was triggered by disapproval of Esperanza's *Out at the Movies* film festival, a queer film series the center had been running annually for six years. Correspondence received by the City Council stressed that Esperanza "intends to use some of the money... to indoctrinate our impressionable youth to [the gay] lifestyle." Esperanza's city funding was cut from $62,531 to zero.

"I love homosexuals," declared right-wing activist Jack Finger, railing against Esperanza at a September, 1997, City Council meeting. "What I absolutely hate is the evil, wicked, child-seducing lifestyle."

San Antonio's gay community did not rally around Esperanza during the uproar. The left-leaning, Latina-headed resource was not a lesbigay organization per se; it represented a range of minorities. Also, relations between its director, Graciela Sanchez, and the wealthy, white gay business establishment had become strained.

Esperanza, in turn, seems to have taken little notice of the San Antonio Four. That situation finally changed in December 2010, when *La Voz de Esperanza*, the center's newsletter, ran an article by Tonya Perkins defending the four women and noting the "homophobia which poisoned San Antonio in the 1990s." At this writing, Esperanza remains the only officially gay-connected entity in Texas or beyond to call attention to the injustice. There has been no self-designated gay publication in San Antonio since 1997; the gay press elsewhere in Texas—including *Dallas Voice*, Houston's *OutSmart*, and *This Week in Texas* (*TWIT*)—has been mostly silent on the San Antonio Four.

Austin-based documentarian Deborah Esquenazi, who is making a film about the San Antonio Four, says local and national LGBTQ organizations have generally ignored her efforts to contact them. "Mostly," she says, "they don't respond to emails and phone calls."

Esquenazi's experience with Gay Inc. echoes that of others—including this writer working on behalf of Bernard Baran—who have tried to enlist the aid of such groups as the Human Rights Campaign in raising awareness of wrongfully convicted queers—or the treatment of queer prisoners, innocent or guilty. Lambda Legal, the primary LGBTQ legal resource nationally, chooses to focus on "impact litigation," not criminal justice.

"Gay people intersect with the criminal justice system in all kinds of ways," says New York activist Bill Dobbs, co-founder of the anti-assimilationist, pro-sex organization Sex Panic. "But when one of us gets accused of a crime, the leadership goes mute. The focus on victims has blinded us to serious injustices."

The San Antonio Four's predicament was mainly brought to light by people and organizations that are not gay-identified. Canadian researcher Darrell Otto discovered the case while sifting through reports on female child molesters, and became certain the women were innocent. He traveled to Texas, established a website (www.fourliveslost.com), wrote articles and blog entries on the subject, and secured the sponsorship of the National Center for Reason and Justice (NCRJ), an organization devoted to reversing wrongful convictions. *Satan's Silence* co-author Debbie Nathan, then a board member of the NCRJ, helped convince the Texas Innocence Project to take the case. Articles began appearing in the *Texas Monthly* and elsewhere.

"At first, I thought, well, maybe those women did it," says Deborah Esquenazi, "but once we'd sifted through the whole case, we were sure they're innocent. My partner and I realized that could be us."

Esquenazi and others who examined the case found the investigation flawed, the evidence meager, and the court proceedings tainted by prejudice. During jury selection, Elizabeth Ramirez's lawyer allowed at least two individuals with moral antipathy to homosexuality to be seated as jurors—including the man elected foreman. At her sister-in-law Anna's trial, where prosecutor Mary Delavan linked lesbianism to abuse of little girls, Rose Vasquez counted at least seventy-five sometimes pointedly derogatory references to lesbians. As the trial progressed, Rose and her husband signed a notarized affidavit stating they overheard a juror discussing "lesbians assaulting two children" at a restaurant with a county employee. Although the affidavit should have caused the juror's removal, the document dropped into a void.

None of the San Antonio Four was subjected to the psychological testing and evaluation processes administered to accused sex offenders in most jurisdictions. Nowhere was it noted that Javier Limon had accused others of molesting his daughters, or that—despite his vocal distaste for lesbians—Javier had been writing love letters to Liz Ramirez, who had rejected him. His letters, which still exist, were never entered into evidence. There were also unacknowledged inconsistencies in the girls' unevenly rehearsed testimony. At Elizabeth Ramirez's trial, Vanessa swore her aunt had held a gun to her head while she talked with her father on the phone and told him all was well. During the trial of the other three women, Vanessa said Anna Vasquez held the gun.

As Darrell Otto notes in his blog, "Most juries find child witnesses to be highly credible, in spite of the fact that it has now been shown that children often lie on the witness stand, for a variety of reasons."

At sex abuse trials, children have been accorded privileges that sometimes trump the rights of the accused, including special seating arrangements concealing them from their alleged abusers, closed courtrooms, and testimony by CCTV or by proxy. At many of these trials, spoon-fed statements by child witnesses have comprised the prosecution's entire case. Yet there is widespread recognition among social scientists and legal professionals that the familiar exhortation to "believe the children" can render egregious results. In *Jeopardy in the Courtroom*, their 1995 book on child testimony, psychologists Stephen Ceci and Maggie Bruck were among the first to show how aggressive and suggestive questioning of non-abused children can lead to "non-victimized children making false disclosures."

A recent breakthrough for the San Antonio Four was the recantation of Stephanie, Elizabeth Ramirez's younger niece, who now says she was told she would "end up in prison or even get my ass beaten" if she didn't recite a claim of abuse she knew to be untrue. There is now hope that even in Texas, a state where poor and working-class defendants are at a notorious disadvantage, the San Antonio Four will be exonerated as well as freed. It helps that they now have the competent legal representation they lacked at trial.

For the moment, however, the women remain in the maw of the largest—and perhaps most rigidly authoritarian—state penal system in the U.S. According to the March 23, 2012 issue of *Dallas Voice*, Texas leads the nation in prison rape, and "LGBT prisoners are 15 times more likely to be raped." Amid the regimentation and the threat of violence, the women remain resistant to declarations of guilt and shows of remorse that could facilitate parole. Branded "in denial," sex offenders who fail to cooperate with treatment may be vulnerable to one-day-to-life civil commitment.

"[One] condition of parole is to complete a sex offender program...," wrote Anna Vasquez in 2007. "I will not take the coward's way out to just go home."

227

It takes special bravery for queers to negotiate the American criminal justice system, where homophobia seems encoded in the institutional DNA. In a study published in 2004 by *The American Journal of Criminal Justice*, 484 Midwestern university students were polled on attitudes toward lesbians and gay men. Despite most students' inclination to extend some rights to gay people, criminal justice majors were found to have a higher degree of anti-gay prejudice than students majoring in any other field. Homophobia among criminal justice professionals, like racism, vitiates the official charge to serve and protect everyone, without exception.

In U.S. prisons, systemic homophobia often has an evangelical dimension. Born-again Watergate felon Charles Colson's anti-gay Prison Fellowship Ministries has been preaching to literally captive audiences nationwide since 1975. The Kansas correctional system, which matches state prisoners with "faith-based mentors," employs many hard-line fundamentalist Christians, including members of Topeka's Fred Phelps clan, whose website is www.godhatesfags.com. Margie Phelps, Director of Re-entry Planning for the Kansas Department of Correction, is an anti-gay firebrand whose favorite homophobic epithet is "feces eater."

"When I went to prison," says Bernard Baran, who survived rapes and beatings in several facilities, "I suddenly didn't have a name. I was 'Mo,' short for 'Homo.' In the joint, gay people are at the bottom of the heap. If they think you're a gay child molester, you're the lowest of the low."

Baran finally gained his freedom after unedited videos of child interviews—hidden from both the jury and his lawyer during his trial—were finally unearthed in 2004 a few months after the sudden death of Berkshire County D.A. Gerard Downing, who had claimed for years the tapes were missing. In 2006, his conviction was overturned on grounds of ineffective assistance of counsel. Baran was freed. In 2009, he won a resounding Appeals Court victory, after which all charges were dropped.

Baran spent twenty-one years and five months in prison. Many of those caught in the child-abuse panic fared better. As the Jordan, Minnesota, case unraveled, all defendants but one were freed. All but two of the Bakersfield defendants were released on appeal. John Stoll, among the last, was released in 2004 when four of his supposed victims, who had been pressured into telling investigators what they wanted to hear, finally recanted. The Amiraults were freed under onerous conditions enabling prosecutors to save face, but at least permitted to return home. Margaret Kelly Michaels's conviction was overturned five years into a forty-seven-year sentence. Others, including the allegedly child-murdering West Memphis Three, have walked out of prison in a state of near or total vindication.

Others remain behind bars. Among them are some of the priests caught in the wide net of the Roman Catholic sex-abuse scandal. These include gay ex-priest Paul Shanley, 81, convicted in 2004 on the unsubstantiated "recovered memories" of a steroid addict. (Street lore falsely credits Shanley with founding and participating in NAMBLA; he did, on the other hand, found the Boston chapter of Dignity, which has disowned him.) A number of dubious, unresolved sex-abuse cases persist in Texas. Besides the San Antonio Four, there is the 1992 SRA case of Austin day-care proprietors Fran and Dan Keller, now serving forty-eight-year sentences.

Those still in prison have, however, acquired a growing number of queer advocates. Additional rays of hope have appeared the form of queer-specific prisoner outreach efforts like Black and Pink, and events like the watershed 2010 Chicago symposium "What's Queer About Sex Offenders? Or, Are Sex Offenders the New Queers?" Increasingly, queer activists recognize the ways in which the prison industrial complex degrades us all. There is a growing awareness that in the U.S., many people are serving time for crimes they did not commit, and that everyone trapped in the world's most populous and retentive chain of gulags is subject to cruel and unusual punishment.

But there is a long way to go. In working exclusively on behalf of putative victims, the LGBTQ mainstream has been strengthening and refining the powers of a system that has traditionally nurtured and sheltered homophobic bias, a system that has long been the surest, sharpest means of keeping sexual minorities in line.

"Worst of the Worst"?

Queer Investments in Challenging Sex Offender Registries

ERICA R. MEINERS, LIAM MICHAUD, JOSH PAVAN, AND BRIDGET SIMPSON

POINTS OF DEPARTURE

OVER THE PAST THIRTY YEARS, Canada and the United States have afforded select gays and lesbians more rights, both symbolic and substantial. Simultaneously, most mainstream gay and lesbian organizations have disengaged from the issues of prisons and policing. Resisting police brutality, pushing back against the criminalization of non-heteronormative sexualities, and fighting carceral expansion have each disappeared from queer rights organization's ostensible agendas. Given that most queers are no longer viewed as the "worst of the worst sexual offenders," mainstream gay and lesbian organizations have disengaged from questions of criminalization in order to "move on"

This piece first appeared in issue thirteen of the Canadian journal Upping the Anti *(uppingtheanti.org) in 2011.*

to other issues like marriage and military inclusion. Meanwhile, sex workers, the HIV positive, barebackers, and other sexually marginalized groups have become increasingly isolated. With carceral expansion becoming an important priority for Canada's governments, and with "sex offenders" increasingly being used to legitimate "tough on crime" policies and prison growth, intersectional interventions on prison issues that include a queer analysis are needed now more than ever.

Federal and provincial governments in Canada are currently set to expend massive amounts of capital to enlarge the carceral apparatus by constructing new prisons and expanding existing ones. This development is accompanied by increased policing, new surveillance technologies, post-release reporting and registration requirements, and other punitive tools that activists and academics have described as a "soft extension" of the prison industrial complex into everyday life. "Sex offenders" and public notification systems have played a pivotal role in bolstering demands for increased surveillance of public places, extensive post-release requirements, and—at times—community notification. The anxieties propagated by "sex offenders" increase the policing of sexually marginalized people, increase the number of charges and convictions, and lengthen prison terms. These fears also spur electoral campaign promises, moral panics that collude with racialized and heteronormative agendas, and persistent punitive requirements that require various levels of government to appear "tough on crime." In turn, these responses lead to demands for new prisons. As notification technologies shift from print to online databases, offender information has begun to circulate increasingly rapidly and widely. Activists attempting to counter misinformation are often shut out from these platforms and potential roles for a critical independent media are circumvented. The potential for broader based community mobilizations is thus limited.

Although there has been some opposition to tough-on-crime social policy in Canada over the past few years, the organized left has been largely silent on this particular front; even activists traditionally critical of crime-and-punishment approaches have allowed themselves to be seduced by the state's ideas about the "sex offender."

Linking the targeting of homosexuals in the past to contemporary sex offender registries should not be mistaken for a romantic appeal to celebrate outlaw sexualities. Nor do queer peoples' histories of being labeled "sex offenders" guarantee an automatic political affinity with those who are currently being criminalized.[1] However, these histories are intertwined with contemporary carceral growth. While select queers are no longer explicitly targeted by public policies, new "sexual offender" legislation does increase queer vulnerability and queer exposure to imprisonment. Meanwhile, the most significant forms of sexual violence (intimate and familial violence) become obscured by the state's focus on "stranger danger" and "dangerous sexual offenders." Equally obscured are the endemic rates of sexual (and other forms of) violence that incarcerated people—overwhelmingly poor, indigenous, and people of colour—are subjected to within prisons. Most importantly, the state's response to "sex offenders" does not address persistent interpersonal sexual violence, which is perpetrated largely by men, and which largely harms women and children.

As justice organizers, educators, advocates, abolitionists, and (in some cases) as survivors of violence, we engage in an analysis of the state's response to sexual and gendered violence with care. We view this moment of carceral expansion as an opportunity to map overlaps between queer and abolitionist politics and to support community-based responses to state and interpersonal sexual violence.

SEX OFFENDER REGISTRIES AND CARCERAL EXPANSION

Over 2.3 million people are now incarcerated in prisons and jails across the United States. This works out to one in every 99.1 adults. Compared to all other nations, the U.S. has the highest rate of imprisonment and the largest number of people locked behind bars. Disproportionately, they are people of color and poor people. Since the 1970s, incarceration rates have increased—not because of rising levels of violence or crime but because of (among other things) "three strikes" laws, mandatory minimum sentencing, and the war on drugs.

Canadian prison expansion has followed a similar trajectory. In 1986—just days after a similar announcement by Ronald Reagan—Prime Minister Brian Mulroney announced Canada's own war on drugs. Prison populations exploded, necessitating the construction of new penal institutions across the country. Decades of overcrowding in the provincial and territorial systems also led to the construction of new prisons and additions to existing facilities. The criminalization of the survival economy accounts for an ever-growing proportion of the offenses for which individuals are incarcerated: in 2008–2009, over 90% of incarcerated women were serving time for prostitution, small theft (valued under $5,000), or fraud. Under the federal Conservatives, the Correctional Service of Canada's (CSC) annual budget has increased by $1.385 billion (86.7%), almost doubling since 2005–2006. As of June 2011, various provincial and territorial correctional authorities have announced plans for additions to existing facilities and the construction of twenty-two new prisons.[2]

Prison expansion in the U.S. and Canada is increasingly marketed as a response to the "worst of the worst"—those who commit acts of violence (generally sexual) against the "most innocent," white children. Over the last two decades, sex offender registries (SORs) and community notification laws have been one of the most visible fronts in the expansion of the U.S. carceral state. Public fears about "sex offenders" (SOs) during the 1990s coincided with the construction of supermax, or control-unit, prisons.[3] Although there is no evidence that these registries and notification systems reduce persistent sexual violence against children and women, the policing of public spaces like parks and school grounds have increased along with people's anxieties.

Throughout the 1990s, the U.S. federal government passed laws requiring states to develop SO registries, to increase community notification systems, and to integrate and standardize processes for tracking and identifying those convicted of sexual offenses. In 1996, in response to the abduction and murder of twelve-year-old Polly Klaas (1992) and seven-year-old Megan Kanka (1994) by two men with prior convictions for violent sexual crimes, the federal government passed Megan's Law. The law established a publicly accessible national sex offender registry that circulated information about known "sex offenders" across the nation. It also coordinated the then-emergent state registry systems.

SORs restrict employment, housing, and mobility—particularly in public and private spaces where children congregate. These laws have been tested in and supported by the courts, and more punitive measures continue to be introduced; upheld by the U.S. Supreme Court in a 2005 decision, civil commitment laws have given law enforcement the power to incarcerate those convicted—even after the completion of their formal sentence. Encouraged by media coverage of child abductions, restrictions on convicted sex offenders increase despite the fact that most perpetrators of sexual and other forms of violence against children are family members.

Over the past ten years, there has been a steady push for a more aggressive national sex offender registry in Canada. Initially introduced as a provincial initiative in 2001[4] by the Harris Conservatives in Ontario, Christopher's Law was the political response to the rape and murder of an eleven-year-old boy by a man on statutory release. Under pressure from the provinces, the federal government followed suit in 2004 by establishing the National Sex Offender Registry. In 2007, a 62,000-signature petition was presented to the National Assembly in Québec demanding a province-wide and publicly accessible database. Tied to broader "tough on crime" policy shifts, the Conservatives introduced Bill S-2 (Protecting Victims from Sex Offenders Act) in the spring of 2010. The bill includes provisions that would make registration mandatory, give police preventative access, and require those recently-registered to provide DNA samples. The stated purpose of Bill S-2 is to "strengthen the National Sex Offender Registry and the National DNA Data Bank by enabling police in Canada to more effectively prevent and investigate crimes of a sexual nature." A federal attempt to coordinate emerging provincial registries, The National Sex Offender Registry has yet to solve a single crime.[5]

Despite a thirty-year low in Canadian crime rates[6] and little to no evidence of any rise in violence in Canada, the federal Conservatives introduced a schedule of reforms in 2010 that mirrors failed U.S. criminal justice policies: mandatory minimum sentencing, further criminalization of drug offenses, the elimination of pretrial "two-for-one" credits, and new prison construction. Child "protection" against alleged sexual predators is a central component of current criminal justice reforms in Canada. Bill S-2 and Bill C-22 (Protecting Children from Online Sexual Exploitation Act, which passed first reading in May 2010) are offered to allegedly protect select children. Meanwhile, proposed changes to the Youth Criminal Justice Act will punish more young people. As always, the state's "protection" measures constitute after-the-fact responses and afford no prevention measures. We are thus compelled to question the intent and design of this kind of social policy.

As in the U.S., public fears of the "sex offender" have been leveraged to build the Canadian carceral state. After the Bloc Québécois voted *en masse* against Bill C-268 (which would impose a mandatory minimum sentence for those convicted of child trafficking) in 2009, the federal Conservatives mailed flyers to every resident in each Bloc Québécois riding. Under the headline "Your Bloc MP voted against the protection of children" (in French), the flyer depicted a dark, shadowy man leading a white child from a playground. Concurrently, other print advertisements suggested the Bloc was "soft on pedophiles." In the spring of 2011, the Ontario Progressive Conservatives promised that—if elected—they would make sex offenders wear GPS trackers and make the entire Ontario registry publicly accessible online. Alberta has already implemented a similar GPS tracking pilot project. These moves demonstrate the extent to which public opinion is amenable to highly punitive surveillance and policing where "sex offenders" are concerned. Campaigns for increased criminalization and prison expansion continue to succeed by framing the opposition as "soft" on crime, insensitive to the safety of children, and indifferent to the realities of sexual violence.

In the U.S., opposition to publicly accessible SORs (limited though it is) has been sparked by instances of vigilante violence against accused or convicted sex offenders, targeted harassment and outings, cases of mistaken identity, and limited but detailed investigative journalism that has chronicled the explicitly punitive restrictions on SO movement post-release. In Canada, notable opposition from either the institutional or grassroots left has yet to materialize. This is in large part due to the non-public nature of the Canadian registry, which has allowed it to enact much of the everyday surveillance and restriction of the American registry while avoiding public debates and opposition. By monopolizing mobilizations of disgust and pity, the Canadian state has effectively regulated and managed opposition to how sex offenses are criminalized and administrated.

QUEER INVESTMENTS

The push for the public registration of "sex offenders" evokes familiar queer histories. Many of the frameworks and strategies currently being used to detain, surveil, and punish "sex offenders" are well known by queer activists who have spent decades battling the policing and surveillance of street sex workers, bars and clubs, and bathhouses and other public sexual cultures. Policing in Canada has historically targeted queer people and continues to target sexually marginal and marginalized groups. When select white and affluent gays and lesbians ceased to be the overt targets of policing, and queer organizations moved on to other issues, anti-prison communities lost a formidable ally. As public memory of queer resistances to criminalization evaporated, our communities lost their critical assessment of what constitutes "dangerous sexual behavior." How are these designations made? And who is all this "protection" for?

Gay, lesbian, bisexual, and especially transgender, transsexual, and gender nonconforming communities continue to be overrepresented in the Canadian and U.S. criminal justice system, though this vulnerability is no longer (or rarely) the result of explicitly homophobic state violence. Today, prison justice and abolition activists—and queer organizers—struggle with both the implications of relentless prison growth and our diminished capacity to name, identify, and resist the social processes that underwrite this expansion. Because gay and lesbian community organizations have widely disengaged from criminalization, queers are less equipped to contend with shifting patterns of state violence and new articulations of "sex offenses."

QUEER HISTORIES

Historically, queers have been the targets of criminal persecution and registration. In many jurisdictions, non-reproductive homosexual sexual acts were *by definition* sex offenses and used to restrict access to employment, social benefits, parenting, immigration, and citizenship. Queer historian William Eskridge has reported how, in 1947, the California legislature "unanimously passed a law to require convicted sex offenders to register with the police in their home jurisdictions." Chief

Justice Warren requested that this law be extended to include those convicted of "lewd vagrancy" to ensure that as many homosexuals as possible were included. In 1950, the Federal Bureau of Investigation collected information—including fingerprints—for those charged with sodomy, oral copulation, and lewd vagrancy to create a "national bank of sex offenders and known homosexuals."[7]

However, homosexuals and other "sex offenders" were not uniformly targeted. As Eskridge reports, "in the 1930s, when only 6% of its adult male population was non-white, twenty percent of New York City's sex offenders were black," revealing who was—and continues to be—most vulnerable to policing and sexual surveillance.[8] In a 1965 case that received national attention in Canada, a Northwest Territories man named Everett George Klippert was charged and convicted on several counts of gross indecency for having consensual sex with several men. In his sentencing, he was deemed to be "an incurable homosexual" and therefore a "dangerous sexual offender" to be placed in indefinite preventative detention.[9]

These historical practices have become central to SORs and are also apparent in contemporary policing of marginal or marginalized sexual cultures. This is especially evident when considering how public notification and shaming—often under the guise of public (and, particularly, childhood) "safety"—are used to target and police sexually marginal social spaces and public sexual cultures. Throughout the early 1980s, hundreds of men in Canada and the U.S. were publicly outed after being caught having sex in public bathrooms, bathhouses, and other sites. Following the Toronto bathhouse raids of 1981, the names of men present during the raid were published in *The Toronto Sun* while police contacted their employers. After targeting a group of underage sex workers and their clients in 1994, police in London, Ontario held press conferences to expose a "sex ring" that "passed around boys." In response, the Homophile Association of London, Ontario accused the police of unfairly accusing men, engaging in double standards for gay sex, and promoting exaggerations, distortions, and fear-mongering.[10] Bar and bathhouse raids during the early 2000s (of which there were many) played out similarly.

Public notification and shaming are often legitimated by claims that they protect youth from sexual violence. Nevertheless, for youth engaging in sex work and often for queer youth, protection is negated by the very mechanisms that purport to "protect" youth from sexual exploitation. In 2003, forty Montréal police officers raided Taboo, a gay club featuring stripping and frequented by sex workers and those interested in purchasing non-heterosexual sex. Police arrested and laid indecency charges against four customers and twenty-three young male strippers (including one seventeen year old). Raids of bars frequented by sex workers or that provide space for public sexual cultures are not exceptional in Canada; however the raid at Taboo is significant because it constitutes what Maria-Belén Ordóñez, a Toronto-based anthropologist, has called a "homophobic response that is mainly tied to young sex workers catering to older gay men."[11] The raids, their rationale, and the court proceedings that followed demonstrate how legal enforcement mobilized to protect youth in fact criminalized young people.[12]

FLEXIBILITY OF THE "SEX OFFENDER" CATEGORY

Under Canadian law, the formal "sex offender" designation has gradually been dropped from many sexual practices associated with queers; however, other non-normative sexual practices continue to designated in this way. Sexually deviant archetypes that represent "predatory" or "irresponsible" sexuality—often non-hetero-patriarchal and always deeply racialized—continue to be targeted for state regulation. These include the "welfare queen," the teenaged mom, the HIV+ person who "willfully infects" others, and the sex worker. While "homosexuals" may no longer be the central targets of social policies enforcing sexual normativity, the effects of this policing continue to be felt by many, including queers.

In the U.S., the criminal "sex offender" category is applied inconsistently. In 2010, sex workers in New Orleans were charged under a state-wide law that makes it a crime against nature to engage in "unnatural copulation" (committing acts of oral or anal sex). Conviction meant registration as an SO and having the words "sex offender" stamped on one's driver's license. Meanwhile, out of concern for the futures of the young people, the 3rd U.S. District Court of Appeals in Philadelphia ruled that "sexting" (distribution of pornography) did not warrant felony charges, which would require registration as a sex offender if convicted.[13]

The increasing criminalization of HIV non-disclosure in Canada[14] also demonstrates the uneven and violent application of the "sex of-fender" classifications. From 1998 to 2011, a slate of charges—rang-ing from sexual assault to first-degree murder—were brought against HIV+ individuals for having failed to disclose their HIV status. These charges were overwhelmingly laid against immigrants, men of colour, sex workers, and (increasingly) gay men. Their names and photographs have routinely been published in newspapers, even prior to conviction. In 2008, Vancouver police blanketed the downtown core with posters featuring the picture of a sex worker who was merely suspected of hav-ing transmitted HIV. In Winnipeg in August 2010, police published a Canada-wide arrest warrant for a Sudanese man *suspected* of transmit-ting HIV to two women. And in Ottawa in May 2010, police issued a public warning about a gay man accused of non-disclosure during consensual sex and explicitly labeled him a "sexual predator." Many of the charges brought against HIV+ individuals for not disclosing their status during a sexual encounter—sexual assault, aggravated sex-ual assault, etc.—are grounds for registration on the Canadian SOR. While it remains to be seen to what extent individuals criminalized for non-disclosure will actually be added to the registry (as many of the cases are in progress), recently proposed reforms threaten to add almost all of those facing conviction under HIV-related prosecutions.

The trajectory of HIV criminalization—and, in particular, the tactics of public notification and shaming—reveals how recent legal shifts are firmly rooted in broader historical constructions of the "sex-ual predator." HIV criminalization exacerbates what geographer Ruth Wilson Gilmore has called "group-differentiated vulnerabilities" to criminalization and imprisonment and premature death.[15] In this way, it mirrors prior public panics about sex offenders and homosexuals, which were characterized by public naming, scapegoating, and wide-spread social vilification.[16]

Designation and registration of sex workers as "sex offenders," crim-inalization of sexual non-disclosure of HIV status, and appeals to high-ly punitive surveillance technologies to contain, monitor, and track known "sex offenders" all resemble the ways in which queer sexuality has been policed and managed historically. While gay and lesbian communities may no longer be targeted explicitly, these communities continue to be subject to state violence and "sex offender" panic *as* sex workers, *as* HIV-positive people, and *as* those to whom the "sex offender" designation has been applied.

ERASURE

Registries function to obscure the real sources and sites of sexual violence. Overwhelmingly, the perpetrators of sexual violence against women and children are not strangers. The focus on "stranger danger" functions to displace attention from the real harms: poverty, colonialism, and heteropatriarchy. As anthropologist Roger Lancaster summarizes, "a child's risk of being killed by a sexually predatory stranger is comparable to his or her chance of getting struck by lightning (1 in 1,000,000 versus 1 in 1,200,000)."[17] Despite this reality, U.S. legal scholar Rose Corrigan points out that feminist organizers were largely silent during the implementation of national registries in the U.S. and Canada. In her estimation, "the most threatening aspects of feminist rape law reform—its criticisms of violence, sexuality, family, and repressive institutions—are those that supporters of Megan's Law erase in rhetoric and practice."[18] The "worst of the worst," if there is such a thing, is to be found in our own patriarchal families and neighbourhoods.

In addition to the reality that perpetrators of violence targeting children are rarely strangers, there is no evidence that registries and community notification systems protect children. In Canada, where SORs are non-public and used overwhelmingly to investigate crimes that have already been committed, they cannot—by their own logic—prevent any crime. Criminologists who study these registries have argued that there is no evidence that they have been successful and that their expansion has been "based on a mere verisimilitude of empirical justification."[19] Creating safer and strong communities requires that we challenge the expansion of these registries. By challenging mythic and manufactured sources of sexual violence, we are forced to confront sexual violence in its most widespread, everyday, and intimate forms.

THE CARCERAL STATE

An increase in criminalization means that those most vulnerable—including queers and those involved in survival economies like the sex and drug trade, people living with HIV, and those that challenge age of consent laws—will be caught up in the criminal justice system. More people in the system means more people subjected to racist, gendered, and homophobic judicial proceedings. Conviction means detention and confinement in institutions predicated on gender normativity, compulsory heteronormativity, and colonial and racial oppression. More people will become isolated from communities of affinity and origin and more will be exposed to epidemic rates of HIV and Hepatitis C in prisons that withhold the resources necessary for survival. Expansion of the carceral state also means increased exposure to state and structural violence through interlocking punitive systems like child protection services, immigration enforcement, psychiatric intervention, and related medical violence.

This deepened exposure to state violence also increases vulnerability to sexual violence. According to one U.S. study, 20 percent of inmates in men's prisons are sexually abused at least once while serving their sentence.[20] Among women at some U.S. prisons, the rate is as high as 25 percent. Violence also occurs in ineffective sexual offender "treatment" programs.[21] Not only does the state's claim to offer protection fall terribly short, it actively produces an array of new possibilities for gender and sexual violence.

MYTHIC CHILDREN

SORs are part of the carceral state's push toward a culture of child protection almost wholly focused on sexual innocence. Across the U.S., as select brown and black boys are moved into juvenile detention centers at age eleven, as queer youth are denied meaningful sexual health education, and as pregnant teenagers are pushed out of school, it's clear that "protection" is unevenly accessed. The laws across the U.S. that protect young children from sexual violence—Megan's Law, Jessica's Law, The Adam Walsh Act, the Amber Alert—almost uniformly refer to white children. Almost by definition, constructions of mythic sexual innocence make queers into threats (even in contexts where individual lesbians and gays may be protected). Poll after poll demonstrates that the public perceives pedophilia to be the greatest threat to childhood safety. This perception is intimately linked to fear of the queer. As queer theorist Lee Edelman put it, "the sacralization of the child thus necessitates the sacrifice of the queer."[22] In a heteronormative culture that valorizes sexual innocence, non-normative sexualities are suspect, contagious, and thought to pose risks.

QUEER FUTURES/ABOLITION FUTURES

SORs and the moral and political anxieties they foster are central pathways enabling carceral expansion. The Harper government's recent "tough on crime" legislative changes focused on sex offenses provide yet another example of carceral expansion being enabled by "sex offender" anxieties. Coalitions between queers and prison abolitionists are needed now more than ever as lesbian and gay mainstream organizations restrict their focus to marriage and the military (in the U.S.) and sentencing enhancements for those convicted of hate crimes against gays and lesbians (in Canada). The state's focus on "sex offenders" opens a new front in the regulation of sexual deviance. Proceeding under a banner that effectively inspires loathing and fear, they obscure the historical links between current objectives and homophobic social policy and state violence. Elaborating these links is particularly urgent in the face of current efforts to expand the Canadian carceral state. Most centrally, prison expansion that includes U.S.-style SORs does nothing to make our communities stronger or to reduce or eliminate sexual violence.

Resistance to carceral expansion and SORs must come from a variety of institutional, community, and organizational forces. Organizing against prison expansion requires that we identify how queers are still being harmed by "sex offender" panics and analyze how sexually-related offenses are still being mobilized in the service of the carceral state. Organizing must also support the self-determination of survivors of violence and build accountability for perpetrators without encouraging carceral expansion. Below, we highlight three themes around which to organize these struggles. We believe they offer clear sites for organizing a broader and more effective movement against sexual and state violence. There is other work happening; this list is neither representative nor comprehensive but comprises an assemblage of different models. We learn from a number of organizations doing pieces of this work, and we argue that linking these pieces together can provide a framework for transforming bankrupt notions of state "'protection."

1. *Direct support for youth (and others) doing sex work.* This work is currently being done by groups like Projet d'Intervention auprès des Mineurs-res Prostués-ées (PIAMP)[23] in Montréal and the Young Women's Empowerment Project in Chicago. These organizations support sexual and other forms of self-determination and autonomy, interrupt multiple violences faced by youth criminalized or otherwise marginalized, and challenge the ideas of "predatory sexuality" and childhood innocence that fuel prison expansion. Recognition of youth as potential sexual actors and broader support for sexual self-determination for youth disrupts the state's mobilization of childhood innocence to legitimize further violence and sexual regulation in the name of "protection."

2. *Engagement with sexual violence without turning to the state.* This work is currently being done by groups like Generation Five and the Storytelling and Organizing Project in Oakland and the Challenging Male Supremacy Project in New York. These organizations are working to build community-based reconciliation and develop mechanisms and practices of accountability for those that perpetrate harm. Specifically, they strive to build collective responses to harm that are rooted in queer, anti-racist feminism and that don't create or reproduce vulnerability to state and sexual violence. By examining the sites and sources of sexual violence, these projects offer tools for survivors, elaborate frameworks that connect interpersonal violence to state violence, and develop responses outside of the frameworks of state punishment. These responses are intended to be transformative for survivors, "bystanders," and those that perpetrate harm.

3. *Case support, individual advocacy, and direct support for individuals convicted under SO provisions.* This work is currently being one by groups like the National Center for Reason and Justice in Boston and the Prisoner Correspondence Project in Montréal. The advocacy of these organizations challenges the myth that criminalization actually functions to "catch" the "worst of the worst." Work of this nature exposes how the punitive structures of the carceral state do little to address persistent sexual and gender-based violence. It also shows how socially sanctioned practices of vilification and scapegoating often increase sexual and gender violence through overexposure to imprisonment.

These organizations offer us models for imagining and building a cross-community coalitional politics to confront claims that imprisonment is an effective response to sexual violence. They build processes that contend with sexual and intimate violence while rejecting how the state "sees" and responds to violence and conceives of sexual "crimes." Together, they offer us various points of departure from which to imagine and build abolition futures.

Organizations cited in piece:

Challenging Male Supremacy Project:
leftturn.org/experiments-transformative-justice

Critical Resistance:
criticalresistance.org

Generation Five:
generationfive.org

National Center for Reason and Justice:
ncrj.org

Prisoner Correspondence Project:
prisonercorrespondenceproject.com

Projet d'Intervention auprès des Mineurs-res Prostués-ées:
piamp.net

Storytelling and Organizing Project:
stopviolenceeveryday.org

NOTES

1   Despite its history as a generally white and classed referent and
    its implication in the erasure of transgender and transsexual
    identity, we use the term "queer" to encompass not just gay,
    lesbian, bisexual and transgendered identities but other non-het-
    eronormative and non-gender nonconforming identifications as
    well.

2   For information on Canadian carceral expansion, see Jus-
    tin Piché's work including his website updates at pris-
    onstatecanada.blogspot.com and his 2010 report "Mor-
    atorium Needed on Punishment Legislation" available
    at the Canadian Center for Policy Alternatives website,
    http://www.policyalternatives.ca/publications/monitor/
    moratorium-needed-punishment-legislation.

3   A 2006 study by the Urban Institute charts the rarity of su-
    per-max prisons prior to 1986. However, by "2004, 44 states
    had supermax prisons" (Daniel P. Mears, March 2006). "Evalu-
    ating the Effectiveness of Supermax Prisons," Urban Institute p.
    ii, www.urban.org/ UploadedPDF/411326_supermax_prisons.
    pdf). These institutions—which keep people incarcerated in sol-
    itary confinement cells from twenty-two to twenty-three hours
    a day—were made possible through public discourses about the
    "worst of the worst," criminals thought to constitute an immi-
    nent public danger.

4   While the registry was a new initiative, increased surveillance
    of those categorized as sexual predators was not new. In 1997,
    Bill C-55 was implemented to allow the imposition of long-
    term supervision orders on offenders who are considered
    "likely" to re-offend but who do not meet the criteria for a

"dangerous offender" designation. This had the effect of encompassing many convicted of lower level sex offenses within SO surveillance.

5 Currently, the Canadian registry differs from its American counterpart in a few significant ways: a) the Canadian registry is accessible only to law enforcement officials and not to the general public, b) law enforcement officials may only access it for investigative purposes (i.e. only after a crime has been committed), and c) the decision to add an individual onto the registry is not automatic but instead comes at the request of the Crown Counsel during sentencing.

6 Canadian crime rates, including violent crime rates, have been decreasing steadily every year. In some provinces, the crime severity index in 2008 decreased by as much as 14 percent (Statistics Canada, 2011).

7 William Eskridge. (2008). *Dishonorable Passions: Sodomy Laws in America*. New York: Viking, 82.

8 Ibid, 81.

9 This case, and Tommy Douglas and Pierre Trudeau's stance led to the 1969 decriminalization of homosexuality. (Kirkby, Gareth. 2006. "35 Years and Counting." *Extra West*. Retrieved online at: www.xtra.ca/public/National/ 35_years_and_counting-2303. aspx).

10 HALO the Homophile Association of London Ontario with CLGRO the Coalition for Lesbian and Gay Rights in Ontario. "ON GUARD: A Critique of Project Guardian." September 1996 (HALO, 1996). Retrieved online at: www.clgro.org/pdf/ On_Guard.pdf.

11 Maria-Belén Ordóñez. (2010). "Taboo: Young Strippers and the Politics of Intergenerational Desire." P. 179 in *Sex, Drugs & Rock and Roll: Psychological, Legal and Cultural Examinations of Sex and Sexuality*, edited by Helen Gavin and Jacquelyn Bent. Oxford, UK: Inter-Disciplinary Press.

12 Particularly for youth, state definitions of interpersonal and sexual violence are often complicit in the reproduction of heteronormativity. Through this alignment, anything external to gender

conforming and heteronormative standards is framed as in need of regulation, punishment, and ultimately, containment. This contradiction is not new; state sponsored violence, marginalization, and criminalization has often been legitimated by claiming to offer "protection" to women and (white) womanhood.

13 Carlin DeGuerin Miller (March 24, 2010). "'Sexting' Teens Are Being Labeled Sex Offenders, Lawmakers Look to Change That". CBS News. Retrieved online at: http://www.cbsnews.com/8301-504083_162-20001082-504083.html

14 Canada recently became the first country to lay charges of first-degree murder (as well as the first to secure a conviction) for HIV non-disclosure.

15 Ruth Wilson Gilmore. (2002). "Race and Globalization." In R. J. Johnson, Peter J. Taylor, Michael J. Watts, (Eds)., *Geographies of Global Change: Remapping the World*. Malden, MA., Blackwell Pub., 261.

16 Eric Rofes "The Emerging Sex Panic Targeting Gay Men." Speech given at the National Gay and Lesbian Task Force's Creating Change Conference in San Diego, November 16, 1997.

17 Roger Lancaster. (2011). *Sex Panic and the Punitive State*, University of California Press, 77.

18 Rose Corrigan. (2006). "Making Meaning of Megan's Law." *Law & Social Inquiry* 31, 276.

19 Wayne A. Logan. (2009). "Knowledge as Power: Criminal Registration and Community Notification Laws in America." Stanford University Press, 2009; FSU College of Law, Public Law Research Paper No. 387, 99.

20 Cindy Struckman-Johnson and David Struckman-Johnson. (2000). "Sexual Coercion Rates in Seven Midwestern Prison Facilities for Men." *The Prison Journal*, December 2000 vol. 80 no. 4: 379–390

21 See for example, recent work by Dany LaCombe including "Consumed with Sex: The Treatment of Sex Offenders in Risk Society," *The British Journal of Criminology*, Vol. 48, Issue 1, 55–74 (2008).

22 Lee Edelman. (2004). *No Future: Queer Theory and the Death*

Drive. Durham, Duke University Press Books, 28.

23 Roughly translated, PIAMP stands for Support Project for Minors Practicing Sex Work.

About the Contributors

Bill Andriette has written for and edited a number of gay periodicals, and for twenty years was an editor at *The Guide*, a Boston-based gay magazine shut down by its new owners, Toronto's Pink Triangle Press, in 2010. His work has appeared in such places as *Gay Community News*, *Playboy*, and *Newsday*, and he founded and edited *Gayme*. He studied philosophy at Cornell University, and has written on the intersection of sexuality and economics and the role of sexual demonization as a leitmotif of contemporary Western state legitimacy. He has come to take a dim view of "LGBT" identity politics as a function of Western neoliberal, neo-imperialist, neo-totalitarian tendencies.

Jack Aponte is a queer Boricua butch living in Brooklyn. Jack's preferred gender pronouns are she and her, but she doesn't mind other pronouns, either. Jack began over sharing and stirring shit up on the Internet since the 90s; she blogged for many years at *AngryBrownButch* and, most recently, writes at jackalop.es. Jack is also a worker-owner at Palante Technology Cooperative, a NYC-based worker cooperative that helps community organizations and other nonprofits move forward with the aid of technology. She is involved in organizing and movements for social, economic, and media justice and in queer, trans, and people of color communities.

Sébastien Barraud, MA Anthropology specialized in migrations, ethnics and gay studies. He is an educator and union representative in a primary school. He is also a social worker in a drop-in center for male sex workers. Born in France (1978), he has lived in Montréal since 2007. In 2005, he joined Warning (www.thewarning.info), a think-tank about sexuality, prevention, and the connections of those components with the notions of freedom, pleasure, desire, and norm. He has written more than forty articles on its website and one about the impact of ethnicity for HIV prevention in *Santé gaie* (Peppers Ed.), the first francophone book about gay men's health, published by Warning in 2010. Originally from Paris, Warning is now also present in Brussels, Geneva, and Montréal. In 2009, Sébastien cofounded the Montréal activist collective PolitiQ-queers solidaires! and joined the organization of the Radical Queer Semaine, a ten-day Montréal bilingual queer festival taking place every March. Since 2011, he is also a member of the Canadian Feminist Alliance in Solidarity for sex workers rights. In 2012, he co-created the SéroSyndicat/Blood Union, a Montréal-based group of seropositive and seroconcerned people active in the struggle against serophobia and all forms of criminalization.

Mattilda Bernstein Sycamore (mattildabernsteinsycamore.com) is most recently the author of a memoir, The End of San Francisco (City Lights 2013), and the editor of Why Are Faggots So Afraid of Faggots?: Flaming Challenges to Masculinity, Objectification, and the Desire to Conform (AK Press 2012). Sycamore is also the author of two novels, So Many Ways to Sleep Badly (City Lights 2008) and Pulling Taffy (Suspect Thoughts 2003), and the editor of four additional nonfiction anthologies, including Nobody Passes: Rejecting the Rules of Gender and Conformity (Seal 2006) and That's Revolting! Queer Strategies for Resisting Assimilation (Soft Skull 2008). Sycamore is currently finishing a third novel, Sketchtasy. She loves feedback, so feel free to say hi.

Dwayne Booth has been a freelance writer and cartoonist for twenty-two years, publishing under both his real name and the pen name

Mr. Fish with many of the nation's most reputable and prestigious magazines, journals ,and newspapers. In addition to his weekly cartoon for *Harper's Magazine* and daily contributions to Truthdig.com, he has also contributed to the *Los Angeles Times*, the *Village Voice*, the *Atlantic*, the *Huffington Post*, *The Nation*, *Vanity Fair*, *Mother Jones*, the *Advocate*, *Z Magazine*, Slate.com, and others. In May 2008 he was presented with a first place award by the Los Angeles Press Club for editorial cartooning. In 2010 and 2011 he was awarded the prestigious Sigma Delta Chi Award for Editorial Cartooning from the Society of Professional Journalists. In 2012 he was awarded the Grambs Aronson Award for Cartooning with a Conscience. His most recent books are *Go Fish: How to Win Contempt and Influence People* (Akashic Books 2011) and *WARNING: Graphic Content* (Annenberg Press 2014). He lives in Philadelphia with his wife and twin daughters.

Kate Bornstein is an author, playwright, and performance artist whose work to date has been in service to sex positivity and gender anarchy. Her work on behalf of building a coalition of those who live on cultural margins recently earned her an award from the Stonewall Democrats of New York City, as well as two citations from New York City Council members. Kate's latest book, *Hello, Cruel World: 101 Alternatives To Suicide For Teens, Freaks, and Other Outlaws*, was published in 2007. According to daily email and Twitter, the book is still helping people stay alive. Other published works include the books *Gender Outlaw: On Men, Women and the Rest of Us*; and *My Gender Workbook*. Kate's books are taught in over 150 colleges around the world. Her memoir, *A Queer and Pleasant Danger: The true story of a nice Jewish boy who joins the Church of Scientology, and leaves twelve years later to become the lovely lady she is today* came out on Beacon Press in 2013.

Karma R. Chávez is a teacher in Madison, Wisconsin. She is also involved in several community projects and groups surrounding issues of social, racial and economic justice. She is a member of the Against Equality Collective and a host of the radio program, *A Public Affair* on Madison's community radio station, 89.9 FM WORT

Ryan Conrad is an activist, artist, and scholar from a mill town in central Maine whose work focuses on the intersections between radical queer politics, affect, and the history of HIV/AIDS activism and art. In 2009, he co-founded Against Equality and has edited the collective's pocket-sized anthology series. He is currently a PhD candidate in The Centre for Interdisciplinary Studies in Society and Culture's Humanities Doctoral program at Concordia University in Montréal. His written and visual work is archived on faggotz.org and he can be reached at rconrad@meca.edu.

John D'Emilio has been a pioneer in the developing field of gay and lesbian studies. He is the author or editor of more than half a dozen books, including *Sexual Politics, Sexual Communities: the Making of a Homosexual Minority in the United States*; *Intimate Matters: A History of Sexuality in America* [with Estelle Freedman]; and *Lost Prophet: The Life and Times of Bayard Rustin*. His essay, "Capitalism and Gay Identity," first published in 1983, still gets reprinted almost three decades later. D'Emilio has won fellowships from the Guggenheim Foundation and the National Endowment for the Humanities; was a finalist for the National Book Award; and received the Brudner Prize from Yale University for lifetime contributions to gay and lesbian studies. A former co-chair of the board of directors of the National Gay and Lesbian Task Force, he was also the founding director of its Policy Institute. *Intimate Matters* was quoted by Supreme Court Associate Justice Anthony Kennedy in the 2003 *Lawrence v. Texas* case, the decision that declared state sodomy statutes unconstitutional. When not working, he watches old movies, solves sudoku puzzles, and searches for New York-style pizza in Chicago.

James D'Entremont is a journalist and playwright based in Boston. His plays have been performed in Boston and New York, at regional theaters, and abroad. He is a Fellow of Yaddo, MacDowell, and the Albee Foundation. A longtime anti-censorship activist, he spent much of the 1990s heading the Boston Coalition for Freedom of Expression. More recently, he has joined his partner Bob Chatelle, executive director of the National Center for Reason and Justice, in working on behalf of Bernard Baran and others wrongfully convicted of crimes. He has written for publications ranging from *Index on Censorship* to Passport magazine. From 1996 to 2008, he was a staff writer for the gay men's monthly *The Guide*, contributing articles about censorship issues, sex-abuse controversies, day-care witch hunts, recovered-memory therapy, sex-offender legislation, and sex-offender treatment. His *Guide* assignments included coverage of the Paul Shanley sex-abuse trial.

Deeg is a fat butch lesbian who lives in the SF Bay Area. Deeg has been working as an anti-assimilation, queer liberation activist for about forty years, and believes that the liberation struggle must include fighting against all forms of oppression. Deeg is a member of LAGAI—Queer Insurrection, which has been fighting against imperialism, racism, sexism, and all other bad things since 1983, and is also a member of Queers Undermining Israeli Terrorism (QUIT!). Both LAGAI and QUIT! believe that we need to create a just and free world in which people can be happy, rather than seek "equality" in this wretched straight society.

Kenyon Farrow is a writer and activist. He's the US and Global Policy Director for Treatment Action Group, and a columnist with *RH Reality Check*. The former Executive Director of Queers for Economic Justice is also co-editor of *Letters From Young Activists: Today's Rebels Speak Out*. His work has appeared in several anthologies and new outlets, including TheAtlantic.com, BET.com, *Alternet*, *The Huffington Post*, and *Colorlines*.

Larry Goldsmith is a historian and a former reporter for *Gay Community News* (Boston, Massachusetts), and has been active in anti-war, labor, and LGBT organizations since the late 1970s. He lives in Mexico City, and teaches at the Universidad Nacional Autónoma de México and El Colegio de México.

Imani Henry, Activist, Writer, Performer. After graduating with a BA in Acting from Emerson College in 1992, Imani became a regular in the slam poetry and Queer theater scenes in the cities of Boston and New York. From 2000–2004, Imani was a stage manager, space grantee, and Artist-in-Residence, at the Brooklyn Arts Exchange, where he had the opportunity to write and develop three plays. Imani toured with his multi-media show, *B4T (before testosterone)*, at colleges, conferences, and theaters across the US, Canada, and Europe from 2002–2007. His writing has appeared in several publications including the Lambda award-winning Does Your Mama Know (Red Bone Press), *Voices Rising: Celebrating 20 years of Black LGBT Writing* (Other Countries 2007), *Marxism, Reparations and the Black Freedom Struggle* (World View Forum Publishing), and the newly released, *Against Equality: Prisons Will Not Protect You* (Against Equality Publishing). Since 1993, Imani has been a journalist for the progressive weekly *Workers World Newspaper.* Currently Imani is working on the 2014 launch of his multi-media performance project, on the gentrification of Brooklyn, NY entitled **Before It's Gone: Take it B(l)ack.** Follow me on twitter.com/imanihenry, http://www.oocities.com/imani_henry/, or check out iacenter.org

ah am crunch. "**jamal**" is de name given ta me by mah mother. "**rashad**"—by my cousin, Tammy. an "**jones**" was imposed on mah kin by de system of white supremacist erasure an enslavement dat brought us ta dis place on slaveships. ah am queer, black, magic, an aquarius, a taught male, moving, water, flesh, making a path out of addiction through discovering recovery, optimistic, a story teller, a drag performer, other'd in thought (most of de time), an a crotch load of other things. all equal. some constant. ah like to read an ta "read". ta build, create, write, listen, kiki wid folk of all ages. ah love little people, walking, nina simone, essex hemphill, an reminding folk dat ah am from Washington D.C. ah am currently an unemployed teacher- writin' an performin' in Oakland CA, where ah have lived fo four years. ah have been published an book'd ta perform an advertise. ah am gettin away from de tendency ta make a biography a list of achievements. ah want you ta some spirit in me. ah look forward ta de future of dis world- cause ah look forward wat ah feel. ah feel goodness comin. fo me, writin creates dat goodness. writin is power fo me. it is de ability ta create dimensions, move through hard emotion, reach fokl an reach yourself. writin' (in watever for) is de backbone of mah self help practice. writin' is spirit.

MJ Kaufman is primarily a playwright. Originally from Portland, Oregon, MJ attended Wesleyan University and recently received an MFA in playwriting from the Yale School of Drama. He has received awards and commissions from the Program for Women in Theater, the Playwrights Foundation, the National Foundation for Advancement in the Arts, Young Playwrights Inc., New Harmony Project, and the Huntington Theatre, where he is also a playwriting fellow. MJ was awarded the 2010 Jane Chambers Prize in Feminist Theatre for his play, *A Live Dress*. His work has also been performed in Russian in Moscow. MJ received the 2013 ASCAP Cole Porter Prize in Playwriting. MJ is currently an Artist in Residence at Mascher Arts Coop, a member of The Foundry, and Clubbed Thumb Emerging Writers Group.

Deena Loeffler is a Midwestern transplant to the East Coast, where there is more sunshine but less snow. She is a health services researcher during the day and a member of the editorial collective for Against Equality. In her free time, her activism centers on farm and domestic animals, and she often does freelance editing for friends. She is a fan of public transportation, vegan ice cream, and the serial comma.

Cecilia Cissell Lucas received her MA and PhD from the Social and Cultural Studies program at UC Berkeley's Graduate School of Education. Her interdisciplinary dissertation sits at the intersection of Education, Ethnic Studies, and Performance Studies, and examines issues related to white U.S. citizens' engagement with racial justice and decolonization projects. She also has a BFA in Theater from the University of Illinois at Urbana-Champaign, and spent almost five years working as the Assistant Director of Albany Park Theater Project, creating original plays with an ensemble of youth and adult artists based on real-life stories from Chicago's Albany Park neighborhood. She is currently working as a Lecturer at UC Berkeley, teaching in the Global Poverty and Practice Minor and Peace and Conflict Studies department, and developing a play based on her dissertation.

Jason Lydon is a Unitarian Universalist community minister in Boston, Massachusetts. He founded Black and Pink after a short six-month prison sentence and has been working in the movement to abolish the prison industrial complex for over a decade. When not organizing with others to overthrow imperialism, white supremacy, capitalism, and heteropatriarchy you can find Jason watching far too many movies or riding bikes. You can email him: Jason@blackand-pink.org

Into bee keeping, jam making, and running, **Erica R. Meiners** is the author *Flaunt It! Queers organizing for public education and justice* (2009), *Right to be hostile: schools, prisons and the making of public enemies* (2009) the forthcoming *Intimate Labour*, and articles in *AREA Chicago, Meridians, Academe, Social Justice, Women's Studies Quarterly*, and No More Potlucks. A Professor of Education and Gender and Women's Studies at Northeastern Illinois University, she is a member of her labor union, University Professionals of Illinois, and actively involved in a number of non-traditional and popular education projects including an anti-prison teaching collective, a high school project for people exiting prisons and jail, and radical education at Stateville Prison (http://p-nap.org/).

Liam Michaud works as a streetworker at CACTUS-Montréal, doing HIV and Hep C prevention and advocacy among drug users, sex workers, and those facing criminalization and state violence in Montréal. Over the last eight odd years he's been involved in projects working alongside those surviving the effects of incarceration, including the Prisoner Correspondence Project, and Continuité-famille auprès des détenues. He's doing research on displacement of communities living and working downtown through development and policing, and on failed public health responses to HIV in Québec.

Katie Miles lives in New York, where she works as a labor organizer. She was born and raised in San Francisco

Yasmin Nair is a writer, academic, and activist based in Chicago.

She is a co-founder of Against Equality, and her work can be found at yasminnair.net.

Tamara K. Nopper has a PhD in sociology, adjuncts as a lecturer in Sociology, Asian American Studies, and Urban Studies, and is a writer and editor currently living in Philadelphia. Her areas of teaching, research, and writing are in race politics, urban development, Black-Asian American conflict, immigration, and public policy. Her work can be found at http://tamaranopper.com/ .

Josh Pavan is an Alberta-bred Canadian queen relocated to Montréal where she works as a trade unionist and community organizer. In 2007, he helped start up the Prisoner Correspondence Project, offering queer- and trans-specific support and resources to prisoners. His spare time is spent figuring out political drag as the divine Lady Gaza and defending the honor of misunderstood pop stars.

Therese Quinn is Chair and Associate Professor of Art History and Director of the Museum and Exhibition Studies Program at the University of Illinois at Chicago. She writes about the arts and cultural institutions as sites for democratic engagement and justice work; contributes a regular column to *Yliopisto*, the magazine of the University of Helsinki; and is a founding member of Chicagoland Researchers and Advocates for Transformative Education. Her most recent books are *Art and Social Justice Education: Culture as Commons* (2012, Routledge), *Sexualities in Education: A Reader* (2012, Peter Lang), and *Teaching Toward Democracy* (2010, Paradigm).

Kate Raphael has been a radical queer activist for over twenty-five years. She is a cofounder of QUIT! Queers Undermining Israeli Terrorism and a member of LAGAI-Queer Insurrection, one of the oldest anti-assimilationist queer groups in the world. She spent over a month in Israeli jails for her work supporting Palestinian nonviolent resistance, and is a former grand marshal of the San Francisco LGBT Pride Parade.

Liliana Segura is a journalist and editor writing on prisons and harsh sentencing. She is currently an associate editor at *The Nation Magazine*. lilianasegura.tumblr.com

Bridget Simpson, a Montréal-based invert, has done work with the Prisoner Correspondence Project since 2008.

Dean Spade is an associate professor at the Seattle University School of Law. In 2002, he founded the Sylvia Rivera Law Project, a collective that provides free legal help to low-income people and people of color who are trans, intersex, and/or gender non-conforming and works to build trans resistance rooted in racial and economic justice. He is the author of *Normal Life: Administrative Violence, Critical Trans Politics and the Limits of Law* (2011).

Eric A. Stanley is a President's Postdoctoral fellow in the departments of Communication and Critical Gender Studies at the University of California, San Diego. Along with Chris Vargas, Eric directed the films *Homotopia* and *Criminal Queers*. A coeditor of the anthology *Captive Genders: Trans Embodiment and the Prison Industrial Complex*, Eric's other writing can be found in the journals *Social Text, American Quarterly, Women and Performance,* and *TSQ.*

Craig Willse is an assistant professor of cultural studies at George Mason University, where he is also faculty adviser for Students Against Israeli Apartheid. He lives in Washington, DC.

AK Press is one of the world's largest and most productive anarchist publishing houses. We're entirely worker-run and democratically managed. We operate without a corporate structure—no boss, no managers, no bullshit. We publish close to twenty books every year, and distribute thousands of other titles published by other like-minded independent presses from around the globe.

The Friends of AK program is a way that you can directly contribute to the continued existence of AK Press, and ensure that we're able to keep publishing great books just like this one! Friends pay $25 a month directly into our publishing account ($30 for Canada, $35 for international), and receive a copy of every book AK Press publishes for the duration of their membership! Friends also receive a discount on anything they order from our website or buy at a table: 50% on AK titles, and 20% on everything else. We've also added a new Friends of AK ebook program: $15 a month gets you an electronic copy of every book we publish for the duration of your membership. Combine it with a print subscription, too!

There's great stuff in the works—so sign up now to become a Friend of AK Press, and let the presses roll!

Email friendsofak@akpress.org for more info, or visit the Friends of AK Press website: www.akpress.org/programs/friendsofak